Ordinary Magic

ALSO BY JOHN WELWOOD

Toward a Psychology of Awakening (2000)

Journey of the Heart: Intimate Relationship and the Path of Love (1990)

Challenge of the Heart: Love, Sex, and Intimacy in Changing Times (1985)

Awakening the Heart: East/West Approaches to Psychotherapy and the Healing Relationship (1983)

The Meeting of the Ways: Explorations in East/West Psychology (1979)

Ordinary Magic

 Everyday Life as Spiritual Path

EDITED BY JOHN WELWOOD

SHAMBHALA · *Boston & London* · 1992

Shambhala Publications, Inc.
Horticultural Hall
300 Massachusetts Avenue
Boston, Massachusetts 02115
www.shambhala.com

18   17   16   15   14   13   12   11   10
Printed in the United States of America
⊗ This edition is printed on acid-free paper that meets
the American National Standards Institute Z39.48
Standard.
Distributed in the United States by Random House,
Inc., and in Canada by Random House of Canada Ltd

Library of Congress Cataloging-in-Publication Data

Ordinary magic: everyday life as spiritual path/edited
   by John Welwood.
      p.   cm.
      ISBN-13 978-0-87773-597-7 (alk. paper)
      ISBN-10 0-87773-597-2
      1. Meditation.   2. Awareness.   3. Conduct of life.
   I. Welwood, John, 1943–
   BL627.O73   1992   92-50125
   291.4—dc20   CIP

This book is dedicated to Thich Nhat Hanh, whose life and work are an inspiring example of meditation in action.

Spirituality is completely ordinary. Though we might speak of it as extraordinary, it is the most ordinary thing of all.

Spirituality is simply a means of arousing one's spirit, of developing a kind of spiritedness. Through that we begin to have greater contact with reality.

If we open our eyes, if we open our minds, if we open our hearts, we will find that this world is a magical place. It is magical not because it tricks us or changes unexpectedly into something else, but because it can *be* so vividly and brilliantly.

— CHÖGYAM TRUNGPA

✿ Contents

❂ Introduction

As children we have all felt, at least occasionally, a powerful sense of wonder at being alive in this world. Yet in growing up, we mostly lose that sense of magic. As we become caught up in worldly ambitions and burdens, life becomes increasingly routine, humdrum, and one-dimensional.

Magic, as I am using this term, is a sudden opening of the mind to the wonder of existence. It is a sense that there is much more to life than we usually recognize; that we do not have to be confined by the limited views that our family, our society, or our own habitual thoughts impose on us; that life contains many dimensions, depths, textures, and meanings extending far beyond our familiar beliefs and concepts.

The loss of a sense of the magic and sacredness of life is also happening in our world at large. In traditional cultures living closer to the natural world, people had a more immediate sense of larger forces shaping their lives. Gods and demons were near at hand. And the culture provided rituals and symbols that helped people remember the larger sacred dimension of life in the midst of their daily activities. Walking, eating, lovemaking, working—indeed, every activity and life passage—were endowed with religious or symbolic meanings that helped individuals connect with the larger, universal forces shaping their destiny.

Now that we have become disconnected from the cycles and rhythms of nature, we frequently seem to miss the whole point of being here at all as we rush through the whirlwind of our busy lives. Yet being busy is not the main problem. What does it matter whether we have ten things to do today or just one, since we can do only one thing at a time in any case? The problem with having ten things to accomplish is that while doing one, we are often dreaming or worrying about the success or failure of all ten. The speed and compulsion of our thoughts distract us and pull us away from where we are at each moment.

The word *dis-traction* is particularly useful here. It suggests losing traction, losing our ground—which is precisely what happens when we slip and fall away from being present. It is only in the stillness and simplicity of presence—when we are aware of what we are experiencing, when we are here with it as it unfolds—that we can really appreciate our life and reconnect with the ordinary magic of being alive on this earth.

WAKEFUL PRESENCE

Our society would have us believe that inner satisfaction depends on outer success and achievement. Yet struggling to "get somewhere" keeps us perpetually busy, stressed-out, and disconnected from that essential inner resource—our ability to be fully present—which *could* provide a real sense of joy and fulfillment. Our life is unsatisfactory only because we are not living it fully, because instead we are pursuing a happiness that is always somewhere else, other than where we are right now.

Nonetheless, many of us do manage to carve out some niche in our life where we *can* be fully present; and this is usually where we wind up feeling most fulfilled. Indeed, the things in life we most enjoy—lovemaking, beauty, creativity, sports or strenuous exercise, new and challenging situations—are those that bring us here most fully. Artists often feel most alive when their work demands their total attention. Great athletes become still and centered in themselves when playing because they are totally on the spot, having to keep their attention on the game at every moment. All real enjoyment, success, and excellence depend on this ability to be present.

Presence is like the air we breathe; it is essential for our life, yet so transparent and intangible that we rarely give it particular attention or importance. For instance, as a writer I can easily become distracted by the results and rewards of writing—the finished product—and fail to see that what I value most about it is that it helps me focus and connect with myself more fully in the present moment. Yet when I give more attention to the product than to the here-and-now experience of writing, I lose my enjoyment and much of my effectiveness. Similarly, if athletes become distracted by hopes and fears about winning or losing, they will lose their stillness, their presence, and most likely the game as well. Or if lovers focus on the performance and outcome of sex, they will enjoy it less and may not even be able to "perform" at all.

Cultivating the capacity to be fully present—awake, attentive, and responsive—in all the different circumstances of life is the essence of spiritual practice and realization. Those with the greatest spiritual realization are those who are "all here," who relate to life with an expansive awareness that is not limited by any fixation on themselves or their own point of view. They don't shrink from any aspect of themselves or life as a whole.

ORDINARY SPIRITUALITY

The word *spirituality*, like the word *magic*, often carries with it rarefied and otherworldly associations. That is because the life of the spirit has become divorced from so-called "real life" in the world. For much of history, in both Eastern and Western culture, spiritual practice has been the province of priests, monks, and nuns—those who have renounced ordinary life and retired to a monastery or hermitage. Meanwhile, the world of family life, daily work, business, and commerce has gone its own way, becoming increasingly disconnected from a sense of larger spiritual values.

Yet we can no longer afford the luxury of a spirituality that is separate from the world. Even if we had the time and inclination for such a pursuit, the increasingly precarious condition of our planet and its inhabitants cries out for greater involvement and concern than ever before. The difficult problems facing us on all sides—the environmental crisis, the breakdown of family and community, the loss of humanity's sacred traditions and values, the decline of education, the widening gulf between rich and poor, the increasing speed and stress of modern living—call for a new vision of human purpose that goes beyond just getting and spending.

Human life on this planet can survive and prosper only if there is a radical shift in consciousness. We need to realize that the purpose of being here is not to conquer and control, but to serve something larger than ourselves: life itself and our fellow beings. To that end, we need to develop a grounded spirituality, one that can affect the quality of life on this planet through being thoroughly committed to the here-and-now.

Of course, this is a tremendous challenge because the distractions of our world are more pervasive and seductive than ever before. We have created powerful entertainment industries designed to lure us away from the present moment and fill our minds with fantasies of some other more glamorous life we could be leading. Whenever we want to tune out of our own life, all we have to do is to press a button and tune in a high-gloss facsimile of life fabricated by "newsmakers," television personalities, and advertising agents. Everywhere we turn, the engines of materialism are overrunning the earth. The world is driven by the game of buying and selling, which seems to take up more and more of everyone's time. Even in countries with strong indigenous sacred traditions, such as India, Bhutan, or Thailand, the youth seem more interested in Western consumer goods than in preserving what's left of the sanity in their own culture.

Yet we cannot simply blame our materialistic culture for our predicament, since our society is as much the product of our distraction as its cause. The forces of distraction are within us, and they have been with us for thousands of years. In the ancient psychologies of the East, which developed out of precise meditative attention to the workings of the mind and emotions, these forces are described by the term *samsara*, which literally means "spinning," or "whirling." It just so happens that our technologies, which speed up the pace of life (cars, planes, computers, faxes) and fill up any gaps of free time (television, car phones, portable radios) have set us spinning and whirling at a much faster rate than ever before. And the faster we spin, the more addicted we become to our speedy pace.

How then can we cultivate a ground of sanity and presence so that we do not spin mindlessly out of control, destroying the simple beauty of our life and collectively hurtling over the brink of planetary disaster? Perhaps we could look to those masters of whirling—the Persian dervishes—for some clues. I recently had the privilege of watching a dervish perform his ancient, sacred ritual. As he began to whirl, it was amazing to see the top half of his body spinning at a dizzying speed, with his arms outstretched to heaven, in a state of total abandon. This was all the more remarkable because at the same time the lower half of his body—his pelvis, legs, and feet—was in such total, precise contact with the ground below. It was as though two entirely different kinds of consciousness were operating in him at the same time. It struck me that his dance was an external portrait of how we need to live if we are to ride the energy of our whirling lives without being thrown off center. We can only let go, open up, and dance with life's energies when we establish a strong, reliable connection with our ground.

This book is about how to find our ground in the midst of everyday life, how to develop greater presence of mind, heart, body, and spirit, and how to bring this into whatever activity we are engaged in. The writings assembled here teach us that any activity can provide an opportunity to tap into our deeper being and bring forth its essential qualities of openness and joy, clarity and compassion. They also show how any activity is more creative, enjoyable, powerful, and effective when done in this spirit.

To find a ground of sanity and presence amid the whirling distractions of our lives, we need a way to cultivate and draw upon the sharp, laserlike quality of our awareness, which is the only thing that can cut through the thick layers of our distraction. Meditation—the practice of mindfulness, awareness, or presence—provides such a way. If we want to taste the fullness and richness of being alive, we need to learn to practice meditation in action.

The idea of meditation often intimidates people. It conjures up notions of otherworldly withdrawal, appearing to be the specialized occupation of a chosen few who have the time and inclination for a religious life. But the perspective presented here is quite different. We could define meditation simply as the practice of becoming more fully awake and present. It is nothing more esoteric than that. The contributors to this book regard mindful or contemplative awareness as the key to life, the spice that brings out all the varied flavors of human existence, the doorway to rediscovering the inherent magic of being alive.

Meditation is extremely down-to-earth because it helps us connect with the actual textures of our experience, in all their variety and profundity. Because it puts us in touch with the life in and around us, this kind of awareness practice is the quintessence of spirituality.

LIVING IN TWO WORLDS

Spirituality, as Chögyam Trungpa simply defines it, is "a means of arousing one's spirit, of developing a kind of spiritedness" that allows us "to have greater contact with reality."[1] In this sense, spiritual practice need not be associated with religious observances or traditions, or with otherworldly pursuits. Indeed, every great spiritual tradition contains teachings, often hidden in its core, about overcoming the separation between worldly and spiritual life. This deeper wisdom insists that the vertical search—for meaning, transcendence, or depth—bears real fruit only when it intersects with the horizontal search—understanding how to live in the body, on the earth, in families, or in the marketplace, with dignity and compassion. The Jewish tradition regards the body as the sacred temple of the soul; the Star of David is composed of two overlapping triangles, one pointing toward heaven, one toward earth. In the Christian tradition the cross is a sacred symbol of the meeting of horizontal and vertical, spirit and flesh, temporal and eternal. And Zen and Vajrayana Buddhism teach that *samsara*—the world of spinning confusion—is inseparable from *nirvana*—the realization of freedom, truth, and inner peace.

To be human is to live in two worlds. Our posture, with our head raised to heaven, and our feet planted firmly on the earth, perfectly expresses our dual nature. So if we seek only to transcend this world, or if we only succumb to it, we lose half of our humanness. The human soul becomes impoverished when we try to escape the contradiction at the core of our nature. It evolves and develops through living in the polar tension between heaven and earth, spirit and animal, expansion and contraction. Indeed, we can never be fully present unless we recognize and honor all of who we are, including both our expansiveness *and* our limitations.

The most powerful kind of spiritual practice, then, involves bringing these two sides of our nature together—cultivating our larger expansive presence in the midst of our daily round, while also facing and working with all the obsta-

---

1. Chögyam Trungpa, "Theism and Nontheism," in *Speaking of Silence: Christians and Buddhists on the Contemplative Way*, edited by Susan Walker (New York: Paulist Press, 1987) p. 152.

cles that stand in the way of that. Here, in the intersection where the two sides of our nature meet, we can begin to re-member the sacred, or magical, quality of existence.

Practicing Mindfulness and Awareness

Being present is the simplest thing there is, and yet amid all the distractions of our world it is also one of the most difficult. Therefore it requires a disciplined approach, at least at first, to cut through the habitual state of distraction that has dominated our awareness for so many years.

Since the writings in this book focus primarily on mindfulness in action, we should briefly review what a formal practice of awareness may involve. The first step is to settle down, assume an upright posture, and bring attention to the immediate flow of our moment-to-moment experience. The simplest method is following the breath while labeling one's thoughts, when they arise, as thoughts, in order to distinguish them from direct, nonconceptual perception and awareness. The point is to return to the present whenever we become caught in mental distractions. Different traditions practice this in different ways and call it by various names: nondual or choiceless awareness, contemplation, vipassana, zazen, self-remembering.

As we start to practice awareness, we soon discover how much of our lives we spend dreaming. Normally we have no problem noticing our night-dreams or those vivid excursions into fantasy that we call daydreams. What we usually don't notice is that we are dreaming most of the time. These mini-dreams may only last ten or twenty seconds. Our mind is constantly imagining reality, and substituting that imagination for direct perception.

The practice of mindfulness helps us distinguish between thought and awareness, thinking and being. There is a tremendous difference between thinking and actually believing, "life is hell," and the awareness that we are having thoughts that life is hell. Through paying closer attention to our experience, we can begin to make a subtle, yet crucial distinction between our shifting judgments about reality—"This peacefulness is good . . . This anger is bad . . . I can't wait 'til this is over . . . She's interesting . . . He's such a bore . . ."—and the vivid, ineffable qualities of immediate experience itself— the peacefulness, the anger, the impatience, or the "isness" of another person, before we put them into any interpretive boxes at all.

If reality operated entirely according to our ideas and beliefs about it, then learning the right concepts would be all we would need in order to know how to live. On one level, reality does appear to be strictly determined, since we can discover predictable laws that allow us to make stable plans and calculations. Yet on another level, reality can never be entirely determined, measured, characterized, or pinned down at all. Can we really say we know what mind is, what matter is, what life is, what a person is? When the subatomic physicists failed to pin down the basic constituents of the material world, they recognized this slippery quality of reality and had to invent a new "law" to account for it: the "uncertainty principle."

We actually experience this indeterminacy all the time without noticing or fully appreciating it. In Buddhism, it is termed *shunyata*, which is usually translated as "emptiness," but which Herbert Guenther translates more precisely as "the open dimension of being."[2] This is the dimension where magic happens, where ordinary things are suddenly seen as more than what they usually appear to be. Our friends are much more than the images and expectations we have of them. Our mind is unfathomable. Our most basic needs and aspirations are often difficult to grasp. And our feelings about things are unpredictable, changing direction as often as the wind. The open dimension of being is a wild card that reality continually introduces into our experience.

2. Herbert V. Guenther and Chögyam Trungpa, *The Dawn of Tantra* (Boston: Shambhala Publications, 1975) p. 30.

Meditation is a gateway into this open dimension. The more we sit with our present experiencing, the more we find that it is brimming with energy and clarity. Everything is happening here, and only here: the feelings in our body, the nourishment of the breath, the textures of our thought, the desire to live more fully, the pain of our disappointments, the speed of our busyness, the love we feel for another, the play of the wind in the trees. When we relax our attempt to get a hold on life, we start to appreciate the richness contained in the simplest things.

Increased awareness also helps us relate in a new way to the thoughts and emotions that usually imprison us. Instead of just being enveloped in their grip, we can begin to notice their dynamic experiential textures. Usually when I'm angry at someone, I become caught up in a stream of negative thoughts directed at that person. When I become aware of this, however, I can explore the texture of the anger and negativity instead: its tight, dark, obsessive, and hammering quality. As I feel that painful quality, my attachment to it begins to loosen, and the anger becomes less stuck and solid. It is more like a wild horse I need to learn to ride, a high-energy partner I must learn to dance with. Realizing this helps me wake up in the middle of my angry thoughts, come back to my breath, and connect with the ground of just being here once more.

Coming back to the present moment is simple enough. What makes it difficult is our investment in habitual attitudes and identities, which we maintain by telling ourselves familiar stories about "the way things are." These stories often operate in the background of the mind, as part of an ongoing stream of subconscious gossip we keep up with ourselves. Stories, in this definition, are belief systems that determine how we perceive and react to things. If I believe that "It's a cold, cruel world," then I will interpret events in that light and act accordingly. And the more I act as though it's a cold, cruel world, the more the world actually appears to be that way.

Thus believing that our stories are reality creates a distorted reality. And this causes us to keep losing our ground—that simple presence and open awareness that is our true nature. If awareness is like the sun, which illumines whatever it shines on, the dense fabric of our stories is like a cloud cover blocking and obscuring its natural radiance and clarity.

Only awareness can free us from our thoughts. In the moment we become aware that our thoughts are just thoughts, rather than reality itself, we wake up from their spell and can return to presence. It is empowering to discover that we are not enslaved by our thoughts, by how our mind interprets reality. When this happens, it feels as though we just left a stuffy room and stepped outdoors into cool, invigorating air. This sudden taste of freedom provides a glimpse of ordinary magic.

According to the meditative traditions, awareness is inherently free or "self-liberated." It is often likened to a sparkling, clear mirror, which has no intrinsic bias for or against anything, but generously reflects whatever it encounters. Awareness is also spacious, like the sky stretching endlessly in every direction. It is fluid as well. Like a zoom lens, it can either move back from any state of mind we are caught in—providing a larger perspective on what is happening—or zero in on the subtlest details. But just as it takes practice to play a musical instrument fluidly, we must at first intentionally *practice* awareness if we want it to flow more freely and shine more brightly. In the Zen tradition, this is called "polishing the mirror."

When we practice awareness instead of spinning out in thought, we "find our seat": We discover nowness, our most trustworthy ground and support. The French term, "He is not in his seat," indicates someone who has lost his composure and confidence. Riders also use the term "a good seat" to describe the quality of settling into the saddle and connecting with the horse underneath. The classic meditation posture—sitting still in an upright, balanced way—lets us ride the wild horse of the mind without losing our seat. As we begin to see through our habitual mind-sets, our attempts to control our experience, we start meeting life more directly and making the shift in consciousness our world so desperately needs.

MEDITATION IN ACTION

Yet the ultimate proof and test of meditation is how we put it into practice—whether it helps us live in a more creative, helpful, and compassionate way. Most people who have done an intensive meditation retreat for a few days, weeks, or months find their mind becoming clearer and their heart becoming more open. Yet upon returning to their everyday responsibilities, they often feel just as stuck in old patterns and thoughts as they ever were.

This is to be expected. It is much easier to be mindfully present when we set aside a special time and place for it than when we're in the midst of our busy lives. Yet if we are going to live in this world, rather than in a monastery, we need to learn how to use any activity or life situation as an opportunity to experience a deeper contact with reality and a more powerful quality of presence. How can our daily life become a continual opportunity to expand awareness, work creatively with the challenges facing us, free ourselves from old dysfunctional patterns, and relate to ourselves and others more compassionately? These are the questions this book addresses.

The first section explores how to polish the mirror of awareness in daily life. The second section shows how creativity requires mindfulness and how mindfulness in turn heightens creativity. The third section explores how meditative awareness is essential for healing and well-being. And the final section discusses different ways in which a meditative approach to life affects our relationships with others, with society, and with the world at large.

This is a book of reminders. My intention and desire in

putting it together has been to provide refreshment for people whenever they feel lost, confused, tired, unsure of what their life is about or where they're going. Practically every page reminds you to look again, consider your actions more closely, and see your life in a larger context. Those who have no meditation experience or who seek a deeper connection with the spiritual dimension of their life should find inspiration here to move in that direction. And experienced meditators will find encouragement and guidance here about how to extend their practice and let it touch every aspect of their daily life.

Though putting a book together can often feel like a chore, working on this one had none of that quality because these writings kept reminding me to wake up and practice what they are talking about. May you find the same kind of inspiration here!

PART
ONE

❀ *Everyday Meditation*

Just to be is a blessing.
Just to live is holy.

—Rabbi Abraham Heschel

❊ Introduction

At any moment, whatever we are experiencing, only one of two things is ever happening: either we are being with what is, or else we are resisting what is. Being with what is means letting ourselves have and feel our experience, just as it is right now. When we choose to be actively present with what is, we radiate a powerful energy that is most compelling. This is where genuine creativity, health, and communication, as well as spiritual power, arise from.

Yet oddly enough, we rarely let ourselves simply have our experience. We are usually resisting it instead—trying to manipulate it and make it something other than it is. As children, we first learned to resist our experience as a way of coping with what seemed like overwhelming influences in the world around us. Because we were so open and sensitive to begin with, we learned to shut down and turn away from what we were feeling, as a way to avoid feeling pain. Yet when we contract ourselves against the painful aspects of our experience, we actually stop being.

As a verb, the word *be-ing* means actively coming-into-presence, energetically connecting and engaging with what is, here and now. When we habitually contract against an area of our experience, such as anger, it's as though we create a hole or dead spot in our being. Then when anger arises—in ourselves or in others—we go dead and become somewhat dysfunctional in this area. And the more dead spots we have in our being, the less freely and flexibly we respond to life's challenges and opportunities.

Whenever we resist what is, we become tense and contracted; we're not much fun to be around. In fact, even *we* don't enjoy being around ourselves. No wonder we check out and wander off into distractions—seeking entertainment, driving ourselves to achieve, resorting to drugs and alcohol, desperately striving to be some other way than we are, living in fantasies of future happiness. All these forms of distraction are ways of trying to fill up the void that is left when we don't let ourselves be.

So the first step on any path of personal or spiritual development is to become aware of how we contract and turn away from our experience. Spiritual practice involves both becoming aware of this resistance and discovering that it is all right to open ourselves to life, that we can handle it, and that we will grow and expand by doing so.

To bring spiritual practice into daily life we can only start with where we are. The first step in cultivating a more open, wakeful presence in our lives involves settling down, as Thich Nhat Hanh suggests in the opening chapter. Once we settle down, the sun of our awareness can begin to shine forth. The first thing it illumines is the river of our perceptions, constantly flowing and changing. To be mindful does not mean stopping this river of thoughts and feelings, but rather bringing them into the light of consciousness. When we do this, we start to settle down, not because we necessarily feel tranquil, but because we are not resisting what is happening. Then whatever we do—whether it is washing the dishes, drinking tea, or confronting problems in our work or relationships— becomes more interesting, a teaching, a meditation in itself. The sun of awareness is what can bring out all the rich and varied colors of our daily life.

One way that our culture subtly encourages us to resist our experience is by rewarding those activities that are glamorous and fascinating, while devaluing the simple, ordinary activities that make up much of daily life. (Basic but necessary tasks such as farming, cooking, or teaching usually receive the least financial reward and social recognition.) However, as psychologist Karlfried Graf von Dürckheim points out, daily repetitive tasks, such as driving the car, walking, or waiting in line at the grocery checkout, provide excellent opportunities for inner work and development.

When we try to escape from irritating situations, such as waiting in line, by reading a magazine or spacing out, we actually stop being. And the more we go unconscious in these situations, the more of our lives we spend in a state of deadness or non-being. On the other hand, when we regard everything that happens to us as part of our path, we can make use of even the most dull, repetitive activities as a form of spiritual practice. For instance, we might use waiting in line as an opportuntity to pay attention, to ride the wild horse of our impatience, or to explore our resistance to this experience. Then it may serve to remind us of the challenge and humor of living in two worlds; here we are, a spark of the divine, standing in a supermarket line!

Chögyam Trungpa echoes this theme in the next chapter. He emphasizes that to bring spirituality into everyday life we must relate properly to the earth. In New Age circles these days, it is common to imagine that spirituality is an ascent above the ordinary to some "higher" plane of reality. Yet that approach does not help us cultivate respect for and attention to the concrete, ordinary details of our lives. If we rush through our meal, leave grease on the plates when we wash them, or don't respect another person's feelings, we are not relating properly to the earthly dimension of life. How we handle these concrete details reflects our state of mind, and therefore gives us immediate feedback about who we are, where we are in our development, and what obstacles stand in our way. What can help us relate to life's little details with greater clarity and respect is bringing the spacious, mirrorlike quality of our awareness into whatever we are doing at each moment. That is also how to bring together heaven and earth, the two sides of our nature.

Buddhist nun Pema Chödrön suggests that we also join heaven and earth when we can simultaneously hold in our heart life's pain and sadness along with its power and joy, without having a bias toward one side or the other. Though this is not easy to do, it does open us to life's vastness and depth. The music or art that affects us most deeply is never just happy or sad, but always combines these two qualities. Like art, ritual is a conscious act that points beyond itself to the larger rhythms of the whole. Pema's recounting of the poignant meeting between Queen Victoria and the Sioux Black Elk beautifully portrays how ritual, as a sacred language transcending our limited conceptual or cultural frameworks, brings the two sides of our existence together. In this sense, relating to ordinary activities—waking up in the morning, cooking, sweeping the floor—as ritual helps us bring a deeper quality of awareness into everyday life.

If awareness is like the sun, then attention, or focused awareness, is like a flame that can burn through our egocentric confusion, as the American Zen teacher Charlotte Joko Beck points out. But when our attention is scattered and distracted, this is like burning soft coal, which scatters soot all around. We keep making messes out of situations, and having to go back and clean up these messes. Being mindful, on the other hand, is like burning hard coal. When we attend to the details of each situation, our actions leave no messy, sticky residues. Hard as this may be to grasp, the Buddha, or awakened mind in each person, *is* whatever we are experiencing in the moment—the wind in the trees, the traffic on the freeway, the confusion we are feeling—if we but surrender to it. Surrendering to it means experiencing it fully, giving it our full attention, without struggling against it or trying to make it something other than it is. In opening to what is, without strategies or agendas, we touch what cannot be grasped—a moment of nowness, sharp and thin as a razor's edge. And walking on this razor's edge cuts through the struggle between self and other that separates us from a more immediate presence to life.

In the next chapter, Krishnamurti's descriptions of the landscapes and situations he is in, interwoven with his reflections, portray a clear, meditative attention to detail, to what he calls the sacredness of pure fact—pure experience not interpreted or packaged by the busy thinking mind. To really see what is around us, we must have access to an awareness that can be humble and innocent in the face of what is.

In the final chapter of this section, A. H. Almaas asks the crucial question that lies at the heart of all psychological and spiritual well-being: "Are you here?" He suggests that most of us betray and abandon ourselves by not recognizing and appreciating our true being, by not letting ourselves be what we truly are: "a presence that impregnates the present and fills our body." Having abandoned ourselves, we then try to fill up the yawning void that remains with material possessions, fleeting pleasures, or temporary worldly successes. But the real challenge of human existence is not about achievement, pleasure, or success. Our most important work is to allow our true nature—our ability to be fully present—to emerge and manifest itself in our lives, and to help others do the same.

1 ❁ *Sunshine and Green Leaves*

THICH NHAT HANH

THANH THUY'S APPLE JUICE

Today three children, two girls and a little boy, came from the village to play with Thanh Thuy (pronounced "Tahn Tui"). The four of them ran off to play on the hillside behind our house and were gone for about an hour when they returned to ask for something to drink. I took the last bottle of homemade apple juice and gave them each a full glass, serving Thuy last. Since her juice was from the bottom of the bottle, it had some pulp in it. When she noticed the particles, she pouted and refused to drink it. So the four children went back to their games on the hillside, and Thuy had not drunk anything.

Half an hour later, while I was meditating in my room, I heard her calling. Thuy wanted to get herself a glass of cold water, but even on tiptoes she couldn't reach the faucet. I reminded her of the glass of juice on the table and asked her to drink that first. Turning to look at it, she saw that the pulp had settled and the juice looked clear and delicious. She went to the table and took the glass with both hands. After drinking half of it, she put it down and asked, "Is this a different glass, Uncle Monk?" (a common term for Vietnamese children to use when addressing an older monk).

"No," I answered. "It's the same one as before. It sat quietly for a bit, and now it's clear and delicious." Thuy looked at the glass again. "It really is good. Was it meditating like you, Uncle Monk?" I laughed and patted her head. "Let's say that I imitate the apple juice when I sit; that is closer to the truth."

Without a doubt, Thuy thought that the apple juice was sitting for a while to clear itself, just like her Uncle Monk. "Was it meditating like you?" I think that Thanh Thuy, not yet five, understands the meaning of meditation without any explanation. The apple juice became clear after resting awhile. In the same way, if we rest in meditation awhile, we too become clear. This clarity refreshes us and gives us strength and serenity. As we feel ourselves refreshed, our surroundings also become refreshed. Children like to be near us, not just to get candy and hear stories. They like to be near us because they can feel this "freshness."

Tonight a guest has come. I fill a glass with the last of the apple juice and put it on the table in the middle of the meditation room. Thuy is already fast asleep, and I invite my friend to sit very quietly, just like the apple juice.

A RIVER OF PERCEPTIONS

We sit for about 40 minutes. I notice my friend smiling as he looks at the juice. It has become very clear. "And you, my friend, are you? Even if you have not settled as thoroughly as the apple juice, don't you feel a little less agitated, less fidgety, less disturbed? The smile on your lips hasn't faded yet, but I think you doubt that you might become as clear as the apple juice, even if we continue to sit for hours.

"The glass of juice has a very stable base. But you, your

sitting is not so sure. Those tiny bits of pulp only have to follow the laws of nature to fall gently to the bottom of the glass. But your thoughts obey no such law. To the contrary, they buzz feverishly, like a swarm of bees, and so you think you cannot settle like the apple juice.

"You tell me that people, living beings with the capacity to think and to feel, cannot be compared with a glass of juice. I agree, but I also know that we can do what the apple juice does, and more. We can be at peace, not only while sitting, but also while walking and working.

"Perhaps you don't believe me, because 40 minutes have passed and you tried so hard but weren't able to achieve the peace you hoped for. Thuy is sleeping peacefully, her breath-ing is light. Why don't we light another candle before contin-uing our conversation?

"Little Thuy sleeps this way effortlessly. You know those nights when sleep eludes you, and the harder you try to sleep the less you can. You are trying to force yourself to be peaceful, and you feel the resistance inside of you. This same sort of resistance is felt by many people during their first experiences with meditation. The more they try to calm themselves, the more restless they become. The Vietnamese think this is because they are victims of demons or bad karma, but really this resistance is born out of our very efforts to be peaceful. The effort itself becomes oppressive. Our thoughts and feelings flow like a river. If we try to stop the flow of a river, we will meet the resistance of the water. It is better to flow with it, and then we may be able to guide it in ways we want it to go. We must not attempt to halt it.

"Keep in mind that the river must flow and that we are going to follow it. We must be aware of every little stream that joins it. We must be aware of all the thoughts, feelings, and sensations that arise in us—of their birth, duration, and disappearance. Do you see? Now the resistance begins to disappear. The river of perceptions is still flowing, but no longer in darkness. It is now flowing in the sunlight of aware-ness. To keep this sun always shining inside of us, illuminating each rivulet, each pebble, each bend in the river, is the practice of meditation. To practice meditation is, first of all, to observe and to follow these details.

"At the moment of awareness we feel we are in control, even though the river is still there, still flowing. We feel ourselves at peace, but this isn't the 'peace' of the apple juice. Being at peace doesn't mean our thoughts and feelings are frozen. Being at peace is not the same as being anesthetized. A peaceful mind does not mean a mind empty of thoughts, sensations, and emotions."

Sunshine and Green Leaves

Beginning meditators usually think they must suppress all thoughts and feelings (often called "false mind") in order to create conditions favorable to concentration and understanding (called "true mind"). They use methods such as focusing their attention on an object or counting their breaths to try to block out thoughts and feelings. Concentrating on an object and counting the breath are excellent methods, but they should not be used for suppression or repression. We know that as soon as there is repression, there is rebellion—repression entails rebellion. True mind and false mind are one. Denying one is denying the other. Suppressing one is suppressing the other. Our mind is our self. We cannot suppress it. We must treat it with respect, with gentleness, and absolutely without violence. Since we do not even know what our "self" is, how can we know if it is true or false, and whether or what to suppress? The only thing we can do is to let the sunlight of awareness shine on our "self" and en-lighten it, so we can look at it directly.

Just as flowers and leaves are only part of a plant, and just as waves are only part of the ocean, perceptions, feelings, and thoughts are only part of the self. Blossoms and leaves are a natural manifestation of plants, and waves are a natural expression of oceans. It is useless to try to repress or stifle them. It is impossible. We can only observe them. Because they exist, we can find their source, which is exactly the same as our own.

The sun of awareness originates in the heart of the self. It enables the self to illuminate the self. It lights not only all thoughts and feelings present. It lights itself as well.

Let us return to the apple juice, quietly "resting." The river of our perceptions continues to flow, but now, in the sunlight of awareness, it flows peacefully, and we are serene. The relation between the river of perceptions and the sun of awareness is not the same as that of an actual river and the actual sun. Whether it is midnight or noon, whether the sun is absent or its penetrating rays are beaming down, the waters of the Mississippi River continue to flow, more or less the same. But when the sun of awareness shines on the river of our perceptions, the mind is transformed. Both river and sun are of the same nature.

Let us consider the relationship between the color of leaves and sunlight, which also have the same nature. At midnight, the starlight and moonlight reveal only the form of the trees and leaves. But if the sun were suddenly to shine, the green color of the leaves would immediately appear. The tender green of the leaves in April exists because the sunlight exists. One day, while sitting in a forest, mimicking the *Prajna Paramita Heart Sutra*, I wrote:

> Sunshine is green leaves
> Green leaves are sunshine
> Sunshine is not different from green leaves
> Green leaves are not different from sunshine
> The same is true of all forms and colors.

As soon as the sun of awareness shines, at that very moment a great change takes place. Meditation lets the sun of awareness rise easily, so we can see more clearly. When we meditate, we seem to have two selves. One is the flowing river of thoughts and feelings, and the other is the sun of awareness that shines on them. Which is our own self?

Which is true? Which false? Which is good? Which bad? Please calm down, my friend. Lay down your sharp sword of conceptual thinking. Don't be in such a hurry to cut your "self" in two. Both are self. Neither is true. Neither is false. They are both true and both false.

We know that light and color are not separate phenomena. In the same way, the sun of self and the river of self are not different. Sit with me, let a smile form on your lips, let your sun shine, close your eyes, if need be, to see your self more clearly.

I just told you to put down your sword of conceptualization and not cut your self into sections. Actually, you couldn't, even if you wanted to. Do you think you can separate the sunshine from the green color of the leaves? You can no more separate the observing self from the self observed.

DARKNESS BECOMES LIGHT

Observe the changes that take place in your mind under the light of awareness. Even your breathing has changed and become "not-two" (I don't want to say "one") with your observing self. This is also true of your thoughts and feelings, which, together with their effects, are suddenly transformed. When you do not try to judge or suppress them, they become intertwined with the observing mind.

From time to time you may become restless, and the restlessness will not go away. At such times, just sit quietly, follow your breathing, smile a half-smile, and shine your awareness on the restlessness. Don't judge it or try to destroy it, because this restlessness is you yourself. It is born, has some period of existence, and fades away, quite naturally. Don't be in too big a hurry to find its source. Don't try too hard to make it disappear. Just illuminate it. You will see that little by little it will change, merging, becoming connected, with you, the observer. Any psychological state which you subject to this illumination will eventually soften and acquire the same nature as the observing mind.

Throughout your meditation, keep the sun of your awareness shining. Like the physical sun, which lights every leaf and every blade of grass, our awareness lights our every thought and feeling, allowing us to recognize them, be aware of their birth, duration, and dissolution, without judging or evaluating, welcoming or banishing them. It is important that you do not consider awareness to be your "ally," called on to suppress the "enemies" that are your unruly thoughts. Do not turn your mind into a battlefield. Do not have a war there; for *all* your feelings—joy, sorrow, anger, hatred—are part of yourself. Awareness is like an elder brother or sister, gentle and attentive, who is there to guide and enlighten. It is a tolerant and lucid presence, never violent or discriminating. It is there to recognize and identify thoughts and feelings, not to judge them as good or bad, or place them into opposing camps in order to fight with each other. Opposition between good and bad is often compared to light and dark, but if we look at it in a different way, we will see that when light shines, darkness does not disappear. It doesn't leave; it merges with the light. It becomes the light.

A while ago I invited my guest to smile. To meditate does not mean to fight with a problem. To meditate means to observe. Your smile proves it. It proves that you are being gentle with yourself, that the sun of awareness is shining in you, that you have control of your situation. You are yourself, and you have acquired some peace. It is this peace that makes a child love to be near you.

A POEM FOR BUTTONING YOUR JACKET

We can be better than a glass of apple juice. Not only can we settle peacefully while sitting still, we can also do it while standing, lying down, walking, or even working. What prevents you from allowing the sun of awareness to shine while you take a walk, make a cup of tea or coffee, or wash your clothes? When I first became a student at the Tu Hieu Monastery, I learned to maintain awareness during all activities—

weeding the garden, raking leaves around the pond, washing dishes in the kitchen. I practiced mindfulness in the way taught by Zen master Doc The in his little manual, *Essentials of the Practice to Apply Each Day*. According to this small book, we must be fully aware of all our actions. While waking up we know that we are waking up; while buttoning our jacket, we know that we are buttoning our jacket; while washing our hands we know that we are washing our hands. Master Doc The composed short poems for us to recite while washing our hands or buttoning our jackets to help us remain firmly rooted in awareness. Here is the poem he wrote for us to recite while buttoning our jacket:

> While buttoning my jacket
> I hope that all beings
> Will keep their hearts warm
> And not lose themselves.

With the aid of verses like this, it is easy for the sun of awareness to shine its light on our physical actions as well as our thoughts and feelings. When I was a child I often heard my mother tell my elder sister that a girl must pay attention to her every movement. I was glad I was a boy who didn't have to pay attention like that. It was only when I began to practice meditation that I realized that I had to pay a thousand times more attention to my movements than my sister had. And not only to my movements, but also to my thoughts and feelings! My mother, like all mothers, knew that a girl who pays attention to her movements becomes more beautiful. Her movements are not jerky, rushed, or clumsy; they become gentle, calm, and graceful. Without knowing it, my mother taught my sister meditation.

In the same way, someone who practices awareness becomes beautiful to see. A Zen master, observing a student ringing the bell, sweeping the yard, setting the table, can guess how ripe that student is, can measure the student's "level of meditation" in his or her manners and personality. This "level" is the fruit of the practice of awareness, and the master calls it "the flavor of Zen."

THREE HOURS FOR A CUP OF TEA

The secret of meditation is to be conscious of each second of your existence and to keep the sun of awareness continually shining—in both the physical and psychological realms, in all circumstances, on each thing that arises. While drinking a cup of tea, our mind must be fully present in the act of drinking the tea. Drinking tea or coffee can be one of our daily pleasures if we partake of it fully. How much time do you set aside for one cup of tea? In coffee shops in New York or Tokyo, people come in, order their coffee, drink it quickly, pay, and rush out to do something else. This takes a few minutes at most. Often there is loud music playing, and your ears hear the music, your eyes watch others gulping down their coffee, and your mind is thinking of what to do next. You can't really call this drinking coffee.

Have you ever participated in a tea ceremony? It may take two or three hours just being together and drinking one or two cups of tea. The time is not spent talking—only being together and drinking tea. Perhaps you think this is irresponsible because the participants are not worrying about the world situation, but you must admit that people who spend their time this way know how to drink tea, know the pleasure of having tea with a friend.

Devoting two hours to a cup of tea is, I agree, a little extreme. There are many other things to do: gardening, laundry, washing dishes, binding books, writing. Perhaps these other tasks are less pleasant than drinking tea or walking in the hills, but if we do them in full awareness, we will find them quite agreeable. Even washing the dishes after a big meal can be a joy.

BATHING A NEWBORN BUDDHA

To my mind, the idea that doing dishes is unpleasant can occur only when you aren't doing them. Once you are standing in front of the sink with your sleeves rolled up and your hands in warm water, it really isn't so bad. I enjoy taking my time with each dish, being fully aware of the dish, the water, and each movement of my hands. I know that if I hurry in order to go and have a cup of tea, the time will be unpleasant, and not worth living. That would be a pity, for each minute, each second of life is a miracle. The dishes themselves and the fact that I am here washing them are miracles! Each bowl I wash, each poem I compose, each time I invite a bell to sound is a miracle, and each has exactly the same value. One day, while washing a bowl, I felt that my movements were as sacred and respectful as bathing a newborn Buddha. If he were to read this, that newborn Buddha would certainly be happy for me, and not at all insulted at being compared with a bowl.

Each thought, each action in the sunlight of awareness becomes sacred. In this light, no boundary exists between the sacred and the profane. I must confess it takes me a bit longer to do the dishes, but I live fully in every moment, and I am happy. Washing the dishes is at the same time a means and an end—that is, not only do we do the dishes in order to have clean dishes, we also do the dishes just to do the dishes, to live fully in each moment while washing them.

If I am incapable of washing dishes joyfully, if I want to finish them quickly so I can go and have a cup of tea, I will be equally incapable of drinking the tea joyfully. With the cup in my hands I will be thinking about what to do next, and the fragrance and the flavor of the tea, together with the pleasure of drinking it, will be lost. I will always be dragged into the future, never able to live in the present moment.

Nourishing Awareness While Working

Our work, which lets us "earn our daily bread," can be done in the same way as the dishes. In my community, I bind books. Using a toothbrush, a small wheel, and a very heavy fire-proof brick (about 4 or 5 pounds), I can bind 200 books in a day. Before binding, I gather all the pages and arrange them numerically around a long table. Then I walk around the table, and when I have walked all around it, I know that I have the correct number of pages for one signature. Walking around the table, I know that I am not going anywhere in particular, so I walk slowly, gathering each page, conscious of each movement, breathing softly, conscious of each breath. I am at peace while assembling the pages, gluing them, and putting the cover on the book. I know I cannot produce as many books in a day as a professional bookbinder or a machine, but I also know that I do not hate my job. If you want a lot of money to spend, you must work hard and quickly, but if you live simply, you can work gently and in full awareness. I know many young people who prefer to work less, perhaps four hours a day, earning a small livelihood, so they can live simply and happily. This may be a solution to our society's problems—reducing the production of useless goods, sharing work with those who have none, and living simply and happily. Some individuals and communities have already proved that it is possible.

You may ask how you can nourish awareness while washing dishes, binding books, or working in a factory or an office. I think you have to find your own answer. Do whatever you can to keep the light of awareness shining inside yourself. You will discover ways that suit you, or you can try some techniques that others have tried—like reciting the short poems of Zen master Doc The, or concentrating on your breathing. You can maintain awareness of each inhalation and exhalation, of each movement of your lungs. When a thought or feeling arises, allow it to flow naturally with your breath. It may help to breathe lightly and a little more slowly than usual as a reminder that you are following your breathing.

THE PRECIOUS SMILE

While following your breathing, you have been able to stay fully conscious for some time. You have succeeded a bit, haven't you? So why not smile? A tiny bud of a smile, just to prove you have succeeded. Seeing you smile, I know immediately that you are dwelling in awareness. Keep this smile always blooming, the half-smile of a Buddha.

This tiny budding smile, how many artists have labored to bring it to the lips of countless statues of the Buddha? Perhaps you have seen them on the faces at Angkor Wat in Kampuchea, or those from Gandhara in northwest India. I am sure the same smile must have been on the faces of the sculptors as they worked. Can you imagine an angry sculptor giving birth to such a smile? Surely not! I know the sculptor who created the "Parinirvana" statue on Tra Cu Mountain in Vietnam. During the six months it took him to create that statue, he remained vegetarian, practicing sitting meditation and studying sutras. Mona Lisa's smile is light, just a hint of a smile. Yet even a smile like that is enough to relax all the muscles on your face, to banish all worries and fatigue. A tiny bud of a smile on your lips nourishes awareness and calms you miraculously. It returns you to the peace you had lost.

When you walk in the hills, or in a park, or along a river bank, you can follow your breath, with a half-smile blooming on your lips. When you feel tired or irritated, you can lie down with your arms at your sides, allowing all your muscles to relax, maintaining awareness of just your breath and your smile. Relaxing in this way is wonderful, and quite refreshing. You will benefit a lot if you practice it several times a day. Your mindful breath and your smile will bring happiness to you and to those around you. Even if you spend a lot of money on gifts for everyone in your family, nothing you could buy them can give as much true happiness as your gift of awareness, breathing, and smiling, and these precious gifts cost nothing.

BREATHING RHYTHMICALLY

When you are too restless or under too much strain to follow your breathing, you can count your breath instead.

Count "one" during the first inhalation and exhalation. Do not lose the thought "one." During the next inhalation and exhalation, count "two," and do not lose it. Continue in this way until you reach "ten," and then start again with "one." If you lose the thread of concentration at any time, you can start again at "one." When you are calm and concentrated, you will be able to follow your breath without counting.

Have you ever cut grass with a scythe? Five or six years ago, I brought a scythe home and tried to cut the grass around my cottage with it. It took more than a week before I found the best way to use it. The way you stand, the way you hold the scythe, the angle of the blade on the grass are all important. I found that if I coordinated the movement of my arms with the rhythm of my breathing, and worked unhurriedly, while maintaining awareness of my activity, I was able to work for a longer period of time. When I didn't do this, I became tired in just ten minutes. One day a Frenchman of Italian descent was visiting my neighbor, and I asked him to show me how to use a scythe. He was much more adept than I, but for the most part he used the same position and movements. What surprised me was that he too coordinated his movements with his breathing. Since then, whenever I see a neighbor cutting their grass with a scythe, I know they are practicing awareness.

Even before having a scythe, I used other tools—picks, shovels, rakes—coordinating my breath and my movement. I have found that except for very heavy labor, such as moving boulders or pushing full wheelbarrows (which make full awareness difficult), most jobs—turning the soil, making furrows, sowing seeds, spreading manure, watering—can be done in a relaxed and mindful way. During the past few years I have avoided tiring myself and losing my breath. I think it is better not to mistreat my body. I must take care of it, treat it with respect as a musician does his instrument. I apply "nonviolence" to my body, for it is not merely a means to practice the Way, it itself is the Way. It is not only the temple, it is also the sage. My gardening and bookbinding tools, I like and respect them very much. I use them while following my breathing, and I feel that these tools and I breathe together in rhythm.

A Poem and a Peppermint Plant

I don't know what job you do every day, but I do know that some tasks lend themselves to awareness more easily than others. Writing, for example, is difficult to do mindfully. I have now reached the point when I know that a sentence is finished. But while writing the sentence, even now, I sometimes forget. That is why I have been doing more manual work and less writing these past few years. Someone said to me, "Planting tomatoes and lettuce may be the gateway to everything, but not everyone can write books and stories and poems as well as you do. Please don't waste your time with manual work!" I have not wasted any of my time. Planting a seed, washing a dish, cutting the grass are as eternal, as beautiful, as writing a poem! I do not understand how a poem can be better than a peppermint plant. Planting seeds gives me as much pleasure as writing a poem. For me, a head of lettuce or a peppermint plant has as much everlasting effect in time and space as a poem.

Singing, Really Singing

We lead extremely busy lives. Even though we do not have to do as much manual labor as people in former times, we never seem to have enough time for ourselves. I know people who say they do not even have enough time to eat or breathe, and it appears to me to be true! What can we do about this? Can we take hold of time with both hands and slow it down?

First, let us light the torch of our awareness and learn again how to drink tea, eat, wash dishes, walk, sit, drive, and work in awareness. We do not have to be swept along by circumstances. We are not just a leaf or a log in a rushing river. With awareness, each of our daily acts takes on a new meaning, and we discover that we are more than machines, that our activities are not just mindless repetitions. We find that life is a miracle, the universe is a miracle, and we too are a miracle.

When we are invaded by confusion and dispersion, we can ask ourselves, "What exactly am I doing right now? Am I wasting my life?" These questions immediately relight our awareness and return our attention to our breathing. A small smile naturally appears on our lips, and each second of our work becomes alive. If you want to sing, please sing! Really sing!

2 ❁ Everyday Life as Practice

KARLFRIED GRAF VON DÜRCKHEIM

When one speaks of the "daily round" the phrase carries overtones of meaning and experience which distinguish it from the holiday. Compared with a holiday, the ordinary day may appear monotonous and grey. The common round of activities always has an unchanging sameness. It is a treadmill of repeated movements and actions, whereas the holiday stands for something unique, joyous, unusual. The ordinary day deadens, whereas the holiday refreshes. If one contrasts the freedom Sunday brings us, the ordinary day feels constrained and rigid; it stands for labor, for a round of doing, in contrast to the leisure promised by Sunday. The ordinary day devours us; on holiday we find ourselves again.

Need this be so? It must be so, alas, as long as we are engulfed by our worldly ego, and so engrossed by worldly undertakings that they completely overshadow our inward self. There is, however, a way out. It needs just a single moment of insight, a flash of understanding of our situation—to make everything change. Such a moment, such a flash will light up not only our outer actions—particularly those most repetitive and familiar—but our inner experience as well.

"What" we do belongs to the world. In the "how," the *way* we do it, we infallibly reveal to ourselves whether our attitude is in harmony with the inner law or in contradiction to it, in accordance with our right form or opposed to it, open to Divine Being or closed to it. What *is* our right "form"? It is none other than that in which we are transparent to Divine Being. And to be transparent means that we are able to experience Divine Being in ourselves and to reveal it in the world.

Let us suppose, for instance, that a letter has to be posted in a mailbox a hundred yards away. If the mouth of the mailbox is all we see in the mind's eye, then the hundred strides we take toward it are wasted. But if we are on the Way and filled with the sense of all that this implies, then even this short walk, providing we maintain the right attitude and posture, can serve to renew us from the well of inner essence.

The same can be true of any daily activity. The more we have mastered some relevant technique, and the smaller the amount of attention needed to perform the task satisfactorily, the more easily may the emphasis be transferred from the exterior to the interior. Whether in the kitchen or working at an assembly-line, at the typewriter or in the garden, talking, writing, sitting, walking or standing, dealing with some daily occurrence, or conversing with someone dear to us—whatever it may be, we can approach it "from within" and use it as an opportunity for the practice of becoming a genuine human being. When this is understood, the truth of the old Japanese adage becomes clear: "For something to acquire religious significance, two conditions alone are necessary: it must be simple, and it must be repetitive."

What does this word "repetitive" signify here? Daily

tasks, by their very familiarity, can serve to free us from the grip of the ego and its quenchless thirst for success. They can also help to make us independent of the world's approval, and open for us the inward way. But this is true not only of familiar tasks. Even the practice and repeated effort needed to master something new can be put to the service of the inner work. In everything one does it is possible to foster and maintain a state of being which reflects our true destiny. When this possibility is actualized the ordinary day is no longer ordinary. It can become an adventure of the spirit. In such a case the eternal repetitions in the exterior world are transformed into an endlessly flowing and circulating inner fountain. Indeed, once repetition is established it will be found that our very habits can be the occasion for inner work. They enable us to make new discoveries and show us that even from the most mechanical actions there may issue forth that creative power which transforms us from within.

The first condition of all "correct practice" is to understand what the phrase "training on the inner way" means. Inner practice begins only after we have achieved technical mastery, in whatever activity it may be—even sport—and consists of endless repetition. Once the technique of some task has been perfected, each repetition of its practice mirrors our whole inner attitude. Every mistake that is made shows us something about ourselves. If this is understood, our efforts to accomplish daily tasks can, at the same time, become inner work on ourselves. Thus by means of this continuous repetition, the true, inward person begins to emerge. In this way the ordinary daily round can be transformed into "practice."

The second condition for this kind of practice is that we must be resolved and prepared to lead our life in the world in accordance with our inner law, and this means living our life in the service of a larger reality. Only by being faithful and committed to this service can we become whole. When all that we know and do becomes a means for the revelation of Greater Life in the world, then the Way may be attained,

and the ordinary day itself becomes one single field of practice. But so long as we try to gain something solely for
ourselves through this practice—whether it be the acquisi-
tion of higher faculties, extraordinary experiences, or tran-
quility, harmony, even our own salvation—we are bound to
miss the Way.

When essential being becomes inward knowing, we feel a
sudden change in ourselves. Relaxed and free, full of
strength and light, we are filled with a new and creative life.
Those things that lie heavily upon us grow lighter; problems
which have been causing anxiety no longer oppress us; and
events that in our ordinary state would plunge us into despair now lose their potency. Where every door seemed
closed, all are now open. We who in ourselves were poor
now feel rich, and in the midst of clamor we are peaceful and
calm. It is as though we were bathed in an invisible light
which warms and shines upon us. We sense about us a
radiance that shimmers through everything. But just as this
radiance can dawn upon us without warning, so can it as
suddenly disappear. We have no power to make it happen,
nor to retain it once it is there. The most we can do is to learn
to become prescient and aware of those attitudes which prepare us for such experiences and also, of course, those which
prevent them.

The world in which we live is not a vale of sorrows which
separates us from the peaks of the divine; rather it is a bridge
which unites us with those peaks. We need but penetrate the
obscuring mists that lie between us and consciousness and
tear down the obstructing walls that bar our way. This neces-
sitates living the ordinary day as practice. No special time
need be set aside for this. Each moment is a summons calling
us to recollect and test ourselves. There is no activity, serving whatever external purpose, that does not contain an
opportunity to dedicate ourselves more ardently to the
search for truth. No matter what we are doing—walking,
standing or sitting, writing, speaking or being silent, attacking something or defending ourselves, helping or serving

others—whatever the task, it is possible to carry it out with a posture and an attitude that will more and more establish the contact with being.

Our happiness depends on the fulfillment of our deepest longings. Our most fundamental longing is for something which in our essential being we already really *are*. Our happiness, therefore, depends on the extent to which we are able to conform to our inner destiny. But such a consummation is only possible insofar as we freely fulfill this intention in our daily life.

3 ✿ Earth and Space

CHÖGYAM TRUNGPA

When you see ordinary situations with extraordinary insight it is like discovering a jewel in rubbish. If work becomes part of your spiritual practice, then your regular, daily problems cease to be only problems and become a source of inspiration. Nothing is rejected as ordinary and nothing is taken as being particularly sacred, but all the substance and material available in life-situations is used.

However, work can also be an escape from creativity. Either you work frantically, filling in all the spaces and not allowing any spontaneity to develop, or else you are lazy, regarding work as something to revolt against, which indicates a fear of creativity. Instead of letting the creative process be, you follow your next preconception, fearing a spacious state of mind. Whenever a person feels depressed or is afraid, or the situation is not going smoothly, immediately he begins polishing a table or weeding the garden, trying to distract himself. He does not want to deal with the underlying problem so he seeks a kind of pleasure of the moment. He is frightened of the space, of any empty corner. Whenever there is an empty wall, he puts up another picture or hanging. And the more crowded his walls are, the more comfortable he feels.

True work is acting practically, relating to the earth directly. You could be working in the garden, in the house, washing dishes or doing whatever demands your attention. If you do not feel the relationship between earth and yourself, then the situation is going to turn chaotic. If you do not feel that every step, every situation reflects your state of mind, and therefore has spiritual significance, then the pattern of your life becomes full of problems, and you begin to wonder where these problems come from. They seem to spring from nowhere because you refuse to see the subtlety of life. Somehow, you cannot cheat, you cannot pretend to pour a cup of tea beautifully, you cannot act it. You must actually feel it, feel the earth and your relationship to it.

The Japanese tea ceremony is a good example of action that is in contact with earth. It begins by deliberately collecting the bowl, the napkin, the brush, the tea, and the boiling water. Tea is served and the guests drink deliberately, with a feeling of dealing with things properly. The ceremony also includes how to clean the bowls, how to put them away, how to finish properly. Clearing away is as important as starting.

It is extremely important to work, as long as you are not using work as an escape, as a way of ignoring the basic existence of a problem, particularly if you are interested in spiritual development. Work is one of the most subtle ways of acquiring discipline. You should not look down on someone who works in a factory or produces materialistic things. You learn a tremendous amount from such people. I think that many of our attitudinal problems about work come from a pseudosophistication of the analytic mind. You do not want to involve yourself physically at all. You want only to work intellectually or mentally.

This is a spiritual problem. Usually people interested in spiritual development think in terms of the importance of mind, that mysterious, high, and deep thing that we have decided to learn about. But strangely enough the profound and the transcendental are to be found in the factory. It may not fill you with bliss to look at it, it may not sound as good as the spiritual experiences that we have read about, but somehow reality is to be found there, in the way in which we relate with everyday problems. If we relate to them in a simple, earthy way, we will work in a more balanced manner, and things will be dealt with properly. If we are able to simplify ourselves to that extent, then we will be able to see the neurotic aspect of mind much more clearly. The whole pattern of thought, the internal game that goes on, becomes much less of a game. It becomes a very practical way of thinking in situations.

Awareness in work is very important. It could be the same sort of awareness one has in sitting meditation, the leap of experiencing the openness of space. This depends very much upon feeling the earth and the space together. You cannot feel earth unless you feel space. The more you feel the space, the more you feel the earth. The feeling of space between you and objects becomes a natural product of awareness, of openness, of peace and lightness. And the way to practice is not to concentrate upon things nor to try to be aware of yourself and the job at the same time, but you should have a general feeling of acknowledging this openness as you are working. Then you begin to feel that there is more room in which to do things, more room in which to work. It is a question of acknowledging the existence of the openness of a continual meditative state. You don't have to try to hold on to it or try to bring it about deliberately, but just acknowledge that vast energy of openness with a fraction-of-a-second flash to it. After acknowledging, then almost deliberately ignore its existence and continue your work. The openness will continue and you will begin to develop the actual feeling of the things with which you are working. The awareness that we are speaking of is not so much a question of constant awareness or of an object of mind, but it is a matter of becoming one with awareness, becoming one with open space. This means becoming one with the actual things with which you are dealing as well. So meditation becomes very easy; it is no longer an attempt to split yourself into different sections and different degrees of awareness, the watcher and the doer. You begin to have a real relationship with external objects and their beauty.

4 ❁ *This Very Moment*

CHARLOTTE JOKO BECK

Many years ago I was a piano major at Oberlin Conservatory. I was a very good student; not outstanding, but very good. And I very much wanted to study with one teacher who was undoubtedly the best. He'd take ordinary students and turn them into fabulous pianists. Finally I got my chance to study with *the* teacher.

When I went in for my lesson I found that he taught with two pianos. He didn't even say hello. He just sat down at his piano and played five notes, and then he said, "You do it." I was supposed to play it just the way he played it. I played it—and he said, "No." He played it again, and I played it again. Again he said, "No." Well, we had an hour of that. And each time he said, "No."

In the next three months I played about three measures, perhaps half a minute of music. Now I had thought I was pretty good: I'd played soloist with little symphony orchestras. Yet we did this for three months, and I cried most of those three months. He had all the marks of a real teacher, that tremendous drive and determination to make the student see. That's why he was so good. And at the end of three months, one day, he said, "Good." What had happened?

Finally, I had learned to listen. And as he said, if you can hear it, you can play it.

What had happened in those three months? I had the same set of ears I started with; nothing had happened to my ears. What I was playing was not technically difficult. What had happened was that I had learned to listen for the first time . . . and I'd been playing the piano for many years. I learned to pay attention. That was why he was such a great teacher: he taught his students to pay attention. After working with him they really heard, they really listened. When you can hear it, you can play it. And finished, beautiful pianists would finally come out of his studio.

It's that kind of attention which is necessary for spiritual practice. We call it samadhi, this total oneness with the object. But in my story that attention was relatively easy. It was with an object that I liked. This is the oneness of any great art, the great athlete, the person who passes well on the football field, the person who does well on the basketball court, anybody like that who has to learn to pay attention. It's that kind of samadhi.

Now that's one kind, and it's valuable. But what we have to do in spiritual practice is much harder. We have to pay attention to this very moment, the totality of what is happening right now. And the reason we don't want to pay attention is because it's not always pleasant. It doesn't suit us.

As human beings we have a mind that can think. We remember what has been painful. We constantly dream about the future, about the nice things we're going to have, or are going to happen to us. So we filter anything happening in the present through all that: "I don't like that. I don't have to listen to that. And I can even forget about it and start dreaming of what's going to happen." This goes on constantly: spinning, spinning, spinning, always trying to create life in a way that will be pleasant, that would make us safe and secure, so we feel good.

But when we do that we never see this right-here-now, this very moment. We can't see it because we're filtering. What's coming in is something quite different. Just ask any ten people who read this book. You'll find they all tell you something different. They'll forget the parts that don't quite catch them, they'll pick up something else, and they'll even block out the parts they don't like. Even when we go to a spiritual teacher we hear only what we want to hear. Being open to a teacher means not just hearing what you want to hear, but hearing the whole thing. And the teacher's not there simply to be nice to you.

So the crux of meditation is this: all we must do is constantly to create a little shift from the spinning world we've got in our heads to right-here-now. That's our practice. The intensity and ability to be right-here-now is what we have to develop. We have to be able to develop the ability to say, "No, I won't spin off up here," to make that choice. Moment by moment our practice is like a choice, a fork in the road: we can go this way, we can go that way. It's always a choice, moment by moment, between our nice world that we want to set up in our heads and what really is. And what really is, when we meditate, is often fatigue, boredom, and pain in our legs. What we learn from having to sit quietly with that discomfort is so valuable that if it didn't exist, it should. When you're in pain, you can't spin off. You have to stay with it. There's no place to go. So pain is really valuable.

Zen training is designed to enable us to live comfortable lives. But the only people who live comfortably are those who learn not to dream their lives away, but to be with what's right-here-now, no matter what it is: good, bad, nice, not nice, headache, being ill, being happy. It doesn't make any difference.

One mark of a mature Zen student is a sense of groundedness. When you meet one you sense it. They're with life as it's really happening, not as a fantasy version of it. And of course, the storms of life eventually hit them more lightly. If we can accept things just the way they are, we're not going to be greatly upset by anything. And if we do become upset it's over more quickly.

Let's look at the sitting process itself. What we need to do is to be with what's happening right now. You don't have to believe me; you can experiment for yourself. When I am drifting away from the present, what I do is listen to the traffic. I make sure there's nothing I miss. Nothing. I just really listen. And that's just as good as a koan, because it's what's happening this very moment. So as meditation practitioners you have a job to do, a very important job: to bring your life out of dreamland and into the real and immense reality that it is.

The job is not easy. It takes courage. Only people who have tremendous guts can do this practice for more than a short time. But we don't do it just for ourselves. Perhaps we do at first; that's fine. But as our life gets grounded, gets real, gets basic, other people immediately sense it, and what we are begins to influence everything around us.

We are, actually, the whole universe. But until you see that clearly, you have to work with what your teacher tells you to work with, having some faith in the total process. It's not only faith, it's also something like science. Others before you have done the experiment, and they've had some results from that. About all you can do is say, "Well, at least I can try the experiment. I can do it. I can work hard." That much any of us can do.

The Buddha is nothing but exactly what you are, right now: hearing the cars, feeling the pain in your legs, hearing my voice; that's the Buddha. You can't catch hold of it; the minute you try to catch it, it's changed. Being what we are at each moment means, for example, fully being our anger when we are angry. That kind of anger never hurts anybody because it's total, complete. We really feel this anger, this knot in our stomach, and we're not going to hurt anybody with it. The kind of anger that hurts people is when we smile sweetly and underneath we're seething.

When you sit, don't expect to be noble. When we give up this spinning mind, even for a few minutes, and just sit with what is, then this presence that we are is like a mirror. We see everything. We see what we are: our efforts to look good, to be first, or to be last. We see our anger, our anxiety, our pomposity, our so-called spirituality. Real spirituality is just being with all that. If we can really be with Buddha, who we are, then it transforms.

Shibayama Roshi said once, "This Buddha that you all want to see, this Buddha is very shy. It's hard to get him to come out and show himself." Why is that? Because the Buddha is ourselves, and we'll never see the Buddha until we're no longer attached to all this extra stuff. We've got to be willing to go into ourselves honestly. When we can be totally honest with what's happening right now, then we'll see it. We can't have just a piece of the Buddha. Buddhas come whole. Our practice has nothing to do with, "Oh, I should be good, I should be nice, I should be this . . . or that." I *am* who I am right now. And that very state of being is the Buddha.

THE FIRE OF ATTENTION

Back in the 1920s, when I was maybe eight or ten years old, and living in New Jersey where the winters are cold, we had a furnace in our house that burned coal. It was a big event on the block when the coal truck rolled up and all this stuff poured down the coal shute into the coal bin. I learned that there were two kinds of coal: one was called anthracite or hard coal, and the other was lignite, soft coal. My father told me about the difference in the way those two kinds of coal burned. Anthracite burns cleanly, leaving little ash. Lignite leaves lots of ash. When we burned lignite, the cellar became covered with soot and some of it got upstairs into the living room.

What does this have to do with our practice? Practice is about breaking our exclusive identification with ourselves. This process has sometimes been called purifying the mind. To "purify the mind" doesn't mean that you become holy or other than you are; it means to strip away that which keeps

a person—or a furnace—from functioning best. The furnace
functions best with hard coal. But unfortunately what we're
full of is *soft* coal. There's a saying in the Bible: "He is like
a refiner's fire." It's a common analogy, found in other religions as well. To sit in meditation is to be in the middle of
a refining fire. Eido Roshi said once, "This meditation hall
is not a peaceful haven, but a furnace room for the combustion of our egoistic delusions." A meditation hall is not a
place for bliss and relaxation, but a furnace room for the
combustion of our egoistic delusions. What tools do we
need to use? Only one. We've all heard of it, yet we use it
very seldom. It's called *attention*.

Attention is the cutting, burning sword, and our practice
is to use that sword as much as we can. None of us is very
willing to use it; but when we do—even for a few minutes—
some cutting and burning takes place. All practice aims to
increase our ability to be attentive, not just in meditation but
in every moment of our life.

There is no special time or place for great realization. As
Master Huang Po said, "On no account make a distinction
between the Absolute and the sentient world." It's nothing
more than parking your car, putting on your clothes, taking
a walk. But if soft coal is what we're burning, we're not going
to realize that. Soft coal simply means that the burning in our
life is not clean. We are unable to burn up each circumstance
as we encounter it. And the culprit is always our emotional
attachment to the circumstance. For example, perhaps your
boss asks you to do something unreasonable. At that moment what is the difference between burning soft coal and
hard coal? Or suppose we are looking for employment—but
the only work we can find is something we dislike. Or our
child gets into trouble at school . . . In dealing with those,
what is the difference between soft coal and hard coal? If
there isn't some comprehension of the difference, we have
wasted our hours in meditation. Most Zen students are chasing after Buddhahood. Yet Buddhahood *is* how you deal
with your boss or your child, your lover or your partner,

whoever. Our life is always absolute: that's all there is. The truth is not somewhere else. But we have minds that are trying to burn the past or the future. The living present—Buddhahood—is rarely encountered.

When the fire in the furnace is banked, and you want a brightly burning fire, what do you do? You increase the air intake. We are fires too. When the mind quiets down we can breathe more deeply and the oxygen intake goes up.

The mind quiets down because we observe it instead of getting lost in it. Then the breathing deepens and, when the fire really burns, there's nothing it can't consume. When the fire gets hot enough, there is no self, because now the fire is consuming everything; there is no separation between self and other.

THE RAZOR'S EDGE

Always we have an illusion of being separate, which we have created. When we're threatened or when life doesn't please us, we start worrying, we start thinking about a possible solution. And without exception there is no person who doesn't do this. We dislike being with life as it is because that can include suffering, and that is not acceptable to us. Whether it's a serious illness or a minor criticism or being lonely or disappointed—that is not acceptable to us. We have no intention of putting up with that or just being that if we can possibly avoid it. We want to fix the problem, solve it, get rid of it. That is when we need to understand the practice of walking the razor's edge. Spiritual practice is about understanding the razor's edge and how to work with it.

The point at which we need to practice walking the razor's edge is whenever we begin to be upset (angry, irritated, resentful, jealous). First, we need to *know* we're upset. Many people don't even know this when it happens. So step number one is, be aware that upset is taking place. When we meditate and begin to know our minds and our reactions, we begin to be aware that yes, we are upset.

That's the first step, but it's not the razor's edge. We're still separate, but now we know it. How do we bring our separated life together? To walk the razor's edge is to do that; we have once again to be what we basically are, which is seeing, touching, hearing, smelling; we have to experience whatever our life is, right this second. If we're upset we have to experience being upset. If we're frightened, we have to experience being frightened. If we're jealous we have to experience being jealous. And such experiencing is physical; it has nothing to do with the thoughts going on about the upset.

When we are experiencing nonverbally we are walking the razor's edge—we are the present moment. When we walk the edge the agonizing states of separateness are pulled together, and we experience perhaps not happiness but joy. Understanding the razor's edge (and not just understanding it, but doing it) is what meditation practice is. The reason it's difficult is that we don't want to do it. We know we don't want to do it. We want to escape from it.

If I feel that I've been hurt by you, I want to stay with my thoughts about the hurt. I want to increase my separation; it feels good to be consumed by those fiery, self-righteous thoughts. By thinking, I try to avoid feeling the pain. The more sophisticated my practice becomes, the more quickly I see this trap and return to experiencing the pain, the razor's edge. And where I might once have stayed upset for two years, the upset shrinks to two months, two weeks, two minutes. Eventually I can experience an upset as it happens and stay right on the razor's edge.

In fact the enlightened life is simply being able to walk that edge all the time. And while I don't know of anyone who can always do this, certainly after years of practice we can do it much of the time. It is joy to walk that edge.

Still, it is necessary to acknowledge that most of the time we want nothing to do with that edge; we want to stay separate. We want the sterile satisfaction of wallowing in "I am right." That's a poor satisfaction, of course, but still we will usually settle for a diminished life rather than experience life as it is when that seems painful and distasteful.

All troublesome relationships at home and work are born of the desire to stay separate. By this strategy we hope to be a separate person who really exists, who is important. When we walk the razor's edge we're not important; we're no-self, embedded in life. This we fear—even though life as no-self is pure joy. Our fear drives us to stay over here in our lonely self-righteousness. The paradox: only in walking the razor's edge, in experiencing the fear directly, can we know what it is to have no fear.

Now I realize we can't see this all at once or do it all at once. Sometimes we jump onto the razor's edge and then hop off, like water dropped on a sizzling frying pan. That may be all we can do at first, and that's fine. But the more we practice, the more comfortable we become there. We find it's the only place where we are at peace. So many people say, "I want to be at peace." Yet there may be little understanding of how peace is to be found. Walking the razor's edge is it. No one wants to hear that. We want somebody who will take our fear away or promise us happiness. No one wants to hear the truth, and we won't hear it until we are ready to hear it.

On the razor's edge, embedded in life, there is no "me" and no "you." This kind of practice benefits all sentient beings and that, of course, is what spiritual practice is about . . . my life and your life growing is wisdom and compassion.

5 ❁ Not Preferring Samsara or Nirvana

PEMA CHÖDRÖN

If you wanted to pare phenomena down, all there would be are stillness and occurrence: space, and that which is continually born out of space, and returns into space—stillness and occurrence. Sometimes it's called the background and the foreground. In any case, what I'd like to talk about is not preferring stillness or occurrence, or, you could say, not preferring the busyness of samsara or the stillness of nirvana.

Usually there is some kind of bias. There are two common forms of human neurosis. One is getting all caught up in worry and fear and hope, in wanting and not wanting, and things: jobs, families, romances, houses, cars, money, vacations, entertainment, the mountains, the desert, Europe, Mexico, Jamaica, the Black Hole of Calcutta, prison, war or peace, and so on. So many of us are caught in all that occurs, somehow captured by occurrence as if we were caught in a whirlpool. In samsara we continually try to get away from the pain by seeking pleasure, and in doing so, we just keep going around and around and around. I'm so hot I open all the windows, and then I'm so cold I put on a sweater. Then it itches, so I put cream on my arms, and then that's sticky, so I go take a bath. Then I'm cold, so I close the window, and on and on and on. I'm lonely, so I get married, and then I'm always fighting with my husband or my wife, so I start another love affair, and then my wife or husband threatens to leave me and I'm caught in the confusion of what to do next, and on and on and on. We are always trying to get out of the boiling pot into some kind of coolness, always trying to escape and therefore never really fully settling down and appreciating. That's called samsara. In other words, somehow we have this preference for occurrence, so we're always working in that framework of trying to get comfortable through political beliefs and philosophies and religions and everything, trying to gain pleasure in all that occurs.

The other neurosis—which is just as common—is to get caught by peace and quiet, or liberation, or freedom. When I was traveling, I met some people who had formed a group based on their belief that a flying saucer was going to come and take them away from all of this. They were waiting for the flying saucers to come and liberate them from the grossness of this earth. They talked about transcending the awfulness of life, getting into the space and the clarity and the blissfulness of not being hindered in any way, just completely free. When the spaceship took them away, they were going to a place where there weren't going to be any problems. This is what we all do in a subtle way. If we have an experience of clarity or bliss, we want to keep it going. That's what a lot of addiction is about, wanting to feel good forever, but it usually ends up not working out. However, it's a very common neurosis, being caught by this wanting to stay out there, wanting to stay in the space, like some friends of mine in the seventies who decided to take LSD every day so they could just stay out there. Sometimes that's expressed by arranging your life in such a way that it's very quiet, very smooth, very simplified; you become so attached to it that you just want to keep it like that. You resist and resent any kind of noisy situation like a lot of children or dogs coming in and messing everything up. There are some people who have tremendous insight into the nature of reality as vast and wonderful—what is sometimes called sacred outlook—but then they become completely dissatisfied with ordinary life. Rather than that glimpse of sacred outlook actually enriching their life, it makes them feel more poverty-stricken all the time. Often the reason that people go from neurosis into psychosis is that they see that spaciousness, how vast things are and how the world actually works, but then they cling to their insight and become completely caught there. It has been said, quite accurately, that a psychotic person is drowning in the very same things that a mystic swims in.

What I'm saying here is that ego can use anything to re-create itself, whether it's occurrence or spaciousness, whether it's what we call samsara or what we call nirvana. There is a bias in many religious groups toward wanting to get away from the earth and the pain of the earth and never having to experience this awfulness again—"Let's just leave it behind and rest in nirvana." Yet as one Buddhist chant puts it, the Buddha "does not abide in nirvana. He abides in the ultimate perfection." One could assume that if he does not abide in nirvana, the ultimate perfection must be some sense of completely realizing that samsara and nirvana are one, not preferring stillness or occurrence but being able to live fully with both.

Recently, in a friend's kitchen I saw on the wall a quotation from one of Chögyam Trungpa Rinpoche's talks, which said: "Hold the sadness and pain of samsara in your heart and at the same time the power and vision of the Great Eastern Sun. Then the warrior can make a proper cup of tea." I was struck by it because when I read it I realized that I myself have some kind of preference for stillness. The notion of holding the sadness and pain of samsara in my heart rang true, but I realized I didn't do that; at least, I had a definite preference for the power and vision of the Great Eastern Sun, the quality of being continually awake. My reference point was always to be awake and to live fully, to remember the Great Eastern Sun. But what about holding the sadness and pain of samsara in my heart at the same time? The quotation really made an impression on me. It was completely true: if you can live with the sadness of human life (what Rinpoche often called the tender heart or genuine heart of sadness), if you can be willing to feel fully and acknowledge continually your own sadness and the sadness of life, but at the same time not be drowned in it, because you also remember the vision and power of the Great Eastern Sun, you experience balance and completeness, joining heaven and earth, joining vision and practicality. We talk about men and women joining heaven and earth, but really they are already joined. There isn't any separation between samsara and nirvana, between the sadness and pain of samsara and the vision and power of the Great Eastern Sun. One can hold them both in one's heart, which is actually the purpose of practice. As a result of that, one can make a proper cup of tea.

Ritual is about joining vision and practicality, heaven and earth, samsara and nirvana. When things are properly understood, one's whole life is like a ritual or a ceremony. Then all the gestures of life are mudra* and all the sounds of life are mantra†—sacredness is everywhere. This is what's behind ritual, these formalized things that get carried down in the religions of different cultures. Ritual, when it's heartfelt, is like a time capsule. It's as if thousands of years ago somebody had a clear, unobstructed view of magic, power, and sacredness, and realized that if he went out each morning and greeted the sun in a very stylized way, perhaps by doing a special chant and making offerings and perhaps by bowing, that it connected him to that richness. Therefore he taught his children to do that, and the children taught their chil-

---

*Symbolic hand gestures that accompany tantric practices to state the quality of different moments of meditation.
†Words or syllables that express the quintessence of various energies.

dren, and so on. So thousands of years later, people are still doing it and connecting with exactly the same feeling. All the rituals that get handed down are like that. Someone can have an insight, and rather than its being lost, it can stay alive through ritual. For example, Rinpoche often said that the dharma, the teachings of the Buddha, are like a recipe for fresh-baked bread. Thousands of years ago someone discovered how to bake bread, and because the recipe was passed down for years and years, you can still make fresh bread that you can eat right now.

What made me think of ritual as the joining of the sadness and pain of samsara with the vision of the Great Eastern Sun was that somehow it's simply using ordinary things to express our appreciation for life. The sun comes up in the morning, we can use the sound of a gong to call us to the shrine room, we can put our hands together and bow to each other, we can hold up our eating bowls with three fingers in the same way that people have been doing for centuries. Through these rituals we express our appreciation for the fact that there's food and objects and the richness of the world.

Genuine, heartfelt ritual helps us reconnect with power and vision as well as with the sadness and pain of the human condition. When the power and vision come together, there's some sense of doing things properly for their own sake. Making a proper cup of tea means that you thoroughly and completely make that tea because you appreciate the tea and the boiling water and the fact that together they make something that's nourishing and delicious, that lifts one's spirit. You don't do it because you're worried that someone's not going to like you if you don't do it right. Nor do you do it so fast that it's over before you even realize that you made a cup of tea, let alone that you drank six cups. So whether it's smoking a cigarette or drinking a cup of tea or making your bed or washing the dishes—whatever it might be—it's ritual in the sense of doing it properly, if you can hold the sadness in your heart as well as the vision of the Great Eastern Sun.

Native peoples have always understood about the seasons, the sun coming up and going down, and the earth, and they have rituals to celebrate all those things. So that no one can miss the fact that we are all connected, puberty rites and all the other ceremonies are well choreographed, like a beautiful dance. The old people know how to do these things and they pass the knowledge on, and that's called lineage. Black Elk was a Sioux holy man in the 1880s, a time when his people were losing heart, losing their spirit, because the way they had always lived, which had given them so much sense of being connected, was being destroyed. Yet it was still early enough that they had not lost all of it. When he was nine years old, he had a vision of how he might save his people, a vision about horses coming from the four directions. In one direction the horses were white, in another direction sorrel, in another direction buckskin, in the last direction black. With them came maidens carrying sacred objects, and the grandfathers singing prophecies. Each direction had its whole ritualistic symbolism. He never told his vision to anyone, because he thought nobody would believe him. But when he was about seventeen years old, he felt he was going a little crazy, so he finally told the medicine man, who immediately understood and said, "We have to act it out." They did the whole thing, painting their bodies in the way he had seen, enacting the entire vision.

When he was in his twenties, things had completely fallen apart. He ended up being in Buffalo Bill's Wild West Show, with some other Indians. They were taken on a "fire-boat" to Europe to do a show in London with all their ponies and their Indian clothing. One night Queen Victoria came to see the show. Now, you wouldn't think there would be much in common between Black Elk, an Oglala Sioux from the Plains in 1886, and Queen Victoria, but that night nobody else came—just Queen Victoria in a shining carriage and her entourage. When the show was finished, she stood up and shook hands with all of them with her little soft hand. He really liked her. Then she bowed to them, and they were so impressed with her and her bearing that the women did something called the tremolo and the men did the whooping, and then they all bowed to her. Black Elk described her as "Grandmother England." She had so much majesty and presence. "She was little and fat and she was good to us." About a month later, she invited them to her Silver Jubilee. As he said, when he and the other native people got to this great big building, everyone was yelling, "Jubilee! Jubilee! Jubilee!" He said he still didn't know what that meant, but then he was able to describe what he saw. First in her golden coach came Queen Victoria, the horses all covered in gold and her clothes all gold like fire. Then in the black coach with the black horses was the queen's grandson, and in the black coach with the gray horses were her relatives. He described all the coaches and all the horses and then all the men arriving in their beautiful clothing, riding on black horses with plumes. The whole ceremony meant something to them. He said that before the Jubilee he felt like a man who had never had a vision, but that seeing all that pomp and circumstance reconnected him with his heart. When Queen Victoria in her golden coach came by the Indians, she had the coach stopped and she stood up and she bowed to them again. Again they threw all their things in the air and whooped and hollered and did the tremolo, and then they sang to Grandmother England. It cheered them up.

Ritual can be the Queen of England or the people of the Great Plains. It somehow transcends time and space. In any case, I think it has something to do with holding the sadness and pain of samsara in your heart and at the same time holding the vision and power of the Great Eastern Sun. Our whole life could be a ritual. We could learn to stop when the sun goes down and when the sun comes up. We could learn to listen to the wind; we could learn to notice that it's raining or snowing or hailing or calm. We could reconnect with the weather that is ourselves, and we could realize that it's sad. The sadder it is, the vaster it is, and the vaster it is, the more our heart opens. We can stop thinking that good practice is when it's smooth and calm, and bad practice is when it's rough and dark. If we can hold it all in our hearts, then we can make a proper cup of tea.

6 ✿ Seeing without the Observer

J. KRISHNAMURTI

It was a clear morning, though soon clouds would be gathering. As one looked out of the window, the trees, the fields were very clear. A curious thing is happening; there is a heightening of sensitivity. Sensitivity, not only to beauty but also to all other things. The blade of grass was astonishingly green; that one blade of grass contained the whole spectrum of color; it was intense, dazzling and such a small thing, so easy to destroy. Those trees were all of life, their height and their depth; the lines of those sweeping hills and the solitary trees were the expression of all time and space; and the mountains against the pale sky were beyond all the gods of man. It was incredible to see, feel all this by just looking out of the window. One's eyes were cleansed.

•

Meditation is this attention in which there is an awareness, without choice, of the movement of all things, the cawing of the crows, the electric saw ripping through the wood, the trembling of leaves, the noisy stream, a boy calling, the feelings, the motives, the thoughts chasing each other and going deeper, the awareness of total consciousness. And in this

attention, time as yesterday pursuing in the space of tomorrow and the twisting and turning of consciousness has
become quiet and still. In this stillness there is an immeasur-
able, not comparable movement; a movement that has no
being, that's the essence of bliss and death and life.

•

There's a sacredness which is not of thought, nor of a feeling
resuscitated by thought. It is not recognizable by thought nor
can it be utilized by thought. Thought cannot formulate it.
But there's a sacredness, untouched by any symbol or word.
It is not communicable. It is a fact.

A fact is to be seen and the seeing is not through the word.
When a fact is interpreted, it ceases to be a fact; it becomes
something entirely different. The seeing is of the highest
importance. This seeing is out of time-space; it's immediate,
instantaneous. And what's seen is never the same again.

•

How few see the mountains or a cloud. They look, make
some remarks and pass on. Words, gestures, emotions prevent seeing. A tree, a flower is given a name, put into a
category and that's that. You see a landscape through an
archway or from a window, and if you happen to be an artist
or are familiar with art, you say almost immediately, it is like
those medieval paintings or mention some name of some
recent painter. Or if you are a writer, you look in order to
describe; if you are a musician, probably you have never seen
the curve of a hill or the flowers at your feet; you are caught
up in your daily practice, or ambition has you by the throat.
If you are a professional of some kind, probably you never
see. But to see there must be humility whose essence is
innocency. There's that mountain with the evening sun on it;
to see it for the first time, to see it, as though it had never
been seen before, to see it with innocency, to see it with eyes
that have been bathed in emptiness, that have not been hurt
with knowledge—to see then is an extraordinary experience.

•

It was a lovely evening, the sky was clear and, in spite of city
light, the stars were brilliant; though the tower was flooded

with light from all sides, one could see the distant horizon and, down below, patches of light were on the river; though there was the everlasting roar of traffic, it was a peaceful evening. Meditation crept on one like a wave covering the sands. It was not a meditation which the brain could capture in its net of memory; it was something to which the total brain yielded without any resistance. It was a meditation that went far beyond any formula, method. In its movement it took everything in, the stars, the noise, the quiet, and the stretch of water. But there was no meditator; the meditator, the observer must cease for meditation to be. The breaking up of the meditator is also meditation; but when the meditator ceases then there's an altogether different meditation.

It was very early in the morning; Orion was coming up over the horizon and the Pleiades were nearly overhead. The roar of the city had quietened and at that hour there were no lights in any of the windows and there was a pleasant, cool breeze.

In complete attention there is no experiencing; there's no center which experiences, nor a periphery within which experience can take place. Attention is not concentration which is narrowing, limiting. Total attention includes, never excludes.

What brings about total attention? Not any method nor any system. Seeing the whole fabric of non-attention is total attention. An attentive mind is an empty mind.

•

Early this morning, the sky was without a cloud; the sun was coming up behind the Tuscan hills, grey with olive, with dark cypress. There were no shadows on the river and the aspen leaves were still. A few birds that had not yet migrated were chattering and the river seemed motionless; as the sun came up behind the river it cast long shadows on the quiet water. But a gentle breeze was coming over the hills and through the valleys; it was among the leaves, setting them trembling and dancing with the morning sun on them. There were long and short shadows, fat ones and little ones on the brown sparkling waters; a solitary chimney began to smoke, grey fumes carrying across the trees. It was a lovely morning, full of enchantment and beauty, there were so many shadows and so many leaves trembling. There was perfume in the air and though it was an autumnal sun there was the breath of spring. A small car was going up the hill, making an awful noise, but a thousand shadows remained motionless. It was a lovely morning.

In the afternoon yesterday, it began suddenly, in a room overlooking a noisy street; the strength and the beauty of the otherness was spreading from the room outward over the traffic, past the gardens, and beyond the hills. It was there immense and impenetrable; it was there in the afternoon, and just as one was getting into bed it was there with furious intensity, a benediction of great holiness. There is no getting used to it for it is always different, there's something always new, a new quality, a subtle significance, a new light, something that had not been seen before. It was not a thing to be stored up, remembered and examined, at leisure; it was there and no thought could approach for the brain was still and there was no time, to experience, to store up. It was there and all thought became still.

The intense energy of life is always there, night and day. It is without friction, without direction, without choice and effort. It is there with such intensity that thought and feeling cannot capture it to mold it according to their fancies, beliefs, experiences, and demands. It is there with such abundance that nothing can diminish it.

•

There were several people in the room, some sitting on the floor and some on chairs; there was the quietness of appreciation and enjoyment. A man was playing on an eight-stringed instrument. He was playing with his eyes closed, delighted as the little audience. It was pure sound and on that sound one rode, far and very deep; each sound carried one deeper. The quality of sound that instrument produced made the journey infinite; from the moment he touched it till the moment he stopped, it was the sound that mattered not the instrument, not the man, not the audience. It had the effect of shutting out all other sound, even the fireworks that the boys were setting off; you heard them crash and crack but it was part of the sound and the sound was everything—the cicadas that were singing, the boys laughing, the call of a small girl and the sound of silence. He must have played for over half an hour and during that entire period the journey, far and deep, continued; it was not a journey that is taken in imagination, on the wings of thought, or in the frenzy of emotion. Such journeys are short, with some meaning or pleasure; this had no meaning and no pleasure. There was only sound and nothing else, no thought, no feeling. That sound carried one through and beyond the confines of time, and quietly it went on into great immense emptiness from which there was no return. What is returning always is memory, a thing that has been, but here there was no memory, no experience. Fact has no shadow, no memory.

•

The clouds were piling up to the south-west driven by a strong wind; they were magnificent, great billowing clouds, full of fury and space; they were white and dark grey, rain-bearing, filling the sky. The old trees were angry with them and the wind. They wanted to be left alone, though they wanted rain; it would wash them again clean, wash away all the dust and their leaves would sparkle again but they didn't like being disturbed, like old people. The garden had so many flowers, so many colors, and each flower was doing a dance, a skip and a jump, and every leaf was astir; even the little blades of grass on the little lawn were being shaken. And two old, thin women were weeding it; two old women, old before their age, thin and worn out; they were squatting upon the lawn, chatting and weeding, leisurely; they weren't all there, they were somewhere else, carried away by their thoughts, though they were weeding and talking. They looked intelligent, their eyes sparkling, but perhaps too many children and lack of good food had made them old and weary. You became them, they were you and the grass and the clouds; it wasn't a verbal bridge over which you crossed out of pity or out of some vague, unfamiliar sentiment; you were not thinking at all, nor were your emotions stirred. They were you and you were they; distance and time had ceased. A car came with a chauffeur and he entered into that world. His shy smile and salute were those of yours and you were wondering at whom he was smiling and whom he was saluting; he was feeling a little awkward, not quite used to that feeling of being together. The women and chauffeur were you and you were they; the barrier which they had built was gone and as the clouds overhead went by, it all seemed a part of a widening circle, including so many things, the filthy road and the splendid sky and the passer-by. It was like a flame that burned its way through everything leaving no mark, no ashes; it wasn't an experience, with its memories, to be repeated. They were you and you were they and it died with the mind.

It is strange, the desire to show off or to be somebody. It seems so impossibly difficult to be simple, to be what you are and not pretend. To be what you are is in itself very arduous. You can always pretend, put on a mask, but to be what you are is an extremely complex affair; because you are always changing; you are never the same and each moment reveals a new facet, a new depth, a new surface. You can't be all this at one moment, for each moment brings its own change. So if you are at all intelligent, you give up being anything. You think you are very sensitive and an incident, a fleeting thought, shows that you are not; you think you are clever, well-read, artistic, moral, but turn round the corner, you find you are none of these things but that you are deeply ambitious, envious, insufficient, brutal, and anxious. You are all these things turn by turn and you want something to be continuous, permanent, of course only that which is profitable, pleasurable. So you run after that and all the many other yous are clamoring to have their way, to have their fulfillment. So you became the battle-field and generally

ambition, with all its pleasures and pain, is gaining, with
envy and fear.

So to be what you are is an extremely arduous affair; if you
are at all awake, you know all these things and the sorrow of
it all. So you drown yourself in your work, in your belief, in
your fantastic ideals and meditations. By then you have
become old and ready for the grave, if you are not already
dead inwardly. To put away all these things, with their contradictions and increasing sorrow, and be nothing is the most
natural and intelligent thing to do. But before you can be
nothing, you must have unearthed all these hidden things,
exposing them and so understanding them. To understand
these hidden urges and compulsions, you will have to be
aware of them, without choice, as with death; then in the
pure act of seeing, they will wither away and you will be
without sorrow and so be as nothing. To be as nothing is not
a negative state; the very denial of everything you have been
is the most positive action.

•

Without the appreciation of beauty and without the sensitive awareness of it, there is no love. This sensitive awareness
of nature, of the river, of the sky, of the people, of the filthy
road, is affection. The essence of affection is sensitivity. But
most people are afraid of being sensitive; to them to be
sensitive is to get hurt and so they harden themselves and so
preserve their sorrow. But being sensitive is not personal and
when it is, it leads to misery. To break through this personal
reaction is to love, and love is for the one and the many; it
is not restricted to the one or to the many. To be sensitive,
all the senses must be fully alive, active. To be sensitively
aware of thought, of feeling, of the world about you, of your
office and of nature, is to explode from moment to moment
in affection. Without affection, every action becomes bur-
densome and mechanical and leads to decay.

•

Under the trees it was very quiet; there were so many birds
calling, singing, chattering, endlessly restless. The branches

were huge, beautifully shaped, polished, smooth, and it was quite startling to see them, and they had a sweep and a grace that brought tears to the eyes and made you wonder at the things of the earth. The earth had nothing more beautiful than the tree and when it died it would still be beautiful; every branch naked, open to the sky, bleached by the sun and there would be birds resting upon its nakedness. But now the tree was alive, marvelous, and there was plenty of shade and the blazing sun never touched you; you could sit there by the hour and see and listen to everything that was alive and dead, outside and inside. You cannot see and listen to the outside without wandering on to the inside. Really the outside is the inside and the inside is the outside and it is difficult, almost impossible to separate them. You look at this magnificent tree and you wonder who is watching whom and presently there is no watcher at all. Everything is so intensely alive and there is only life and the watcher is as dead as that leaf. There is no dividing line between the tree, the birds, and that man sitting in the shade, and the earth that is so abundant. The birds have become silent for it is getting dark and everything is slowly becoming quiet, ready for the night. The brain, that marvellous, sensitive, alive thing, is utterly still, only watching, listening without a moment of reaction, without recording, without experiencing, only seeing and listening.

•

It was a beautiful evening, with the setting sun behind the trees; on that path you were far away from anywhere, there were scattered villages all around but you were far away and nothing could come near you. It was not in space, time, or distance; you were far away and there was no measure. The depth was not in fathoms; there was a depth that had no height, no circumference. An occasional villager passed you by, carrying the few meager things that he had bought in town and as he went by, almost touching you, he had not come near you. You were far away, in some unknown world that had no dimension; even if you wanted to know, you couldn't know it. It was too far away from the known; it had no relationship with the known. It wasn't a thing you experience; there was nothing to be experienced, and besides all experiencing is always in the field of the known, recognized by that which has been. You were far away, immeasurably far, but the trees, the yellow flowers, and the ear of the wheat were astonishingly close, closer than your thought and marvelously alive, with intensity and beauty that could never wither.

The man on the bicycle was singing in a rather hoarse and tired voice, coming back with the rattling empty milk-cans from the city; he was eager to talk to someone and as he passed by he said something, hesitated, recovered and went on. The moon was casting shadows now, dark and almost transparent ones, and the smell of the night was deepening. And around the bend of the path was the river; it seemed to be lighted from within, with a thousand candles; the light was soft with silver and pale gold and utterly still, bewitched by the moon. The Pleiades were overhead and Orion was well up in the sky and a train was puffing up the grade to cross the bridge. Time had stopped and beauty was there with love and death. And on the new bamboo bridge there was no one, not even a dog. The little stream was full of stars.

7 ❂ Are You Here?

A. H. ALMAAS

"Are you here?" Are you really here in this room? I don't mean is your body here, because that is obviously the case. But are *you* here? Do you feel that you are here in the room? Are you aware of being present here, and of your actual experience in this moment? Or are you lost in thoughts, fantasies, plans, emotional reactions? Are you here, or are you busy liking and disliking? Are you here, or are you busy judging yourself and everything else?

Are you here now, or are you trying to be here, making a token effort because this is what we are talking about? Are you aware of everything and everyone around you? Are you aware of your surroundings, or are you lost in a whirlwind of thoughts? When you hear the question, "Are you here?" it's not important in answering that you try to be good or correct. It's important only to sincerely explore for yourself, are you here or not? Are you in your body or oblivious, or only aware of parts of it? When I say, "Are you in your body?" I mean, "Are you completely filling your body?" I want to know whether you are in your feet, or just have feet. Do you live in them, or are they just things you use when you walk? Are you in your belly, or do you just know vaguely that you have a belly? Or is it just for food?

Are you really in your hands, or do you move them from a distance? Are you present in your cells, inhabiting and filling your body? If you aren't in your body, what significance is there in your experience this moment? Are you preparing, so that you can be here in the future? Are you setting up conditions by saying to yourself, "When such and such happens I'll have time, I'll be here"? If you are not here, what are you saving yourself for?

Regardless of the stories you tell yourself, at this moment, this very moment, there is only this moment, here, now. Nothing else exists. For your direct experience, only the here and now is relevant. Only now is real. And it is always like that. At each moment, only that moment exists. So we need to ask why we put ourselves on hold, waiting for the right time, waiting for the right circumstances to arise in the future. Maybe the right time will never come. Maybe the conditions you have in mind will never come together for you. When will you begin to exist then? When will you begin to be here, to live? Regardless of the ideas about past and future that dominate your experience, right at this moment only this moment exists, and only this moment has any significance for you. The most direct and obvious fact of experience is that the moment, the here and now, is all that exists. This is all there is for this moment. Whatever is happening at this moment, that is your life. The future is not your life; it never arrives. What is actually here is always only this moment.

So can you let yourself be? I am not suggesting that you let yourself be to get anything or do anything, even to understand anything. I mean just to be. Are you giving yourself the simple privilege of being, of existence? Why do you think that what you do, what you have, what you get or don't get are more important than just being here? Why are you always wanting to get something or go somewhere? Why not just relax and be here, simply existing in all your cells, inhabiting all your body? When are you going to let yourself descend from your lofty preoccupations, and simply land where you are?

Stop striving after all kinds of things; stop dreaming, scheming, planning, working, achieving, attempting, moving, manipulating, trying to be something, trying to get somewhere. You forget the simplest, most obvious thing, which is to be here. If you are not in your body, you miss the source of all significance, meaning, and satisfaction. How can you feel the satisfaction, if you aren't here? We miss who we are, which is fundamentally beingness, existence. If we are not here, we exist only on the fringes of reality. We don't sufficiently value simply being. Instead, we value what we want to accomplish, or what we want to possess. It is our biggest mistake. It is called the "great betrayal."

We are always looking for pleasure, frantically seeking happiness in many ways, and totally missing the simplest, most fundamental pleasure, which actually is also the greatest pleasure: just being here. When we are really present, the presence itself is made out of fullness, contentment, and blissful pleasure.

Our habits and conditioning lead us to forget the greatest treasure we have, our birthright—the pleasure and lightness of existence. We think that we will have pleasure or delight if we fulfill a certain plan, if a certain dream comes true, if someone we care for likes us, if we take a wonderful trip. This attitude is an insult to who we are. We are the pleasure, we are the joy, we are the most profound significance and the highest value. When we understand this, we see that it's ridiculous to think that we will get pleasure and joy through these external things—by doing this or that, or receiving approval or love from this or that person. We see then that we have been misinformed; we have been barking up the wrong tree.

Happiness, value, and pleasure are not the result of anything. These qualities are part of our fundamental nature. If we simply allow ourselves to be, this is our natural experience. You are the most precious thing in the universe, but you behave as if you are the poorest, most trivial thing there is. It doesn't really take much to see this. Just stop the whirlwind that goes on. Let yourself relax and be there. You can allow yourself to do it wherever you are. You don't have to be in the Canary Islands to be happy. You don't have to be with someone you are in love with, and who loves you, to be happy. Putting these conditions on your happiness is a degrading way of looking at yourself. Sure, you can be happy in the Canaries or with someone you love, but how about the rest of the time?

You abandon yourself, then start looking for satisfaction. You feel that something's missing, so you are always searching, becoming more and more frantic as all the things you acquire or accomplish don't fill you. This whole pattern occurs because you have stopped being. If you just let yourself be there, there is nowhere to go, nothing to look for, because it's all there. It is not that some people are satisfied by being and others not; no, we all feel satisfied when we are ourselves. It is a quality of our human nature. It is our natural endowment. It is the meaning of being a human being. The only thing we need do is to let ourselves be.

If you simply feel yourself at this moment, even if you don't feel your being in a full, satisfying way, you will naturally become aware of what is blocking your being. What is stopping me from being at this moment? Why do I want to go somewhere else? Why am I always thinking about what's going to make me happy? We can become naturally curious, and begin to unravel the beliefs, hopes and fears that create the blocks to being aware of our being.

When we stop to consider, we recognize that happiness is not something we're going to get somewhere, nor is it the result of some action we take. The very fabric of our being-ness is itself what we are always actually looking for. We seek pleasure, joy, happiness, peace, strength, power. But these are simply aspects of our existence. Our nature, our origin is the most precious thing there is. The existence itself is a delight. This existence, this delight, is the very center of reality, all the time.

Because we forget our origin and our true nature, we tend to stay on the fringes of existence and never let ourselves live in and from the center of ourselves. It's quite a tragic story. When teachers tell you that you are asleep, or have gone astray, they mean that you have gone astray from your existence. You are asleep to your beingness. But it's not exactly that you have gone astray in the sense that you were somewhere else, lost, and now you're here. Actually, you were here all the time. You have actually always been here, but you kept looking elsewhere. Your beingness is what senses, what looks, what feels.

We are a beingness, not a thought following another thought. We are something much more fundamental, more substantial than that. We are a beingness, an existence, a presence that impregnates the present and fills our body. We go so far away from ourselves, but what we are looking for is so near. We constantly put our attention on whether the situation is what we want or don't want. Is it good or bad? But the significance of any experience is our mere presence, nothing else. The content of any experience is simply an external manifestation of that central presence.

So what is the point of waiting? What exactly are you waiting for? Is somebody going to give you what you always wanted? Will a train come from Heaven bringing you goodies? But nothing that could ever happen could be as good, as precious, as who you are.

What stops you from being, from being present, is nothing but your hope for the future. Hoping for something to be different keeps you looking for some future fantasy. But it is a mirage; you'll never get there. The mirage stops you from seeing the obvious, the preciousness of Being. It is a great distortion, a great misunderstanding of what will fulfill you. When you follow the mirage you are rejecting yourself.

Of course, when you let yourself be, as you let yourself sink into reality, you might experience unpleasant things; but these are simply the barriers that stop you from being. In time, with presence, they will dissolve. You might experience discomfort, fear, hurt, various negative feelings. These are the things that you're trying to avoid by not being here. But they are just accumulations of what has been swept under the rug of unconsciousness; they are not you. They are what you confront on the way to beingness. When we acknowledge and understand these feelings while being present, they dissolve, because the idea of ourselves that they are based on is not real.

When the illusions dissolve, what is real, your nature, will surface and remain. You go through a process of purification, not because Being itself is sullied, but because you have so many accumulated assumptions and beliefs about reality. If you continue to hope, and tell yourself stories, you will remain asleep, because reality is still the way it is whether you like it or not. The mirage hasn't worked for you yet and it will not work with more persistence. Would you want it any other way? Would you want your happiness to depend on something other than your nature?

Our work is not to get somewhere or to accomplish something, but to allow our Being to emerge. Just inhabit your body. We're not talking about something you do once in a while, when you meditate, and the rest of the time you do the important things in your life. That's how we think: "I'll meditate now, and then get on with my day, get on with my important agenda." What's important? You're important. You don't need to do anything important to be important. You don't have to achieve enlightenment or accomplish any noble action to give importance to your life. You are. That is the most important thing there is. You're very special, always. You are not important because someone thinks you're special, nor because of any unusual capacities or accomplishments. You are important because of your nature; you cannot help being important and precious. Nothing can prove it or disprove it.

You are important because without your actual presence, there is no significance in life, no value in life. When you are conscious of your existence the experience is unmitigated pleasure. This pleasure is there regardless of what you're doing—scrubbing floors, going to the bathroom, creating something wonderful. Every moment is precious, and lived to the fullest. You are not the feelings or the thoughts or the content of your awareness. None of these are who you are. You are the fullness of your Being, the substance of your presence.

PART TWO

✿ Creativity, Work, and Fresh Perception

Let the beauty that we love be what we do.
There are hundreds of ways to kneel and kiss the
ground.

—RUMI

❖ Introduction

The key to everyday life as spiritual practice lies in bringing a full, rich quality of being and presence into whatever we do. Yet "being" and "doing" often seem mutually exclusive. The cultures of the East have cultivated *being* for thousands of years, while rarely, until recently, placing as much emphasis on doing. The cultures of the West have been busy *doing* for thousands of years—building, inventing, conquering the world—while often failing to appreciate that a healthy, fulfilling human life depends on the quality of one's being and presence. To find the spiritual path in our daily life, we need to bring being and doing together. This is precisely what happens in creativity, where the beauty that we love can become what we do.

The basic principles of creativity are the same whether we are painting, writing, doing business, shooting an arrow, or driving a car. These principles also operate in meditative awareness. To be creative in any field of endeavor, we must first let go of fixed ways of thinking that cause us to act in habitual ways, so that we can perceive what is happening freshly and instantly adapt to changing circumstances. This is what Zen master Suzuki Roshi called "beginner's mind."

Every situation is unique, never entirely the same as any other that we have encountered before. Thus to respond creatively, we must be flexible and adaptable. Anyone who has developed expertise in a particular field—whether it is computer programming, fixing cars, medicine, teaching, or writing novels—has learned general rules and principles about what works and what doesn't work. This is an important part of any craft or vocation. Yet when we rely too much on this learning, we block our creativity. In trying to fit new situations into old formulas, we lose the presence and stillness of mind out of which new insights emerge.

Once we let go of old preconceptions, the next essential ingredient in creativity is a willingness to let ourselves rest in a state of "not knowing" for long enough to allow new solutions to come forth. No matter how difficult the problem we are facing is, if we are wakeful and alert in our uncertainty, an answer will eventually emerge. This is because our body-mind totality is tuned into the situations we inhabit in countless subtle and complex ways; the thinking mind, which can only grasp one thing at a time, can hardly keep up with all this. By being still and receptive, instead of busily trying to find solutions, we give our intelligence the time and space it needs to find an appropriate way to proceed.

Many of the chapters in this section are about the martial or fine arts. I include them here not primarily for practitioners or artists, but because these arts illustrate the power of the meditative mind at work. They show us how mindful presence helps us let go of preconceptions, hang out in the unknown, respond quickly to unexpected circumstances, regain balance quickly when it is lost, and see new possibilities in situations that otherwise seem intimidating or hopeless.

In describing what it is like to draw with a meditative eye, artist Frederick Franck shows us what it actually means to see. It means perceiving the isness of things—a flower, a dead rabbit, a homeless person on the street—without putting them into mental pigeonholes. He also acknowledges the struggle that precedes many creative discoveries: prematurely trying to impose order on a situation until at last we give up and allow the creative juices to flow through us again.

Natalie Goldberg urges us to trust our first thoughts when writing, if our words are to have energy and vigor. Yet she also recognizes that this is no easy task. As she puts it, "You must be a great warrior when you contact first thoughts and write from them." To be a warrior in the spiritual, rather than the military sense, involves courage, first of all. Chögyam Trungpa, in his book, *Shambhala: The Sacred Path of the Warrior*, uses the word *warrior* to translate a Tibetan term meaning "one who is brave." A brave is one who practices courage in the face of the unknown.

Our lives are constantly teetering on the edge of this unknown, which is the source of all creativity. What is known—what has worked or not worked before—is already history. What is fresh and alive comes only from the unknown. It takes courage to open ourselves to the immediate isness of the present moment, without holding on to a program or agenda. Yet this is the only way to develop true compassion and tenderness.

Allen Ginsberg takes this further, describing poetry as a "probe" into the immediate isness of human experience. This requires letting the mind loose and paying attention to our perceptions as they arise, without trying to fit them into any idea of how they should be. In this way, poetry, like meditation, becomes a way of releasing ourselves from the bondage of conditioned mind and "cleansing the doors of perception." Poetry, in fact, is the closest we can get to pure, unconditioned awareness within the medium of words. It is a way of describing the actual texture and flow of experience as it arises.

Pianist Mildred Chase applies the same principles to playing her instrument. Music expresses the living flow of our experience; it is creativity in motion. When playing music, it is especially important not to be ahead of yourself. If you anticipate the next note, you cannot give the note you are sounding full expression, so your playing loses vitality. Thus the essence of creative music-making is—what else?—just being.

Dancer Denise Taylor explores how mindfulness of

bodily activity can help us connect with ourselves more sweetly and tenderly. Mindfulness of body does not mean standing back and watching ourselves, like a cat watching a mouse. Nor does it mean self-consciously trying to move in a smooth, polished way. Indeed, trained dancers often move with the least spontaneity. It's a question of paying attention to the aliveness we feel in the ongoing stream of bodily sensations.

Eugen Herrigel's classic essay on Zen archery demonstrates how much strength of presence is required in order to perform even the simplest of actions with accuracy and precision. Herrigel's teacher makes a radical, uncompromising demand: he must not try to shoot the arrow or hit the target. Trying to hit the target is like the goal-directed attitude that we bring to the whirl of our daily lives: Do this in order to be successful; be successful to win approval; win approval so you can feel better; feel better so you can be more successful; and so on.

The key to archery as a spiritual exercise lies in drawing the bow to the point of maximum tension and then allowing the shot to release itself. This is a wonderful analogy for what happens in every creative moment. There are always times in our personal life or work when we face some new challenge, not knowing what to do. The temptation is to jump to a quick solution so that we don't have to feel tension or discomfort. But Herrigel's teacher suggests that this tension must build before right action can ensue. We must wait and let ourselves experience this moment when our old routines no longer work and a new direction has not yet appeared. For example, if we are experiencing a difficulty in an intimate relationship, our first impulse might be to quickly find a solution so that we don't have to feel the tension of not knowing what to do. Allowing ourselves to feel this discomfort produces a certain inner ferment, which every artist and creative person also experiences before giving birth to something new. If we can remain open to this ferment, we feel raw and tender. We drop down to a deeper level of ourselves where we can connect with our partner in a more vital, fulfilling way. Something larger than our ego has become activated, and leads us in a new direction. As the arrow slips from our hand of its own accord can our larger intelligence points the way?

We can also read the next chapter, written by the seventeenth-century Zen master Takuan, either literally or as an analogy for how to work with everyday situations. This piece is taken from letters Takuan wrote to a prominent samurai at a time when the famous swordsmen of Japan became interested in studying Zen. Takuan points out that the greatest danger for a samurai is "stopping the mind"— letting it become fixated on any thought, feeling, perception—with the result that he cannot respond as freely and quickly as he must.

This same principle holds true in every aspect of our lives. If our mind becomes stuck on seeing our life, our partner, or our parents a certain way, we are setting ourselves up for trouble. As Takuan points out, if we focus on only one leaf, we will not see all the leaves on the tree; if we focus on one part of the body, the whole body cannot move fluidly. When the mind "stops," we lose the larger panoramic perspective that can give us all the information we need. Since we will not be fully equipped to deal with the situations we are facing, we will more easily be defeated by them.

Driving a car is one modern equivalent of a martial art. It is certainly the most dangerous thing most of us do every day, and it can often bring us into conflict with unknown, unpredictable adversaries. Therefore the kind of panoramic awareness Takuan speaks of is nowhere more indispensable to our safety than when we are moving along the road at speeds that were unheard-of in his day. As the Bergers point out, for precision, alertness, and quick responsiveness, nothing can match the "natural-self"—that fluid awareness that we all have access to beneath our rigid self-concepts. This fluid awareness also makes driving more interesting, rather than just a boring chore.

In her chapter on craft, Carla Needleman emphasizes an important, yet rarely mentioned aspect of creative work—disillusionment. One of the great obstacles to creativity comes after an initial success at some enterprise, when you think that you "know" how to do it. If learning and growth were that easy, we would all be creative geniuses and enlightened masters. The real test comes when we discover that we don't know very much, that many of our fondest hopes and dreams are but illusions. As a writer I may start out with a brilliant idea, a grand inspiration. But in the process of executing my vision, I may find that the task I have set myself stretches me to my farthest limits and challenges me on every level of my being, forcing me to give up my grandiose notions of myself and eat humble pie. Only then can I really begin to write.

Disillusionment is powerful, as Carla Needleman points out, because it stops thought and brings about "in my whole organism a quiet and a seriousness that unite me as nothing else has the power to." This experience also has an important place in our personal and spiritual development. The path of opening more fully to life forces us to give up our most cherished ideas about ourselves and surrender instead to *what is*. As we uncover aspects of ourselves that are hard to accept, and realize how much work it takes to free ourselves from our conditioning, we may feel disillusioned. Yet this can be an important vehicle on our path, rather than a reason to blame or give up on ourselves, as Chögyam Trungpa points out:

> Disappointment is the best chariot to use on the path of the dharma. It does not confirm the existence of our ego and its dreams. We must surrender our hopes and expectations, as well as our fears, and march directly into disappointment, work with disappointment, go into it and make it our way of life, which is a very hard thing to do. Disappointment is a good sign of basic intelligence. It cannot be compared to anything else: it is so sharp, precise, obvious, and direct. If we can be open, then we

suddenly begin to see that our expectations are irrelevant compared with the reality of the situations we are facing.

In the final chapter of this section, Jean Martine explores her disappointment with her daily job. How many people every day must ask themselves the question she poses here: How do I infuse my daily work with more life and spirit? Longing for the old relation between master and apprentice, she realizes that the only master available to her at her desk in the advertising agency is right there inside her. Not knowing how to tap this inner guidance, most of us live each day as though we have no spiritual nourishment available to us. Yet what if we acknowledged the wise place within each of us that can give us intelligent guidance? Then we could begin to look at our present life circumstances, whatever they may be, as the raw material of our learning. But in order to do this, we must stop regarding ourselves as victims of circumstances, and start to acknowledge that we are not here purely by accident. The master within is trying to help us wake up by confronting us with our current life situation, which contains all the lessons we need to learn in order to grow into more fully developed human beings.

8 ❀ The Way of Seeing

FREDERICK FRANCK

The letter invited me to give what it called "a workshop." The subject: "Creativity in a Non-Creative Environment," whatever that meant. I had never attended such a weekend gathering on campus, let alone "given" one. So I feverishly prepared lectures and a pack of art slides. I would start with an introductory talk on the relationship between drawing, painting, and sculpture. But it all turned out differently.

In that first lecture I asked the rhetorical question, Who is man, the artist? and answered it by saying: He is the unspoiled core of Everyman, before he is choked by schooling, training, conditioning, until the artist within shrivels up and is forgotten. Even in the artist who is professionally trained to be consciously "creative" this unspoiled core shrivels up in the rush toward a "personal style," in the heat of competition to be "in."

And yet, I added, that core is never killed completely. At times it responds to Nature, to beauty, to Life, suddenly aware again of being in the presence of a Mystery that baffles understanding and which only has to be glimpsed to renew our Spirit and to make us feel that life is a supreme gift.

Many years of preoccupation with Zen have kept me awake to that experience of this opening up of life.

Suddenly I noticed that the strangers' faces in front of me began to look less strange. I was making contact, and encouraged by this rapport, I forgot my carefully hatched lecture and started to talk freely about seeing, about drawing as "The Way of Seeing," and about this seeing/drawing as a way of meditation, a way of getting into intimate touch with the visible world around us, and through it . . . with ourselves.

During the question period that followed one of the teachers said: "I'd love to try your seeing/drawing, but how on earth do I start? I can't even draw a straight line!"

"I'll show you tomorrow morning," I promised. The next morning—it was a sunny spring day—I distributed cheap sketchpads and pencils and asked the participants to sit down somewhere on the lawn. "Now, let your eyes fall on whatever happens to be in front of you. It may be a plant or a bush or a tree, or perhaps just some grass. Close your eyes for the next five minutes . . .

"Now, open your eyes and focus on whatever you observed before—that plant or leaf or dandelion. Look it in the eye, until you feel it looking back at you. Feel that you are alone with it on Earth! That it is the most important thing in the universe, that it contains all the riddles of life and death. It does!

"Now, take your pencil loosely in your hand, and while you keep your eyes focused allow the pencil to follow on the paper what the eye perceives. Feel as if with the point of your pencil you are caressing the contours, the whole circumference of that leaf, that sprig of grass. Just let your hand move! Don't check what gets onto the paper, it does not matter at all! If your pencil runs off the paper, that's fine too! You can always start again. Only, don't let your eye wander from what it is seeing, and don't lift your pencil from your paper! And above all: don't try too hard, don't "think" about what you are drawing, just let the hand follow what the eye sees. Let it caress."

They sat and saw and drew for hours, until lunchtime, like good children. A pretentious one in owl glasses was doing a spiky abstraction. I tried to talk her into using her eyes. "Please realize you are *not* 'making a picture,' you are not being 'creative.' We are just conducting an experiment in seeing, in undivided attention! The experiment is successful if you *succeed* in feeling you have become that leaf or that daisy, regardless of what appears on the paper."

A young woman asked, "Why am I so scared?"

"Maybe you are afraid you are making a fool of yourself and that all the others are so much better! Or maybe it frightens you to be all on your own, without radio or TV, without talking. Alone in the world with your clump of grass, alone with your eyes . . ."

The drawings were a revelation, as were the comments of the people who had made them. There was a drawing of a willow that was as awkward as it was lovely. The willow danced like a prima ballerina, or better, it danced as only willows dance. The woman who drew it was white-haired and in her sixties.

"I don't even know how I did it," she said. "I did what you suggested and then it happened. I had never drawn since I quit school."

The one who "couldn't draw a straight line" had traced a complex patch of ivy in a spidery handwriting of exquisite sensitivity.

The abstract lady had persisted in her spiky triangles, but another said, "I have grown geraniums for thirty years, but, believe it or not, I never knew what a geranium looked like, how it was made, until I drew one today."

Someone else said, "I am a widow and live alone, and I often feel lonely. Today I learned that if you really see the things around you, you're not lonely anymore! I may never be any good at it, but I'll go on drawing!" And another: "I have painted for years. I have been in local exhibitions, but today's experience makes me wonder whether I have been deceiving myself, whether I really ever saw, if I really used my eyes. Anyway, it was an unforgettable experience!"

They all agreed: "A wonderful experience!"

In this twentieth century, to stop rushing around, to sit quietly on the grass, to switch off the world and come back to the earth, to allow the eye to see a willow, a bush, a cloud, a leaf, is "an unforgettable experience . . ."

We do a lot of looking: we look through lenses, telescopes, television tubes . . . our looking is perfected every day . . . but we see less and less.

Never has it been more urgent to speak of *seeing*. Ever more gadgets, from cameras to computers, from art books to videotapes, conspire to take over our thinking, our feeling, our experiencing, our seeing. Onlookers we are, spectators . . . "Subjects" we are, that look at "objects." Quickly we stick labels on all that is, labels that stick once and for all. By these labels we recognize everything but no longer *see* anything. We know the labels on all the bottles, but never taste the wine.

Millions of people, unseeing, joyless, bluster through life in their half-sleep, hitting, kicking, and killing what they have barely perceived. They have never learned to *see*, or they have forgotten that man has eyes to *see*, to experience. When man no longer experiences, the organs of his inner life wither away. Alone or in herds he goes on binges of violence and destruction.

Looking and seeing both start with sense perception, but there the similarity ends. When I "look" at the world and label its phenomena, I make immediate choices, instant appraisals—I like or I dislike, I accept or reject what I look at, according to its usefulness to the "Me" . . . this me that I imagine myself to be, and that I try to impose on others.

The purpose of "looking" is to survive, to cope, to manipulate, to discern what is useful, agreeable, or threatening to the Me, what enhances or what diminishes the Me. This we are trained to do from our first day. When, on the other hand, I *see*—suddenly I am all eyes, I forget this Me, am liberated from it and dive into the reality of what confronts me, become part of it, participate in it.

It is in order to really *see*, to *see* ever deeper, ever more intensely, hence to be fully aware and alive, that I draw what the Chinese call "the Ten Thousand Things" around me. Drawing is the discipline by which I constantly rediscover the world.

I have learned that what I have not drawn I have never really seen, and that when I start drawing an ordinary thing, I realize how extraordinary it is, sheer miracle: the branching of a tree, the structure of a dandelion's seed puff. "A mouse is miracle enough to stagger sextillions of infidels," says Walt Whitman. I discover that among the Ten Thousand Things there is no ordinary thing. All that is, is worthy of being seen, of being drawn.

Seeing and drawing can become one, can become *seeing/drawing*. When that happens there is no more room for the labelings of the Me. Every insignificant thing appears as if seen in its three dimensions, in its own space and in its own time. Each leaf of grass is seen to grow from its own roots, each creature is realized to be unique, existing now/here on its voyage from birth to death. No longer do I "look" at a leaf, but enter into direct contact with its life process, with Life itself, with what I, too, really am. I "behold the lilies of the field" . . . and "see how they grow"! Their growing is my growing, their fading I share. Becoming one with the lilies in *seeing/drawing*, I become not less, but more myself. For the time being the split between Me and not-Me is healed, suspended.

What really happens when seeing and drawing become *seeing/drawing* is that awareness and attention become constant and undivided, become contemplation. *Seeing/drawing* is not a self-indulgence, a "pleasant hobby," but a discipline of awareness, of unwavering attention to a world which is fully alive. It is not the pursuit of happiness, but stopping the pursuit and experiencing the awareness, the happiness, of being all there. It is a discipline that costs nothing, that needs no gadgets. All I carry is a pen in my pocket, a sketchbook under my arm. This eye is my lens. This eye is the lens of the heart, open to the world. My hand follows its seeing.

For the artist within (who must exist in everyone, for if man is created in God's image, it can only mean that he is created creative) there is no split between his seeing, art, and "religion" in the sense of realizing his place in the fabric of all that is. These three are inextricably interwoven: they are one.

And since I am writing about *seeing*, and on the heightened awareness of *seeing/drawing*, I must speak of Zen. Zen is definitely not something exotically Oriental, certainly not a fad, and not even a Buddhist sect. The thirteenth-century Zen sage Dogen warns: "Whosoever speaks of Zen as if it were a Buddhist sect or school of thought is a devil."

What then can one say about the Zen experience, which in itself is inexpressible in words?

One can certainly say what it is not. It is *not* a kind of "self-actualization," an expansion of the limited, isolated Me, of the empirical ego. Neither is it a regression, a return into that vegetative ooze of Oneness, before we became aware of our differentiation as separate egos. On the contrary, the Zen experience is the overcoming of the hallucination that the Me is the valid center of observation of the universe. It is a momentary, radical turnabout, *a direct perception of and insight into the presence, into the transiency, the finitude that I share with all beings.*

The Zen experience is at the same time a direct seeing into what I am in reality. It is the healing of the alienation that hides my true identity—which happens on its deepest level to be my identity with all that is born and will die. This insight into my real condition is the Wisdom that is inseparable from compassion.

Zazen, or sitting in meditation, is generally considered an indispensable preparation toward the Zen experience, *satori*. It is a discipline of *pointed mindfulness* as such, persevered in to the point where the in-sight breaks through. In *seeing/drawing* there is a way of awakening the "Third Eye," of focusing attention until it turns into contemplation, and from there to the inexpressible fullness, where the split between the seer and what is seen is obliterated. Eye, heart, hand become one with what is seen and drawn, things are seen as they are—in their "isness." *Seeing/drawing* as a technique of contemplation is, I believe, a way particularly suited to that "Western temperament" which may be no more than a habitually overstimulated nervous system, an "overloaded switchboard." It is the discipline through which I extricate myself from the habitual, the mechanical, the predigested and acquisitive automatisms of our society. I stand face to face with a hill, a bird, a human face— with my self, in unwavering attention.

Blind to the mystery of the being called "cow," we deal in "cattle," "livestock," "beef-futures." Blind to the mystery of every human being, we manipulate "human material," labor forces, battalions.

There is the story of the Buddha holding up a flower to his disciples and asking them to "say a word about it," something "relevant." The disciples looked, looked intently, then tried to outdo one another in the profundity of their remarks. Only Mahakalyapa "saw." He remained silent and smiled an almost imperceptible smile. To *see* is Mahakalyapa's smile.

But why a flower? Why not a dead rabbit? A minnow? A poor old soul? The eye that sees becomes self-aware, it realizes that it is an integral part of the great continuum of all that is. It sees things such as they are. No thing is a mere symbol of anything but itself. A rose is not a symbol of love, nor a rock of strength. A rose is a rose experienced in its suchness. To draw it is to say "Yes" to its and my existence.

When all antennae are out, as they are in *seeing/drawing*, the eye perceives, and a reflex goes from the retina, via what is called "mind" or "heart" to the hand. In *seeing/drawing* all the hand does is to trace a line, to note it down as an unquestioning instrument. How does one make progress in drawing? By making the eye-heart-hand reflex ever more sensitive, so that the hand may become ever more the willing tool of the eye.

Seeing/drawing the Ten Thousand Things is drawing from Nature. But nature is not all meadows, cows, and daisies. It's also streets and buildings, coffee cups and airplanes. A disciple asked, "Is the Nature present everywhere?" He received this answer: "Yes, there is nowhere it is not present!" It is this Nature that Zen points to and aims to confront.

Seeing into one's "own nature," far from being self-analysis as if one were an object—is the perception, the experience, of Nature as it manifests itself in me, outside me. This seeing-into is at the same time the leap out of the isolation of the Me into the community of beings and things, in the absolute present, the Absolute Presence.

You have noticed that until now I have said hardly a word about the how-to of drawing. It is because nearly all hints on this how-to are fraudulent, teach one at best to imitate other people's drawings, to "manufacture" pictures—as if there were not enough mediocre pictures to last for centuries!

And so I speak, again and again, about experiencing firsthand and about the gift of our eyes to really *see.* "If thine eye is single, the whole body shall be full of light . . ." So let *seeing/drawing* be the celebration of experiencing, of the eye in love, instead of the making of pictures to be framed. There is only one person who can teach you: yourself!

While drawing a rock I learn nothing "about" rocks, but let this particular rock reveal its rockiness. While drawing grasses I learn nothing "about" grass, but wake up to the wonder of this grass and its growing, to the wonder that there is grass at all.

Everyone thinks he knows what a lettuce looks like. But start to draw one and you realize the anomaly of having lived with lettuces all your life but never having seen one, never having seen the semi-translucent leaves curling in their own lettuce way, never having noticed what makes a lettuce a lettuce rather than a curly kale. I am not suggesting that you draw each nerve, each vein of each leaf, but that you feel them being there. What applies to lettuce, applies equally to the all-too-familiar faces of husbands . . . wives . . .

The ninth century Zen master Siubi was asked: "What is the secret of Zen?" "Come back when there is nobody around and I shall tell you." The inquirer returned. Siubi took him to a bamboo grove, pointed at the bamboos and said: "See how long these are. See how short these are!"

Suddenly the questioner *saw*, "had a flash of awakening." What did he see? He had a revelation of sheer existence. Where there is revelation, explanation becomes superfluous. Curiosity is dissolved in wonder.

I think of this story whenever I draw grasses and weeds along the roadside: "See how long this one, see how bent this one, see how straight, how curved, how twisted . . ."

There are many such stories. A scholar asked Hui-t'ang to be initiated in Zen. He felt the master had been holding back its central secrets from him.

On a walk in the mountains, while the laurels were in full bloom and their fragrance filled the air, Hui-t'ang asked: "Do you smell it?" The scholar nodded. "You *see!*" exclaimed the master, "I am hiding nothing from you." The eyes of the scholar were opened.

"What is the Buddha-nature?" the ninth-century sage Joshu was asked. He answered: "The cypress tree in the courtyard!" A riddle? "Split the tree and you will find me, raise the stone and I am there," Jesus said. Without any doubt he had seen the "I am Who I am" revealed in tree and stone, and spoke of this experience.

It is precisely this experience which made Joshu's eye see the Buddha-nature in the cypress tree and which makes us see into the tree's real Being. One might go so far as to say that the tree becomes self-aware in us. There is only that tree, being tree.

This apple tree is not the first one I have drawn, perhaps the thousandth. As my pen follows the trunk, I feel the sap rise through it from roots to spreading branches. I feel in my toes how roots grip earth. In the muscles of my torso I feel the tree's upward groping, its twisting, struggling, its reaching against all resistances, towards the sun. In my arms I sense how the branches must wrest themselves away from the parental trunk, to find their own way, fight against the elements. My fingers become the slender shoots that probe the sky.

One draws best what one knows best. The first thing in America that "drew itself" for me was an apple orchard on Long Island, which recalled one in Holland, where I grew up.

Every so often, I just have to return to Holland, drawn not by friends, by people, but by the flat meadows under the endless sky of my childhood. I have walked and skated through that landscape forever. I know it so well, I have it in my bones. There nothing intervenes with what the eye perceives. The hand moves in perfect freedom and innocence. The landscape draws itself.

Years later when drawing in America, in Africa, in Asia, in Australia, suddenly overwhelmed by human features, vegetation, animals, architectural forms never drawn before, the eye caught stagefright—how does one draw an African jungle? An emu? Noh-action? A wallaby? A Japanese market, an Ethiopian child?

I learned: just give the eye a little time to overcome its panic, to calm down until the hand dares trust it again, for alien forms do not stay alien very long. The exotic does not exist except on travel posters. Clouds and trees, insects, birds, butterflies, and grass and graves underfoot are everywhere, and human faces, after all, disclose themselves as being human very soon.

And the cities: Paris, Vienna, Tokyo, Rome, Delhi—they are not just places I have visited, they have become hometowns by seeing/drawing. Each one has its own atmosphere. How does one "catch" that atmosphere, so that a detail from a drawing of Rome cannot be mistaken for one of Paris? Atmospheres build themselves up out of a million imperceptible micro-details, elements often too minute, too fleeting for the conscious mind to pick up, but which the eye-heart-hand reflex notes down, so that the buildings, and even the faces that form themselves on the paper, become unmistakably Roman, Indian, Parisian, or Japanese.

In order to draw a horse, draw horses until you practically become a horse—not "horses in general," but always that particular horse you are drawing at a given moment. Until you feel the tense curving of its neck in your own neck!

And I have been a cow, eyes all soul, tinged with sudden jerks of fright and suspicion at that blinding white drawing pad, have felt in my slow, contemplative cow's skull flashes of warning, felt my eyes slide sideways, reconnoitering for escape routes. No, a cow is not a rectangle on legs.

While I am *seeing/drawing*, I take hold of the thing, until it fills my total capacity for experience. Once I have thus taken possession of a hill, a body, a face, I let go, let it go free again, as if I were releasing a butterfly. Yet it remains mine forever. After much *seeing/drawing* my eye goes on drawing whether my hand draws or not. From morning till night, my eye draws the Ten Thousand Things.

Perhaps I have given the impression that the moment I take pen in hand a stillness falls within, that the eye-heart-hand reflex can be switched on and off at will? Nothing could be less true. On the contrary, at the beginning of a drawing session, I am more often than not in a state of acute agitation, even panic. The first few drawings I do of a model are often nervous scribbles, for the eye cannot focus yet, the hand doesn't obey. It is as if I collided with the model in mid-distance and we are having a fight. I resent her, find fault with her poses, her smirk, her frown, in an exacerbation of that "normal" hostility we reserve for strangers who make excessive demands on us. The me, the ego, is straining too hard ... sometimes this period of despair goes on for hours. Hand keeps fighting eye. The eye is shifty, it does not see—it looks. The brain meddles with every stroke. Then, provided I don't give up, I may yet overcome this horror, may lose that meddlesome me, and something else may take over.

This hostile, touchy, idiosyncratic me has calmed down, something in the model at last begins to speak to me: the sadness of her glance, a birthmark perhaps. I *see* again! The eye no longer jerks in half-sleep. Anxieties, memories, day-dreams cease.

The good drawings I do are hardly mine. Only the bad ones are mine for they are the ones where I can't let go, am caught in the me-cramp. "If the good drawings are not yours, if it is not the ego that draws them, do you mean to say that they are done by the Absolute?" someone is bound to ask ironically.

That which draws in *seeing/drawing* is that which I really am, but which I cannot possibly define and label. It simply defines itself by the way it draws. *Seeing/drawing* therefore is an impossible effort as long as the ego tries to force it. Once the ego lets go, it becomes effortless.

What is called "Buddhahood" has through the ages also been spoken of as the "True Self," the "Essence of Mind," the "Original Face," the "Cosmic Unconscious," the "True-Man-Without-Label," the "Heart," the "Buddha-nature," the "Unborn" . . . Its awakening has been called "realization," "Enlightenment," "Satori," or in Christian language the "birth of God in the soul"—something not to be experienced sometime later in a distant future, but now/here, in the present.

A monk asked: "What is this 'True-Man-Without-Label'?" Rinzai came down from his pulpit, grabbed the monk and shouted: "Speak! Speak!" What could be the correct answer to Rinzai's "Speak! Speak!"? Since I am not that monk, I can't answer for him. But for myself? I grab my pen and draw! The Suchness of things calls out, calls me by name and shouts, Speak! Speak! I respond, I draw.

Where this True-Man-Without-Label is awakened, the Buddha is present and "I am before Abraham was," and before scripture was written: at the root source of all revelations, where all men are totally equal.

One day I stood in the grottoes of Lascaux, France, where thirty thousand years ago the cavemen of Aurignac had drawn the magnificent bulls on the rock walls. Face to face with these most ancient of drawings, I saw how these prehistoric artists had seen directly into the very life center of the animals, had grasped it with the full humanity of their eyes and hands. Here the True-Man-Without-Label was already at work in *seeing/drawing*, giving his answer to Rinzai's "Speak! Speak!" Zen and culture were already present, and from Lascaux, via *Vedas* and *Upanishads*, via Gospels and sutras, via Chuang Tzu and Lao Tzu, Buddha and Jesus, Hui-Neng, Rembrandt, Bach, and numberless others, mostly forgotten, the True-Man-Without-Label—our deepest longing, our own reality—speaks to us.

Seeing/drawing is beyond words, beyond silence—for the True Self cannot be expressed by either the use of words or of silence. The sense perception, the activity of the reflex eye-heart-hand, is still, as in Lascaux, the leap from a platitudinous world to one of mystery. All is suddenly suffused with meaning. Once this leap has been made, once wonder and awakening have flashed upon us, we inevitably fall back into our half-sleep—but with a difference, for a radical change in perception and feeling has taken place. Through the multiplicity of forms and appearances the Structure of Reality was mirrored, and disclosed itself, unconfused by concepts, opinions, labels, and prejudices. The relatedness between self and the universe has been restored.

9 ✿ *Writing Fearlessly*

NATALIE GOLDBERG

FIRST THOUGHTS

*F*irst thoughts have tremendous energy. It is the way the mind first flashes on something. The internal censor usually squelches them, so we live in the realm of second and third thoughts, thoughts on thought, twice and three times removed from the direct connection of the first fresh flash. For instance, the phrase, "I cut the daisy from my throat" shot through my mind. Now my second thought, carefully tutored in 1 + 1 = 2 logic, in politeness, fear, and embarrassment at the natural, would say, "That's ridiculous. You sound suicidal. Don't show yourself cutting your throat. Someone will think you are crazy." And instead, if we give the censor its way, we write, "My throat was a little sore, so I didn't say anything." Proper and boring.

First thoughts are also unencumbered by ego, by that mechanism in us that tries to be in control, tries to prove the world is permanent and solid, enduring and logical. The world is not permanent, is ever-changing and full of human suffering. So if you express something egoless, it is also full of energy because it is expressing the truth of the way things are. You are not carrying the burden of ego in your expression, but are riding for moments the waves of human consciousness and using your personal details to express the ride.

In Zen meditation you sit on a cushion called a zafu with your legs crossed, back straight, hands at your knees or in front of you in a gesture called a mudra. You face a white wall and watch your breath. No matter what you feel—great tornadoes of anger and resistance, thunderstorms of joy and grief—you continue to sit, back straight, legs crossed, facing the wall. You learn to not be tossed away no matter how great the thought or emotion. That is the discipline: to continue to sit.

The same is true in writing. You must be a great warrior when you contact first thoughts and write from them. Especially at the beginning you may feel great emotions and energy that will sweep you away, but you don't stop writing. You continue to use your pen and record the details of your life and penetrate into the heart of them. Often in a beginning class students break down crying when they read pieces they have written. That is okay. Often as they write they cry, too. However, I encourage them to continue reading or writing right through the tears so they may come out the other side and not be thrown off by the emotion. Don't stop at the tears; go through to truth. This is the discipline.

Why else are first thoughts so energizing? Because they have to do with freshness and inspiration. Inspiration means "breathing in." Breathing in God. You actually become larger than yourself, and first thoughts are present. They are not a cover-up of what is actually happening or being felt. The present is imbued with tremendous energy. It is what is. My friend who is a Buddhist said once after coming out of a meditation retreat, "The colors were so much more vibrant afterward." Her meditation teacher said, "When you are present, the world is truly alive."

WRITING AS A PRACTICE

This is the practice school of writing. Like running, the more you do it, the better you get at it. Some days you don't want to run and you resist every step of the three miles, but you do it anyway. You practice whether you want to or not. You don't wait around for inspiration and a deep desire to run. It'll never happen, especially if you are out of shape and have been avoiding it. But if you run regularly, you train your mind to cut through or ignore your resistance. You just do it. And in the middle of the run, you love it. When you come to the end, you never want to stop. And you stop, hungry for the next time.

That's how writing is, too. Once you're deep into it, you wonder what took you so long to finally settle down at the desk. Through practice you actually do get better. You learn to trust your deep self more and not give in to your voice that wants to avoid writing. It is odd that we never question the feasibility of a football team practicing long hours for one game; yet in writing we rarely give ourselves the space for practice.

When you write, don't say, "I'm going to write a poem." That attitude will freeze you right away. Sit down with the least expectation of yourself; say, "I am free to write the worst junk in the world." You have to give yourself the space to write a lot without a destination. I've had students who said they decided they were going to write the great American novel and haven't written a line since. If every time you sat down, you expected something great, writing would always be a great disappointment. Plus that expectation would keep you from writing.

My rule is to finish a notebook a month. Simply to fill it. That is the practice. My ideal is to write every day. I say it is my ideal. I am careful not to pass judgment or create anxiety if I don't do that. No one lives up to his ideal.

In my notebooks I don't bother with the side margin or the one at the top: I fill the whole page. I am not writing anymore for a teacher or for school. I am writing for myself first and I don't have to stay within my limits, not even margins. This gives me a psychological freedom and permission. And when my writing is on and I'm really cooking, I usually forget about punctuation, spelling, etc. I also notice that my handwriting changes. It becomes larger and looser.

Often I can look around the room at my students as they write and can tell which ones are really on and present at a given time in their writing. They are more intensely involved and their bodies are hanging loose. Again, it is like running. There's little resistance when the run is good. All of you is moving; there's no you separate from the runner. In writing, when you are truly on, there's no writer, no paper, no pen, no thoughts. Only writing does writing—everything else is gone.

One of the main aims in writing practice is to learn to trust your own mind and body; to grow patient and nonaggressive. Art lives in the Big World. One poem or story doesn't matter one way or the other. It's the process of writing and life that matters. Too many writers have written great books and gone insane or alcoholic or killed themselves. This process teaches about sanity. We are trying to become sane along with our poems and stories.

Chögyam Trungpa, Rinpoche, a Tibetan Buddhist master, said, "We must continue to open in the face of tremendous opposition. No one is encouraging us to open and still we must peel away the layers of the heart." It is the same with this way of practice writing: We must continue to open and trust in our own voices and process. Ultimately, if the process is good, the end will be good. You will get good writing.

ELKTON, MINNESOTA: WHATEVER'S IN FRONT OF YOU

I walk into the classroom in Elkton, Minnesota. Early April the fields around the school are wet, unplowed, not seeded yet. And the sky is deep gray. I tell the twenty-five eighth-graders that I am a Jew after I hear that *rabbis* is one of their spelling words. None of them has ever seen a Jew before. I am aware that everything I do now for the next hour represents "Jew." I walk in eating an apple: all Jews now will eat apples. I tell them I have never lived in a small town: now no Jew has ever lived in the country. One student asked if I knew anyone in a concentration camp. And we talk about the Germans: many are of German descent.

They are very warm and there's a beautiful depth of vulnerability about them. They know what well the water they drink comes from, that their cat who ran away two years ago will not return, how their hair feels against their heads as they run. I don't have to give them any rules about poetry. They live in that place already. Close to things. So I ask them, "Where do you come from, who are you, what makes you?" I tell them I'm from the city but I know these fields. In writing you can know everything. You can be here and know the streets of New York. You can have parts of others live in you: "I am the wing of the crow that left and will not return."

So this is one way to generate writing. I didn't have a plan before I went into class. I tried to be present, unafraid, open, and the situation gave me the subject. I know this is true wherever I go. The trick is to keep your heart open. In an inner-city school in downtown Manhattan I might come to a class armored with all kinds of ready-to-fix writing exercises, because I would be more scared. I was brought up in New York and have heard many stories. That would be a loss for everyone, mostly for myself. If I'm afraid, my writing's bent, untruthful to what is real. "But there is cause for fear there!" No, that's going in with a preconceived idea.

How to generate writing ideas, things to write about? Whatever's in front of you is a good beginning. Then move out into all streets. You can go anywhere. Tell me everything you know. Don't worry if what you know you can't prove or haven't studied. I know the fields around Elkton because I say I do and because I want to walk out into them forever.

Don't worry that forever might be the one week you're there as resident poet or salesman for a tractor company or a traveler on the way west. Own anything you want in your writing and then let it go.

WE ARE NOT THE POEM

The problem is we think we exist. We think our words are permanent and solid and stamp us forever. That's not true. We write in the moment. Sometimes when I read poems at a reading to strangers, I realize they think those poems are me. They are not me, even if I speak in the "I" person. They were my thoughts and my hand and the space and the emotions at that time of writing. Watch yourself. Every minute we change. It is a great opportunity. At any point, we can step out of our frozen selves and our ideas and begin fresh. That is how writing is. Instead of freezing us, it frees us.

The ability to put something down—to tell how you feel about an old husband, an old shoe, or the memory of a cheese sandwich on a gray morning in Miami—that moment you can finally align how you feel inside with the words you write; at that moment you are free because you are not fighting those things inside.

LISTENING

Several years ago I took a singing lesson from a Sufi singing master, and he told me there is no such thing as tone-deafness. "Singing is ninety percent listening. You have to learn to listen." If you listen totally, your body fills with the music, so when you open your mouth the music automatically comes out of you.

Writing, too, is ninety percent listening. You listen so deeply to the space around you that it fills you, and when you write, it pours out of you. If you can capture that reality around you, your writing needs nothing else. You don't only listen to the person speaking to you across the table, but simultaneously listen to the air, the chair, and the door. And go beyond the door. Take in the sound of the season, the sound of the color coming in through the windows. Listen to the past, future, and present right where you are. Listen with your whole body, not only with your ears, but with your hands, your face, and the back of your neck.

Listening is receptivity. The deeper you can listen, the better you can write. You take in the way things are without judgment, and the next day you can write the truth about the way things are. Jack Kerouac in his list of prose essentials said, "Be submissive to everything. Open. Listening." He also said, "No time for poetry, but exactly what is." If you can capture the way things are, that's all the poetry you'll ever need.

ENGENDERING COMPASSION

I am on a Greek island right now: the Aegean Sea, cheap rooms on the beach, nude swimming, little tavernas where you sit under dried bamboo sipping ouzo, taste octopus, watch the great sun set. I am thirty-six and my friend who is with me is thirty-nine. It is the first time either of us has been to Europe. We take in everything, but only halfway because we are busy always, always talking. I tell her about my dance recital when I was six years old in a pink tutu; how my father, who sat in the front row, broke down weeping when he saw me. She tells me how her husband in a Catholic school in Nebraska came late for a play that he was the star of and how the nuns had all the schoolchildren on their knees praying that he would appear.

On Tuesday I decide I need to be alone. I want to walk around and write. Everyone has a great fear in life. Mine is loneliness. Naturally our great fear is usually the one most important to overcome to reach our life's dreams. I am a writer. Writers spend a lot of time alone writing. Also, being an artist in our society makes us lonely. Everyone else leaves in the morning for work and structured jobs. Artists live outside that built-in social system.

So I have chosen to spend the day alone because I always want to push my boundaries. It's noon, very hot. I am not going to the beach and everything is closed here at midday. I begin to wonder what I am doing with my life. Whenever I get disoriented or not sure of myself, it seems I bring my whole life into question. It becomes very painful. To cut through, I say to myself, "Natalie, you planned to write. Now write. I don't care if you feel nuts and lonely." So I begin. I write about the nearby church, the boat in the harbor, my table in the cafe. It isn't great fun. I am wondering when my friend will return. She doesn't come back with the five-o'clock boat.

I can't speak Greek. I am all by myself and notice my environment much more acutely. The four old men at the next table take the long string out of the back of every green bean they have piled on the table. The one facing the ocean argues with the man to his left. An old woman in black near the wharf bends to pull up her long stocking. I wander to a beach I didn't know before and begin reading *Green Hills of Africa* on a sand bar as the sun sets. I notice a taverna that sells fresh tuna. I am attempting to connect with my environment. I miss my friend very much, but through my panic I break through to a kinship with the sand, the sky, my life. I walk back along the beach.

When we walk around Paris, my friend is afraid of being lost and she is very panicky. I don't fear being lost. If I am lost, I am lost. That is all. I look on my map and find my way. I even like to wander the streets of Paris not particularly knowing where I am. In the same way I need to wander in the field of aloneness and learn to enjoy it, and when loneliness bites, take out a map and find my way out without panic, without jumping to the existential nothingness of the world, questioning everything—"Why should I be a writer?"—and pushing myself off the abyss.

So when we write and begin with an empty page and a heart unsure, a famine of thoughts, a fear of no feeling—just begin from there, from that electricity. This kind of writing is uncontrolled, is not sure where the outcome is, and it begins in ignorance and darkness. But facing those things, writing from that place, will eventually break us and open us to the world as it is. Out of this tornado of fear will come a genuine writing voice.

While I was in Paris I read *Tropic of Cancer* by Henry Miller. In the second-to-last chapter Miller rages on about a school in Dijon, France, where he is stuck teaching English, about the dead statues and students who would become dentists and engineers, the cold bone winter and the whole town pumping out mustard. He is furious that he must be there. Then right at the end of the chapter, he sits, late at night, outside the college gates in perfect peace, surrendering himself for the moment to where he is, knowing nothing is good or bad, just alive.

To begin writing from our pain eventually engenders compassion for our small and groping lives. Out of this broken state there comes a tenderness for the cement below our feet, the dried grass cracking in a terrible wind. We can touch the things around us we once thought ugly and see their special detail, the peeling paint and gray of shadows as they are— simply what they are: not bad, just part of the life around us—and love this life because it is ours and in the moment there is nothing better.

10 ❁ *Meditation and Poetics*

ALLEN GINSBERG

Real poetry practitioners are practitioners of mind awareness, or practitioners of reality, expressing their fascination with a phenomenal universe and trying to penetrate to the heart of it. Poetics isn't mere picturesque dilettantism or egotistical expressionism for craven motives grasping for sensation and flattery. Classical poetry is a "process," or experiment—a probe into the nature of reality and the nature of the mind.

Major works of twentieth-century art are probes of consciousness—particular experiments with recollection or mindfulness, experiments with language and speech, experiments with forms. Modern art is an attempt to define or recognize or experience perception—pure perception.

A few Buddhist dharma phrases correlate charmingly with the process of Bohemian art of the twentieth century—notions like "Take a non-totalitarian attitude," "Express yourself courageously," "Be outrageous to yourself," "Don't conform to your idea of what is expected but conform to your present spontaneous mind, your raw awareness."

You need a certain deconditioning of attitude—a deconditioning of rigidity and unyieldingness—so that you can get to the heart of your own thought. That's parallel with traditional Buddhist ideas of renunciation—renunciation of hand-me-down conditioned conceptions of mind. It's the meditative practice of "letting go of thoughts"—neither pushing them away nor inviting them in, but, as you sit meditating, watching the procession of thought forms pass by, rising, flowering and dissolving, and disowning them, so to speak: you're not responsible any more than you're responsible for the weather, because you can't tell in advance what you're going to think next.

So it requires cultivation of tolerance toward one's own thoughts and impulses and ideas—the tolerance necessary for the perception of one's own mind, the kindness to the self necessary for acceptance of that process of consciousness and for acceptance of the mind's raw contents, as in Walt Whitman's "Song of Myself."

The specific parallel to be drawn is to Keats's notion of "negative capability," written out in a letter to his brother. He was considering Shakespeare's character and asking what kind of quality went to form a man of achievement, especially in literature. "Negative capability," he wrote, "is when a man is capable of being in uncertainties, mysteries, doubts, without any irritable reaching out after fact and reason." This means the ability to hold contrary or even polar opposite ideas or conceptions in the mind without freaking out—to experience contradiction or conflict or chaos in the mind without any irritable grasping after facts.

The really interesting word here is "irritable," which in Buddhism we take to be the aggressive insistence on eliminating one concept as against another, so that you have to take a meat-ax to your opponent or yourself to resolve the contradictions.

As part of "purification" or "deconditioning" we have the need for clear seeing or direct perception—perception of a young tree without an intervening veil of preconceived ideas;

the surprise glimpse, let us say, or insight, or sudden Gestalt, or I suppose you could say satori, occasionally glimpsed as esthetic experience.

In our century Ezra Pound and William Carlos Williams constantly insist on direct perception of the materials of poetry, of the language itself that you're working with. The slogan here—and henceforth I'll use a series of slogans derived from various poets and yogis—is one out of Pound: "Direct treatment of the thing." How do you interpret that phrase? Don't treat the object indirectly or symbolically, but look directly at it and choose spontaneously that aspect of it which is most immediately striking—the striking flash in consciousness or awareness, the most vivid, what sticks out in your mind—and notate that.

Pound was calling for direct perception, direct contact without intervening conceptualization, a clear seeing attentiveness, which, as you may remember, echoing in your brain, is supposed to be one of the marks of Zen masters, as in their practice of gardening, tea ceremony, flower arranging or archery.

That idea was relatively rare in late-nineteenth-century academic Western poetry, though Pound also drew from advanced Western models—old Dante to the French modernist poets Jules Laforgue, Tristan Corbière and Rimbaud. The tradition was initiated by Baudelaire, who had updated the poetic consciousness of the nineteenth century to include the city, real estate, houses, carriages, traffic, machinery. As Walt Whitman said, "Bring the muse into the kitchen."

Another slogan that evolved around the same time as Pound's and with the same motif was William Carlos Williams' famous "No ideas but in things." He repeats it in his epic *Paterson*, a little more clearly for those who haven't understood: "No ideas but in facts." Just the facts, ma'am. Don't give us your editorial; no general ideas. Just "give me a for instance"—correlate the conception with a real process or a particular action or a concrete thing, localized, immediate, palpable, practicable, involving direct sense contact.

In one of the immortal bard's lyrics, divine Shakespeare gives you nothing but things:

> When icicles hang by the wall
> And Dick the shepherd blows his nail
> And Tom bears logs into the hall,
> And milk comes frozen home in pail . . .
> And Marian's nose looks red and raw. . . .

That was Shakespeare's vivid presentation of unmistakable winter. You don't need to make the generalization if you give the particular instances. A poet is like a Sherlock Holmes, assembling the phalanx of data from which to draw his editorial conclusion. William James' notion was of "the solidity of specificity." Kerouac's phrase for it was, "Details are the life of prose." To have it you've got to have "direct treatment of the thing." And that requires direct perception— mind capable of awareness, uncluttered by abstraction, the veil of conceptions parted to reveal significant details of the world's stage.

Williams has another way of saying it—homely advice to young poets and American art practitioners: "Write about things that are close to the nose." There's a poem of his, much quoted by Buddhist poets, called "Thursday."

> I have had my dream—like others—
> and it has come to nothing, so that
> I remain now carelessly
> with feet planted on the ground
> and look up at the sky—
> feeling my clothes about me,
> the weight of my body in my shoes,
> the rim of my hat, air passing in and out
> at my nose—and decide to dream, no more.

Just try! Actually that one single poem is the intersection between the mind of meditation—the discipline of meditation, letting go of thoughts—and the Yankee practice of poetry after William James, where the poet is standing there, feeling the weight of his body in his shoes, aware of the air passing in and out of his nose.

We might make a little footnote here that "spirit" comes from the Latin *spiritus*, which means "breathing," and that the spiritual practices of the East are primarily involved with meditation, and that meditation practices usually begin with trying to increase one's awareness of the space around you, beginning with the fact that you're breathing. So generally you follow your breath, in Zen or in Tibetan style. It's a question of following the breath out from the tip of the nose to the end of the breath and then following it back into the stomach, perhaps, or the lower abdomen. So it's sort of charming that Williams arrived at this concept on his own: "air passing in and out at my nose—and decide to dream no more."

Another Pound phrase that leads the mind toward direct treatment of the thing, or clear seeing, is: "The natural object is always the adequate symbol." You don't have to go chasing after far-fetched symbols because direct perception will propose efficient language to you. And that relates to another very interesting statement, by the Tibetan lama poet Chögyam Trungpa: "Things are symbols of themselves." Pound means that the natural object is identical with what it is you're trying to symbolize in any case. Trungpa is saying that if you directly perceive a thing it's completely there, completely itself, completely revelatory of the eternal universe that it's in, or of your mind as it is.

In Kerouac's set of thirty slogans called "Belief & Technique for Modern Prose" there are a few mind-arrows, or mind-pointers, which are instructions on how to focus in, how to direct your mind to see things, whether it's "an old teacup in memory," or whether you're looking out a window, sketching verbally. Kerouac advised writers: "Don't think of words when you stop but to see picture better." William Blake's similar slogan is: "Labor well the Minute

Particulars, attend to the Little-ones." It's very pretty actually; take care of the little baby facts. Blake continues:

He who would do good to another, must do it in Minute
  Particulars
General good is the plea of the scoundrel hypocrite & flatterer:
  For Art and Science cannot exist but in minutely organized
  Particulars

A classic example of William Carlos Williams in America seeing minute particulars clearly, precisely, thoroughly, is in the most famous and most obvious of Imagist poems, "The Red Wheelbarrow."

> so much depends
> upon
>
> a red wheel
> barrow
>
> glazed with rain
> water
>
> beside the white
> chickens.

That's considered the acme Imagist poem of direct perception. I think it was written in the twenties. It's not much, actually. Williams didn't think it was so much; he said, "An inconsequential poem—written in 2 minutes—as was (for instance) The Red Wheelbarrow and most other short poems." But it became a sort of sacred object.

Why did he focus on that one image in his garden? Well, he probably didn't focus on it—it was just there and he saw it. And he remembered it. Vividness is self-selecting. In other words, he didn't prepare to see it, except that he had had a life's preparation in practicing awareness "close to the nose," trying to stay in his body and observe the space around him. That kind of spontaneous awareness has a Buddhist term for it: "the Unborn." For where does a thought come from? You can't trace it back to a womb, a thought is "unborn." Perception is unborn, in the sense that it spontaneously arises. Because even if you tried to trace your perceptions back to the source, you couldn't.

To catch the red wheelbarrow, however, you have to be practiced in poetics as well as practiced in ordinary mind. Flaubert was the prose initiator of that narrowing down of perception and the concretization of it with his phrase "The ordinary is the extraordinary." There's a very interesting formulation of that attitude of mind in writing poetry by the late Charles Olson, in his essay "Projective Verse." Here's what Olson says:

> ONE PERCEPTION MUST IMMEDIATELY AND DIRECTLY LEAD TO A FURTHER PERCEPTION.... In any given poem always, always one perception must, must, must [as with the mind] MOVE INSTANTER ON ANOTHER!

I interpret that set of words—"one perception must move instanter on another"—as similar to the dharmic practice of letting go of thoughts and allowing fresh thoughts to arise and be registered, rather than hanging onto one exclusive image and forcing Reason to branch it out and extend it into a hung-up metaphor. That was the difference between the metaphysically inspired poetry of the thirties to the fifties in America after T. S. Eliot and the Open Form, practiced simultaneously by Ezra Pound and William Carlos Williams and later by Charles Olson and Robert Creeley. They let the mind loose. Actually, that's a phrase by one of the founders of our country: "The mind must be loose." That's John Adams, as reported by Robert Duncan in relation to poetics.

So we have, as a ground of purification, letting go—the confidence to let your mind loose and observe your own perceptions and their discontinuities. You can't go back and change the sequence of the thoughts you had; you can't revise the process of thinking or deny what was thought, but thought obliterates itself anyway. You don't have to worry about that, you can go on to the next thought.

Robert Duncan once got up and walked across the room and then said, "I can't revise my steps once I've taken them." He was using that as an example to explain why he was interested in Gertrude Stein's writing, which was writing in the present moment, present time, present consciousness: what was going on in the grammar of her head during the time of composition without recourse to past memory or future planning.

Mediators have formulated a slogan that says, "Renunciation is a way to avoid conditioned mind." That means that meditation is practiced by constantly renouncing your mind, or "renouncing" your thoughts, or "letting go" of your thoughts. It doesn't mean letting go of your whole awareness—only that small part of your mind that's dependent on linear, logical thinking. It doesn't mean renouncing intellect, which has its proper place in Buddhism, as it does in Blake. It doesn't mean idiot wildness. It means expanding the area of awareness, so that your awareness surrounds your thoughts, rather than that you enter into thoughts like a dream. Thus the life of meditation and the life of art are both based on a similar conception of spontaneous mind. They both share renunciation as a way of avoiding a conditioned art work, or trite art, or repetition of other people's ideas.

Poets can avoid repetition of their obsessions. What it requires is confidence in the magic of chance. Chögyam Trungpa phrased this notion, "Magic is the total delight in chance." That also brings magic to poetry: chance thought, or the unborn thought, or the spontaneous thought, or the "first thought," or the thought spoken spontaneously with its conception—thought and word identical on the spot. It requires a certain amount of unselfconsciousness, like singing in the bathtub. It means not embarrassed, not jealous, not involved in one-upmanship, not mimicking, not imitating, above all not self-conscious. And that requires a certain amount of jumping out of yourself—courage and humor and openness and perspective and carelessness, in the sense of burning your mental bridges behind you, outreaching yourself; purification, so to speak, giving yourself permission to utter what you think, either simultaneously, or immediately thereafter, or ten years later. That brings a kind of freshness and cleanness to both thought and utterance.

When I met Chögyam Trungpa in San Francisco in 1972 we were comparing our travels and our poetry. He had a heavy schedule and a long itinerary, and I said I was getting fatigued with mine. He said, "That's probably because you don't like your poetry."

So I said, "What do you know about poetry? How do you know I don't like my poetry?"

He said, "Why do you need a piece of paper? Don't you trust your own mind? Why don't you do like the classic poets? Milarepa made up his poems on the spot and other people copied them down."

That's actually the classical Buddhist practice among Zen masters and Tibetan lamas, like the author of "The Hundred Thousand Songs of Milarepa." These songs are the most exquisite and hermetic as well as vulgar and folk-art-like works in all of Tibetan culture—classic folk poetry, known by every Tibetan. But Milarepa never could write. The method, again, was spontaneous mind, on-the-spot improvisation on the basis of meditative discipline.

What Trungpa said reminded me of a similar exchange that I had with Kerouac, who also urged me to be more spontaneous, less worried about my poetic practice. I was always worried about my poetry. Was it any good? Were the household dishes right, was the bed made? I remember Kerouac falling down drunk on the kitchen floor of 170 East Second Street in 1960, laughing up at me and saying, "Ginsberg, you're a hairy loss." That's something that he made up on the spot, a phrase that just came out of his mouth, and I was offended. A hairy loss! If you allow the active phrase to come to your mind, allow that out, you speak from a ground that can relate your inner perception to external phenomena, and thus join Heaven and Earth.

11 ❂ *Just Being at the Piano*

MILDRED CHASE

Nowhere is it more important to be in the here and now than in playing the piano. The slightest lapse in attention will affect every aspect of how I realize the recreation of a piece of music. One note, coming a hair's breadth late in time, may distort the expression of a phrase. It is impossible to be self-conscious and totally involved in the music at the same time. Consciousness of the self is a barrier between the player and the instrument. As I forget my own presence, I attain a state of oneness with the activity and become absorbed in a way that defies the passage of time.

Each time we play, we are new beings, and the performance that was fitting yesterday does not have the ring of truth today—even if we were to identically duplicate it. Spontaneity in playing is all important; only a recording will sound the same each time it plays.

In my own experience, I had to dare to let go of a way of playing that was secure, based upon years of study. In letting go of a way of playing that had held up well enough in concerts, I often wondered if I was losing my way, never to find it again and never to reach another that I could accept in its place. It was easy to become discouraged. Yet all this was necessary in order to allow the insights which proved to be the missing parts in my training. These were parts that only I could fill in, that could be learned only from myself. What I discovered gave me that sense of deeper involvement in my music that I had known to be missing. Through this process of growth I finally began to realize the true reward of my art: living in a constant state of discovery and increased awareness.

I am now able to reach a state of being at the piano from which I come away renewed and at peace with myself, having established a harmony of the mind, heart, and body. This does not diminish my performance in any way, either in style or in communicativeness. In fact, it is quite the opposite. The heightened awareness and the sense of harmony that I take away with me from the instrument benefit the people with whom I interact, and the other activities that occupy me. We bring to our music from our lives and take from our music to the rest of our living.

I no longer feel tormented as I used to when I am unable to fit in my hours of practice. Now even if I have only fifteen minutes at the piano on an extremely busy day, if I can reach this state of harmony in my playing even briefly, I leave the instrument knowing that I have experienced the heightened moment, and to touch on it will nourish the rest of the day.

Just being at the piano—egoless—is to reach that place where the only thing that exists is the sound and moving toward the sound. The music on the page that was outside of you is now within you, and moves through you; you are a channel for the music, and play from the center of your being. Everything that you have consciously learned, all of your knowledge, emanates from within you. There is a sense of oneness in which the heart of the musician and the heart of the composer meet, in which there is no room for self-conscious thought. You are at one with yourself and the act, and feel as if the playing has already happened and you are effortlessly releasing it. The music is in your hands, in the air, in the room, the music is everywhere, and the whole universe is contained in the experience of playing.

12 ❀ Coming Home to the Body

DENISE TAYLOR

In teaching movement and improvisation, I have found that when the mind is fully present with an activity, a radiance, a visually perceptible authenticity emerges. Both performer and audience sense this undeniable quality of presence. I call it "the authentic moment." In this moment the ordinary is experienced as remarkable.

Such moments come naturally to the untrained mover, who isn't sure what to do; since there are no familiar reference points, the mind is forced to stay in the immediate vicinity—which is the present moment. This naturalness can also be refined and developed. The practice of mindfulness—learning to discern sensations in the body in stillness and movement—can help us learn to be in our body in a more natural, spontaneous way.

The Buddha gave four primary postures for meditation: standing, sitting, walking, and lying down. We are always in one of these or on the way to one, so they are continually available to us as vehicles for mindfulness. We get up from bed; reach for a glass in the cupboard; lean over to scrub the toilet; sit down at a table; cross our legs; look into the sky. Being "on the way"—in transition between these postures— also provides a potential focus for the mind.

To turn our attention to the movement of our bodies is an act of love, in the sense of self-regard. When people used to say, "You have to love yourself first," I was never sure what this meant. I needed a tangible method. Techniques like visualization or writing affirmations never worked for me. But feeling my feet on the ground, the heat in my chest, the constriction in my head when I'm angry, the air over my bare feet as I walk, the sensation of my body turning in water— these all give me a sense that I am here, like it or not. There's no mistaking what is happening and there's no way to do it wrong. I am moving through the world with a sense of watching sweetly over it all. I am actually with myself, like a good friend, as I walk, run, dance, or sit down.

Of course, this doesn't work if we are trying to sit in the chair with perfect posture, to dance artfully, or to run faster than the day before. Trained performers often struggle to reenact a genuineness they once felt, to relive a moment of past inspiration, instead of opening themselves to the rawness and vulnerability of the unknown present. To be at home in our body, it is important to open to the sensations of our movement without a lot of comment, without trying to live up to an image or to engage in a self-improvement campaign.

Letting things unfold in this way is at the heart of all improvisation that is fresh and alive. There is no one self-consciously doing it. It is as though we had just entered a theater and come upon a rehearsal in progress. It has a magical, one-of-a-kind, never-to-be-seen-again quality. Even if someone had a video camera and shot the scene for later viewing, it wouldn't capture that authentic moment, which arose spontaneously out of our state of mind, the time of day, our receptivity to what we saw and felt—a thousand elements, none of which can be grasped or held onto.

Authentic expression often begins with quirky, jagged

edges. When we are grappling to express some profound truth in ourselves, our speech often becomes faltering, full of holes. Similarly, spontaneous movement can have a craggy quality, and is often a bit messy. We must give up the struggle to maintain our composure, to look good, and to cover up our moments of being at a loss. This requires a willingness to surrender and *fall* into the next movement, without preconceptions about how we will look. Falling requires letting go, as when we fall asleep or fall in love. If we refuse to fall, our body becomes rigid and our movements become premeditated.

We must also be willing to let ourselves "do it wrong," and let our awkwardness be witnessed. To be seen like this may feel uncomfortable for the performer, but the spectator often finds it gripping and engaging. When we enter directly into our own discomfort, and let that be seen, this connects us with others. Although we may imagine them judging us, those who witness us in this moment of "falling apart" will often feel a tremendous sense of goodwill and intimacy with us.

Mindfulness practice trains us to drop into the body again and again. What we find when we look around in the body are sensations. All the drama of our thought, feeling, and action begins with sensations. Through mindfulness we train ourselves to be in the body to receive them. To be present with the sensations in our body is not an act of will. It is a kind of equanimity or grace. In such moments we feel our activity belonging to life. We wash the dishes as a holy act. We turn the key in the lock and know what the wrist is doing. Feeling our body turn away from the cold weather, we catch ourselves and consciously rise up to meet it. The choice to be aware is often an act of courage.

The essential practice here, which I learned from my meditation teacher, Ruth Denison, is to return to whatever presents itself in our experience from moment to moment, to feel the actual physical sensation of our aliveness. Movement invites attention, asks us to practice devotion to ourselves, not in a self-centered way, but as an act of loyalty. Instead of abandoning ourselves, we can learn to inhabit ourselves. The body is tremendously homesick for us, and it waits patiently for our return. Though we have ignored its invitations for years and years, when we do say yes, now, it bounds forward with great exuberance and know-how. We find that we need no training in being fully alive, that we only lacked the determination to feel our aliveness. And here it is.

13 ✿ Zen Archery

EUGEN HERRIGEL

The next thing to be learned was the "loosing" of the arrow.

"All that you have learned hitherto," said the Master one day, "was only a preparation for loosing the shot. We are now faced with a new and particularly difficult task, which brings us to a new stage in the art of archery." So saying, the Master gripped his bow, drew it and shot. Only now, when expressly watching out for it, did I observe that though the right hand of the Master, suddenly opened and released by the tension, flew back with a jerk, it did not cause the least shaking of the body. At least in the case of the Master the loose looked so simple and undemanding that it might have been child's play.

The effortlessness of a performance for which great strength is needed is a spectacle of whose aesthetic beauty the East has an exceedingly sensitive and grateful appreciation. But ever more important to me was the fact that the certainty of hitting seemed to depend on the shot's being smoothly loosed. I knew from rifle-shooting what a difference it makes to jerk away, if only slightly, from the line of sight. All that I had learned and achieved so far only became intelligible to me from this point of view: relaxed drawing of the bow, relaxed holding at the point of highest tension, relaxed loosing of the shot, relaxed cushioning of the recoil—did not all this serve the grand purpose of hitting the target, and was not this the reason why we were learning archery with so much trouble and patience? Why then had the Master spoken as if the process we were now concerned with far exceeded everything we had practiced and accustomed ourselves to up till now?

However that may be, I went on practicing diligently and conscientiously according to the Master's instructions, and yet all my efforts were in vain. Often it seemed to me that I had shot better before, when I loosed the shot at random without thinking about it. Above all I noticed that I could not open the right hand, and particularly the fingers gripping the thumb, without exertion. The result was a jerk at the moment of release, so that the arrow wobbled. Still less was I capable of cushioning the suddenly freed hand. The Master continued undeterred to demonstrate the correct loose; undeterred I sought to do like him—with the sole result that I grew more uncertain than ever.

The Master was evidently less horrified by my failure than I myself. Did he know from experience that it would come to this? "Don't think of what you have to do, don't consider how to carry it out!" he exclaimed. "The shot will only go smoothly when it takes the archer himself by surprise. It must be as if the bowstring suddenly cut through the thumb that held it. You mustn't open the right hand on purpose."

There followed weeks and months of fruitless practice. I could take my standard again and again from the way the Master shot, see with my own eyes the nature of the correct loose; but not a single one succeeded. If, waiting in vain for the shot, I gave way to the tension because it began to be unendurable, then my hands were slowly pulled together, and the shot came to nothing. If I grimly resisted the tension till I was gasping for breath, I could only do so by calling on the arm and shoulder muscles for aid. I then stood there immobilized—like a statue, I mocked the Master—but tense, and my relaxedness was gone.

Perhaps it was chance, perhaps it was deliberately arranged by the Master, that we one day found ourselves together over a cup of tea. I seized on this opportunity for a discussion and poured my heart out.

"I understand well enough," I said, "that the hand mustn't be opened with a jerk if the shot is not to be spoiled. But however I set about it, it always goes wrong. If I clench my hand as tightly as possible, I can't stop it shaking when I open my fingers. If, on the other hand, I try to keep it relaxed, the bowstring is torn from my grasp before the full stretch is reached—unexpectedly, it is true, but still too early. I am caught between these two kinds of failure and see no way of escape." "You must hold the drawn bowstring," answered the Master, "like a little child holding the proffered finger. It grips it so firmly that one marvels at the strength of the tiny fist. And when it lets the finger go, there is not the slightest jerk. Do you know why? Because a child doesn't think: I will now let go of the finger in order to grasp this other thing. Completely unself-consciously, without purpose, it turns from one to the other, and we would say that it was playing with the things, were it not equally true that the things are playing with the child."

"Maybe I understand what you are hinting at with this comparison," I remarked. "But am I not in an entirely different situation? When I have drawn the bow, the moment comes when I feel: unless the shot comes at once I shan't be able to endure the tension. And what happens then? Merely that I get out of breath. So I must loose the shot whether I want to or not, because I can't wait for it any longer."

"You have described only too well," replied the Master, "where the difficulty lies. Do you know why you cannot wait for the shot and why you get out of breath before it has come? The right shot at the right moment does not come because you do not let go of yourself. So long as that is so, you have no choice but to call forth something yourself that ought to happen independently of you, and so long as you call it forth your hand will not open in the right way—like the hand of a child. Your hand does not burst open like the skin of a ripe fruit."

I had to admit to the Master that this interpretation made me more confused than ever. "For ultimately," I said, "I draw the bow and loose the shot in order to hit the target. The drawing is thus a means to an end, and I cannot lose sight of this connection. The child knows nothing of this, but for me the two things cannot be disconnected."

"The right art," cried the Master, "is purposeless, aimless! The more obstinately you try to learn how to shoot the arrow for the sake of hitting the goal, the less you will succeed. You think that what you do not do yourself does not happen."

"What must I do, then?" I asked thoughtfully.

"You must learn to wait properly."

"And how does one learn that?"

"By letting go of yourself, leaving yourself and everything yours behind you so decisively that nothing more is left of you but a purposeless tension."

"So I must become purposeless—on purpose?" I heard myself say.

"No pupil has ever asked me that, so I don't know the right answer."

"And when do we begin these new exercises?"

"Wait until it is time."

This conversation—the first intimate talk I had had since the beginning of my instruction—puzzled me exceedingly. Now at last we had touched on the theme for whose sake I had undertaken to learn archery. Was not this letting go of oneself, of which the Master had spoken, a stage on the way to emptiness and detachment? Had I not reached the point where the influence of Zen on the art of archery began to make itself felt? What the relation might be between the purposeless waiting-capacity and the loosing of the shot at the right moment, when the tension spontaneously fulfilled itself, I could not at present fathom.

The first step along this road had already been taken. It had led to a loosening of the body, without which the bow cannot be properly drawn. If the shot is to be loosed right, the physical loosening must now be continued in a mental and spiritual loosening, so as to make the mind not only agile, but free.

In order that this actionless activity may be accomplished instinctively, the soul needs an inner hold, and it wins it by concentrating on breathing. This is performed consciously and with a conscientiousness that borders on the pedantic. The breathing in, like the breathing out, is practiced again and again by itself with the utmost care.

Care has only to be taken that the body is relaxed whether standing, sitting, or lying, and if one then concentrates on breathing one soon feels oneself shut in by impermeable layers of silence. One only knows and feels that one breathes.

This exquisite state of unconcerned immersion in oneself is not, unfortunately, of long duration. It is liable to be disturbed from inside. As though sprung from nowhere, moods, feelings, desires, worries, and even thoughts incontinently rise up, in a meaningless jumble, and the more far-fetched and preposterous they are, and the less they have to do with that on which one has fixed one's consciousness, the more tenaciously they hang on. It is as though they wanted to avenge themselves on consciousness for having, through concentration, touched upon realms it would otherwise never reach. The only successful way of rendering this disturbance inoperative is to keep on breathing, quietly and unconcernedly, to enter into friendly relations with whatever appears on the scene, to accustom oneself to it, to look at it equably and at last grow weary of looking.

This state, in which nothing definite is thought, planned, striven for, desired, or expected, which is at bottom purposeless and egoless, was called by the Master truly "spiritual." It is in fact charged with spiritual awareness and is therefore also called "right presence of mind." This means that the mind or spirit is present everywhere, because it is nowhere attached to any particular place. And it can remain present because, even when related to this or that object, it does not cling to it and thus lose its original mobility. Like water filling a pond, which is always ready to flow off again, it can work its inexhaustible power because it is free, and be open to everything because it is empty. This state is essentially a primordial state, and its symbol, the empty circle, is not empty of meaning for him who stands within it.

Out of the fullness of this presence of mind, disturbed by no ulterior motive, the artist who is released from all attachment must practice his art. Archery thus becomes a ceremony which exemplifies the "Great Doctrine."

It is this mastery of form that the Japanese method of instruction seeks to inculcate. Practice, repetition, and repetition of the repeated with ever increasing intensity are its distinctive features for long stretches of the way.

A painter seats himself before his pupils. He examines his brush and slowly makes it ready for use, carefully rubs ink, straightens the long strip of paper that lies before him on the mat, and finally, after lapsing for a while into profound concentration, in which he sits like one inviolable, he produces with rapid, absolutely sure strokes a picture which, capable of no further correction and needing none, serves the class as a model.

A flower master begins the lesson by cautiously untying the bast which holds together the flowers and sprays of blossom, and laying it to one side carefully rolled up. Then he inspects the sprays one by one, picks out the best after repeated examination, cautiously bends them into the form which exactly corresponds with the role they are to play, and finally places them together in an exquisite vase. The completed picture looks just as if the Master had guessed what Nature had glimpsed in dark dreams.

Why doesn't the teacher allow these preliminaries, unavoidable though they are, to be done by an experienced pupil? Does it lend wings to his visionary and plastic powers if he rubs the ink himself, if he unties the bast so elaborately instead of cutting it and carelessly throwing it away? And what impels him to repeat this process at every single lesson, and, with the same remorseless insistence, to make his pupils copy it without the least alteration? He sticks to this traditional custom because he knows from experience that the preparations for working put him simultaneously in the right frame of mind for creating. The meditative repose in which he performs them gives him that vital loosening and equability of all his powers, that collectedness and presence of mind, without which no right work can be done. Sunk without purpose in what he is doing, he is brought face to face with that moment when the work, hovering before him in ideal lines, realizes itself as if of its own accord.

As in the case of archery, there can be no question but that these arts are ceremonies. More clearly than the teacher could express it in words, they tell the pupil that the right frame of mind for the artist is only reached when the preparing and the creating, the technical and the artistic, the material and the spiritual, the project and the object, flow together without a break.

Day by day I found myself slipping more easily into the ceremony which sets forth the "Great Doctrine" of archery, carrying it out effortlessly or, to be more precise, feeling myself being carried through it as in a dream. Thus far the Master's predictions were confirmed. Yet I could not prevent my concentration from flagging at the very moment when the shot ought to come. Waiting at the point of highest tension not only became so tiring that the tension relaxed, but so agonizing that I was constantly wrenched out of my self-immersion and had to direct my attention to discharging the shot. "Stop thinking about the shot!" the Master called out. "That way it is bound to fail." "I can't help it," I answered, "the tension gets too painful."

"You only feel it because you haven't really let go of yourself. It is all so simple. You can learn from an ordinary bamboo leaf what ought to happen. It bends lower and lower under the weight of snow. Suddenly the snow slips to the ground without the leaf having stirred. Stay like that at the point of highest tension until the shot falls from you. So, indeed, it is: when the tension is fulfilled, the shot *must* fall, it must fall from the archer like snow from a bamboo leaf, before he even thinks it."

In spite of everything I could do or did not do, I was unable to wait until the shot "fell." As before, I had no alternative but to loose it on purpose.

One day I asked the Master: "How can the shot be loosed if 'I' do not do it?"

" 'It' shoots," he replied.

"I have heard you say that several times before, so let me put it another way: How can I wait self-obliviously for the shot if 'I' am no longer there?"

" 'It' waits at the highest tension."

"And who or what is this 'It'?"

"Once you have understood that, you will have no further need of me. And if I tried to give you a clue at the cost of your own experience, I would be the worst of teachers and would deserve to be sacked! So let's stop talking about it and go on practicing."

Weeks went by without my advancing a step. At the same time I discovered that this did not disturb me in the least. Had I grown tired of the whole business? Whether I learned the art or not, whether I experienced what the Master meant by 'It' or not, whether I found the way to Zen or not—all this suddenly seemed to have become so remote, so indifferent, that it no longer troubled me. Several times I made up my mind to confide in the Master, but when I stood before him I lost courage; I was convinced that I would never hear anything but the monotonous answer: "Don't ask, practice!" So I stopped asking, and would have liked to stop practicing, too, had not the Master held me inexorably in his grip. I lived from one day to the next, did my professional work as best I might, and in the end ceased to bemoan the fact that all my efforts of the last few years had become meaningless.

Then, one day, after a shot, the Master made a deep bow and broke off the lesson. "Just then 'It' shot!" he cried, as I stared at him bewildered. And when I at last understood what he meant I couldn't suppress a sudden whoop of delight.

"What I have said," the Master told me severely, "was not praise, only a statement that ought not to touch you. Nor was my bow meant for you, for you are entirely innocent of this shot. You remained this time absolutely self-oblivious and without purpose in the highest tension, so that the shot fell from you like a ripe fruit. Now go on practicing as if nothing had happened."

Only after a considerable time did more right shots occasionally come off, which the Master signalized by a deep bow. How it happened that they loosed themselves without my doing anything, how it came about that my tightly closed right hand suddenly flew back wide open, I could not explain then and I cannot explain today. The fact remains that it did happen, and that alone is important.

The Master proceeded to give us a demonstration of target-shooting: both arrows were embedded in the black of the target. Then he bade us perform the ceremony exactly as before, and, without letting ourselves be put off by the target, wait at the highest tension until the shot "fell." The slender bamboo arrows flew off in the right direction, but failed to hit even the sandbank, still less the target, and buried themselves in the ground just in front of it.

"Your arrows do not carry," observed the Master, "because they do not reach far enough spiritually. You must act as if the goal were infinitely far off. For master archers it is a fact of common experience that a good archer can shoot further with a medium-strong bow than an unspiritual archer can with the strongest. It does not depend on the bow, but on the presence of mind, on the vitality and awareness with which you shoot. In order to unleash the full force of this spiritual awareness, you must perform the ceremony differently: rather as a good dancer dances. If you do this, your movements will spring from the center, from the seat of right breathing. Instead of reeling off the ceremony like something learned by heart, it will then be as if you were creating it under the inspiration of the moment, so that dance and dancer are one and the same. By performing the ceremony like a religious dance, your spiritual awareness will develop its full force."

I do not know how far I succeeded in "dancing" the ceremony and thereby activating it from the center. I no longer shot too short, but I still failed to hit the target. This prompted me to ask the Master why he had never yet explained to us how to take aim. There must, I supposed, be a relation of sorts between the target and the tip of the arrow, and hence an approved method of sighting which makes hitting possible.

"Of course there is," answered the Master, "and you can easily find the required aim yourself. But if you hit the target with nearly every shot you are nothing more than a trick archer who likes to show off. For the professional who counts his hits, the target is only a miserable piece of paper which he shoots to bits. The "Great Doctrine" holds this to be sheer devilry. It knows nothing of a target which is set up at a definite distance from the archer. It only knows of the goal, which cannot be aimed at technically, and it names this goal, if it names it at all, the Buddha." After these words, which he spoke as though they were self-evident, the Master told us to watch his eyes closely as he shot. As when performing the ceremony, they were almost closed, and we did not have the impression that he was sighting.

Obediently we practiced letting off our shots without taking aim. At first I remained completely unmoved by where my arrows went. Even occasional hits did not excite me, for I knew that so far as I was concerned they were only flukes. But in the end this shooting into the blue was too much for me. I fell back into the temptation to worry. The Master pretended not to notice my disquiet, until one day I confessed to him that I was at the end of my tether.

"You worry yourself unnecessarily," the Master comforted me. "Put the thought of hitting right out of your mind! You can be a Master even if every shot does not hit. The hits on the target are only the outward proof and confirmation of your purposelessness at its highest, of your egolessness, your self-abandonment, or whatever you like to call this state. There are different grades of mastery, and only when you have made the last grade will you be sure of not missing the goal."

"That is just what I cannot get into my head," I answered. "I think I understand what you mean by the real, inner goal which ought to be hit. But how it happens that the outer goal, the disk of paper, is hit without the archer's taking aim, and that the hits are only outward confirmations of inner events—that correspondence is beyond me."

"You are under an illusion," said the Master after awhile, "if you imagine that even a rough understanding of these dark connections would help you. These are processes which are beyond the reach of understanding. Do not forget that even in Nature there are correspondences which cannot be understood, and yet are so real that we have grown accustomed to them, just as if they could not be any different. I will give you an example which I have often puzzled over. The spider dances her web without knowing that there are flies who will get caught in it. The fly, dancing nonchalantly on a sunbeam, gets caught in the net without knowing what lies in store. But through both of them 'It' dances, and inside and outside are united in this dance. So, too, the archer hits the target without having aimed—more I cannot say."

Much as this comparison occupied my thoughts—though I could not of course think it to a satisfactory conclusion—

something in me refused to be mollified and would not let me go on practicing unworried. An objection, which in the course of weeks had taken on more definite outline, formulated itself in my mind. I therefore asked: "Is it not at least conceivable that after all your years of practice you involuntarily raise the bow and arrow with the certainty of a sleepwalker, so that, although you do not consciously take aim when drawing it, you must hit the target—simply cannot fail to hit it?"

The Master, long accustomed to my tiresome questions, shook his head. "I do not deny," he said after a short silence, "that there may be something in what you say. I do stand facing the goal in such a way that I am bound to see it, even if I do not intentionally turn my gaze in that direction. On the other hand I know that this seeing is not enough, decides nothing, explains nothing, for I see the goal as though I did not see it."

"Then you ought to be able to hit it blindfolded," I jerked out.

The Master turned on me a glance which made me fear that I had insulted him and then said: "Come to see me this evening."

I seated myself opposite him on a cushion. He handed me tea, but did not speak a word. So we sat for a long while. There was no sound but the singing of the kettle on the hot coals. At last the Master rose and made me a sign to follow him. The practice hall was brightly lit. The Master told me to put a taper, long and thin as a knitting needle, in the sand in front of the target, but not to switch on the light in the target-stand. It was so dark that I could not even see its outlines, and if the tiny flame of the taper had not been there, I might perhaps have guessed the position of the target, though I could not have made it out with any precision. The Master "danced" the ceremony. His first arrow shot out of dazzling brightness into deep night. I knew from the sound that it had hit the target. The second arrow was a hit, too. When I switched on the light in the target-stand, I discovered to my amazement that the first arrow was lodged full in the middle of the black, while the second arrow had splintered the butt of the first and plowed through the shaft before embedding itself beside it. I did not dare to pull the arrows out separately, but carried them back together with the target. The Master surveyed them critically. "The first shot," he then said, "was no great feat, you will think, because after all these years I am so familiar with my target-stand that I must know even in pitch darkness where the target is. That may be, and I won't try to pretend otherwise. But the second arrow which hit the first—what do you make of that? I at any rate know that it is not 'I' who must be given credit for this shot. 'It' shot and 'It' made the hit. Let us bow to the goal as before the Buddha!"

The Master had evidently hit me, too, with both arrows: as though transformed over night, I no longer succumbed to the temptation of worrying about my arrows and what happened to them.

One day the Master cried out the moment my shot was loosed: "It is there! Bow down to the goal!" Later, when I glanced towards the target—unfortunately I couldn't help myself—I saw that the arrow had only grazed the edge. "That was a right shot," said the Master decisively, "and so it must begin. But enough for today, otherwise you will take special pains with the next shot and spoil the good beginning." Occasionally several of these right shots came off in close succession and hit the target, besides of course the many more that failed. But if ever the least flicker of satisfaction showed in my face the Master turned on me with unwonted fierceness. "What are you thinking of?" he would cry. "You know already that you should not grieve over bad shots; learn now not to rejoice over the good ones. You must free yourself from the buffetings of pleasure and pain, and learn to rise above them in easy equanimity, to rejoice as though not you but another had shot well. This, too, you must practice unceasingly—you cannot conceive how important it is."

During these weeks and months I passed through the hardest schooling of my life, and though the discipline was not always easy for me to accept, I gradually came to see how much I was indebted to it. It destroyed the last traces of any preoccupation with myself and the fluctuations of my mood. "Do you now understand," the Master asked me one day after a particularly good shot, "what I mean by 'It shoots,' 'It hits'?"

"I'm afraid I don't understand anything more at all," I answered, "even the simplest things have got in a muddle. Is it 'I' who draw the bow, or is it the bow that draws me into the state of highest tension? Do 'I' hit the goal, or does the goal hit me? Is 'It' spiritual when seen by the eyes of the body, and corporeal when seen by the eyes of the spirit—or both or neither? Bow, arrow, goal and ego, all melt into one another, so that I can no longer separate them. And even the need to separate has gone. For as soon as I take the bow and shoot, everything becomes so clear and straightforward and so ridiculously simple. . . ."

"Now at last," the Master broke in, "the bowstring has cut right through you."

14 ❁ The Art of Sword

TAKUAN SOHO

In terms of martial art, when you first notice the sword that is moving to strike you, if you think of meeting that sword, your mind will stop at the sword in just that position, your own movements will be undone, and you will be cut down by your opponent. This is what *stopping* means—the mind is being detained by some matter.

Although you see the sword that moves to strike you, if your mind is not detained by it and you meet the rhythm of the advancing sword; if you do not think of striking your opponent and no thoughts or judgments remain; if the instant you see the swinging sword your mind is not the least bit detained and you move straight in and wrench the sword away from him; the sword that was going to cut you down will become your own, and, contrarily, will be the sword that cuts down your opponent.

If you put your mind in the rhythm of the contest, your mind can be taken by that as well. If you place your mind in your own sword, your mind can be taken by your own sword. Your mind stopping at any of these places, you become an empty shell.

In Buddhism, we call this stopping of the mind *delusion*.

When facing a single tree, if you look at a single one of its red leaves, you will not see all the others. When the eye is not set on any one leaf, and you face the tree with nothing at all in mind, any number of leaves are visible to the eye without limit. But if a single leaf holds the eye, it will be as if the remaining leaves were not there.

•

If one puts his mind in the action of his opponent's body, his mind will be taken by the action of his opponent's body.

If he puts his mind in his opponent's sword, his mind will be taken by that sword.

If he puts his mind in thoughts of his opponent's intention to strike him, his mind will be taken by thoughts of his opponent's intention to strike him.

If he puts his mind in his own sword, his mind will be taken by his own sword.

If he puts his mind in his own intention of not being struck, his mind will be taken by his intention of not being struck.

If he puts his mind in the other man's stance, his mind will be taken by the other man's stance.

What this means is that there is no place to put the mind.

A certain person once said, "No matter where I put my mind, my intentions are held in check where my mind goes, and I lose to my opponent. Because of that, I place my mind just below my navel and do not let it wander. Thus am I able to change according to the actions of my opponent."

This is reasonable. But viewed from the highest standpoint of Buddhism, putting the mind just below the navel and not allowing it to wander is a low level of understanding, not a high one.

If you consider putting your mind below your navel and not letting it wander, your mind will be taken by the mind that thinks of this plan. You will have no ability to move ahead and will be exceptionally unfree.

This leads to the next question, "If putting my mind below my navel leaves me unable to function and without freedom, it is of no use. In what part of my body, then, should I put my mind?"

I answered, "If you put it in your right hand, it will be taken by the right hand and your body will lack its functioning. If you put your mind in the eye, it will be taken by the eye, and your body will lack its functioning. If you put your mind in your right foot, your mind will be taken by the right foot, and your body will lack its functioning.

"No matter where you put it, if you put the mind in one place, the rest of your body will lack its functioning."

"Well, then, where does one put his mind?"

I answered, "If you don't put it anywhere, it will go to all parts of your body and extend throughout its entirety. In this way, when it enters your hand, it will realize the hand's function. When it enters your foot, it will realize the foot's function. When it enters your eye, it will realize the eye's function.

"If you should decide on one place and put the mind there, it will be taken by that place and lose its function. If one thinks, he will be taken by his thoughts.

"Because this is so, leave aside thoughts and discrimination, throw the mind away from the entire body, do not stop it here and there, and when it does visit these various places, it will realize function and act without error."

Putting the mind in one place is called *falling into one-sidedness*. To be arrested by anything, no matter what, is falling into one-sidedness and is despised by those traveling the Way.

When a person does not think, "Where shall I put it?" the mind will extend throughout the entire body and move about to any place at all.

The effort not to stop the mind in just one place—this is discipline. Not stopping the mind is object and essence. Put nowhere, it will be everywhere. Even in moving the mind outside the body, if it is sent in one direction, it will be lacking in nine others. If the mind is not restricted to just one direction, it will be in all ten.

The Right Mind is the mind that does not remain in one place. It is the mind that stretches throughout the whole body and being.

The Confused Mind is the mind that, thinking something over, congeals in one place.

When the Right Mind congeals and settles in one place, it becomes what is called the Confused Mind. When the Right Mind is lost, it cannot function properly. For this reason, it is important not to lose it.

In not remaining in one place, the Right Mind is like water. The Confused Mind is like ice, and ice is unable to wash hands or head. When ice is melted, it becomes water and flows everywhere, and it can wash the hands, the feet, or anything else.

If the mind congeals in one place and remains with one thing, it is like frozen water and is unable to be used freely: ice that can wash neither hands nor feet. When the mind is melted and is used like water, extending throughout the body, it can be sent wherever one wants to send it.

•

When you dance, the hand holds the fan and the foot takes a step. When you do not forget everything, when you go on thinking about performing with the hands and the feet well and dancing accurately, you cannot be said to be skillful. When the mind stops in the hands and the feet, none of your acts will be singular. If you do not completely discard the mind, everything you do will be done poorly. Completely forget about the mind and you will do all things well.

15 ❁ *Driving Meditation*

KEVIN BERGER AND
TODD BERGER

AWARENESS AND EXPERIENCE

*P*ersonality, good or bad, has nothing to do with driving. Driving has to do with, quite simply, awareness and experience. In driving there is only an unbroken but discontinuous stream of moments of experience and awareness—unbroken in that no moment, like no snowflake, is like any other.

If you can truly be aware of where you are at this moment and experience everything there is to experience within this moment of space and time called "now," then you are "seeing into your natural-self." And in Zen lingo, to see into our natural-self means to use it—to put it into action.

Natural-self is what remains when you still your mind and ignore all the images of personality. Following this, natural-self relies only on experience and awareness in its interaction with the world. Through experience and awareness you gain access to your natural driving ability, and through further experience and awareness you gain confidence in your natural ability, until, finally, you are that ability.

Experience and awareness may, in fact, be all that natural-self is made up of. No one is quite sure what natural-self happens to be. Like a virtual particle in physics, it cannot be seen, only inferred.

DISCIPLINE AND PRACTICE:
MOVING MEDITATION

In driving, the discipline that is needed is called *Moving Meditation*. This discipline takes a certain amount of hard work, yet if we can muster the motivation to practice it for a while, say ten or fifteen minutes per outing, we can be assured of being a happier, safer, more mindful and efficient driver—a Zen Driver.

Moving Meditation is a practice that allows room for our natural-self to unfold, while filtering out image-attachments and other delusions that would rush in if given half a chance. It is, so sayeth the Diamond Sutra, "not dwelling on any object, yet the mind arises."

This arising mind gives way to our two basic guides to achieving true Zen Driving: awareness and experience. Moving Meditation, then, is what helps us get in touch with, improve, and heighten awareness/experience. Trusting our natural-self, practicing Moving Meditation, we focus on being *aware* of everything around us, while we experience, *feel*, everything we do and everything that happens around us.

NO SEEING

With a clear, still mind, free of all "perceptual prejudices," we are nothing but pure awareness/experience. What we're creating with Moving Meditation is a new way of perceiving, practicing what in Zen is called *no seeing*. That is, we look—simply observe—without qualification. "When seeing is no seeing there is real seeing," Suzuki tells us. Real seeing is when we forgo any "specific act of seeing into a definitely circumscribed state of consciousness."

To practice Moving Meditation you must fully accept where you now find yourself, here in your car. Divest yourself of all expectation, standards of comparison, and technique; take that clear, observing, unobstructed state of being, and keep on driving! Now, instead of sitting erect and attentive in a quiet stationary place like a Zendo or meditation hall, you are now sitting erect and attentive in your moving vehicle. You are now meditating as you move along. Do not be ruled by anything inside or outside of you. See and experience without intrusion, but when an intrusion does rear its ugly head in the form of anger, an opinion, some driver cutting you off, simply acknowledge the stray image and return your focus to being aware of everything around you. Now, driving along, be intimately involved in the action and be aware that everything around you is happening for the first time. Everything is constantly changing, each traffic situation requiring its own set of responses. Nothing is left to rote. Keep your mind, body, and senses wide awake, and as you drive along know that all that you *see* is as new as a baby's smile, no matter how many times you *think* you have seen it before.

Real or TV?

Using this newfangled vision allows you to realize that everything beyond your windshield has never happened before, does not fit into any concept, any thought, any memory image; each moment is one of ongoing, first-hand discovery. Practicing Moving Meditation allows you to experience your here-now involvement in all of the action around you. It's only when you lose your immediate awareness and experience that a black veil hangs over your perceptions, causing you to revert back to old patterns and images, transforming your windshield into a TV screen. As with TV, you are then sitting separate from what you are watching. And like everything on TV, what you see from behind the wheel appears either preprogrammed (a product of the past) or rehearsed and minutely structured. Conversely, by practicing Moving Meditation while driving, everything is seen as happening now, fresh, for the first time. But to the extent that your perceptions of what lies beyond your windshield are preprogrammed by thought—laden by conditioned image-filters—you are then that much removed from the actual driving experience. What you are then seeing, and acting upon, might as well be a TV program.

As you drive through your immediate neighborhood everything seems familiar: you stare out of your car and feel that you have seen this particular show a thousand times before. Same old homes, same streets, same kids, same sky, same earth, same problems, same grind. Every view is imbued with endless memories and associations, things that originate solely inside your head and color your perceptions. These images dilute your awareness, take you out of the immediate experience of your surroundings, and make your trip, short as it may be, unsatisfying and boring: a rerun. Also, considering that most accidents occur on "familiar" terrain, driving passively through your neighborhood can be a bit on the dangerous side.

Driving in your car, traveling through a TV show of your own making, is similar to what Castaneda's Don Juan referred to as operating from a "bubble of perception." According to the old sorcerer, we live inside a sphere or bubble, its inside surface as smooth and polished as a mirror, ". . . and what we witness on its round walls is our own reflection. . . . The thing reflected is our view of the world. That view is first a description, which is given to us from the moment of our birth until all our attention is caught by it and the description becomes a view." For many drivers, getting in their cars is not an opening of awareness and experience, but is like climbing into a bubble of perception.

A SAMURAI AWARENESS

Beginning with awareness, the discipline and practice is simply to *focus* on maintaining a 360-degree picture of everything around you at all times. Be aware that you are driving in a multidimensional reality where things are happening on every conceivable level. Sustain a full samurai 360-degree watch. Be aware of any and all possible situations. Let precious little escape your attention. Be aware of your speed, your surroundings; stretch your awareness in all directions, as far ahead, as far behind, and as far to the sides as you can see. There is no trick to developing this degree of awareness, nothing fancy in its use. You quite simply do whatever you need to do to sustain it. Keep glancing in the rearview and side mirrors, turn your head, turn your whole body; do, in fact, whatever's comfortable, just as long as you retain that 360-degree picture in your head. Just as long as you know as certainly as you can know anything exactly what is ahead of you and around you at any given instant!

This awareness is always a here-now affair. Awareness goes from instant to instant; you never anticipate or assume you know what another driver is going to do, for that is slipping out of awareness and into troublesome thought, which is how you get bushwacked! You cannot think your way out of a situation; thought is a thousand times *slower* than natural-self, non-action a thousand times *quicker* than deliberate action. Nothing can match the alacrity, acumen, decisiveness, and alertness of natural-self. And all you need to do to have it is to use it!

Be aware—focus on awareness.

Take account of and gather into your pure awareness everything outside you, everything within your field of vision and senses, anything that in the slightest way comes within the proximity of the skin of your car. Be aware of the sights and sounds and feelings in your path and slipstream. The white lines and Botts Dots that make your tires bump when you cross them. The shapes and shades of the cars keeping pace with you. Be aware of the color of traffic lights as far ahead as your vision carries. What is the traffic scene ahead of you? Behind you? Who's walking the sidewalks? In what direction do the shadows of the trees fall? How briskly is the wind blowing? How close are you to other cars? All this happens spontaneously as you drive along and practice Moving Meditation: you don't latch onto any of it. Nothing sticks in your mind, but nothing escapes it. Watch the eyes of the other drivers. Keep up a "running commentary" on the activity around you: the Mustang twenty feet behind you, gaining; the blue Toyota forty feet behind you, dropping back; the truck one hundred feet ahead of you, changing lanes; the motorcycle you hear on your tail to the left; that kid on the bike approaching an upcoming intersection; the dog in the window of that white house, just sitting there, watching.

No one can teach you this awareness. All you need is the intention or motivation and you will automatically do it. The mind is fully capable of retaining a circular picture while in motion; you don't have to physically look in any one particular direction at any one particular instant to know what's there. Just keep up a constant vigilance and your mind will "remember" a full moving picture. This ability allows you to move comfortably and fluidly through traffic, and, just in case, provides an out for quick emergencies. Accidents are, in theory, out there waiting for you. According to the Traffic Safety Council, two of the top four causes of automobile accidents are inattention and improper lookout—in different terms, poor awareness. If, however, you actively maintain the level of awareness implied by Moving Meditation, you automatically *know* what is out there waiting. You know where it is, you know how far away it is, and since all is in motion, you are able automatically to calculate how long it takes before all things converge.

But you not only want to be aware of what's going on outside of you, you also want to tune in to what is taking place inside of you. Be aware as you drive along of what comes up as extraneous mind chatter, especially those opinions, judgments, criticisms, and emotional valences stirred up by the action around you. Here are a few of the more common ones: "What a jerk!" "You bimbo!" "The light doesn't get any greener, buddy!" "Go any slower, lady, and you might as well walk!" All this incessant inner prattle moves you off center and out of your natural-self. Be aware of self-judgments as well. Go easy on yourself. Keep your focus on your surroundings.

An Impartial Participant

How can we avoid becoming uptight driving monsters and angry Road Rambos? What can we do with anger and frustration when they come sneaking up on us in our rearview mirror?

When confronting any driving situation, you do not want to react aggressively out of ego (the "me-versus-them" theory of driving), nor do you want to be a passive victim of fate and chance. "The basic difference between an ordinary man and a warrior," Don Juan tells Castaneda, "is that a warrior takes everything as a challenge, while an ordinary unaware man takes everything either as a blessing or a curse." What you want is to have no *personal investment* in any aspect of driving. No ego-ness, no victim-ness, no mind, no form, no thought, no image-attachments of any kind. "Everything that happens, and above all, what happens to me, should be observed impartially, as though on the deepest level it did not concern me," writes Herrigel. To drive from a place of pure, impartial awareness/experience divested of any sense of separate "me" is to cut off at the source any sour feelings for our fellow drivers. To rely solely on awareness and experience is to rise above every shot at our emotions from others—to be beyond petty grievances both inside and outside of ourselves. Centered in awareness/experience, traffic flows around you, and you move along as in a natural slipstream.

So now, driving along, you're suddenly startled by this high-speed, high-performance machine that comes flying out of nowhere and, within a hair's breadth, deftly zips around you. It doesn't cause you to swerve or brake, but still, as you watch it disappear into the horizon, how do you react? If you

have any reaction at all you are not driving from pure aware-
ness/experience. Consider, again, that there is no territory
you need to protect, no ego that need be offended, no value
system that calls for an emotional judgment. So, what's to
react to? Some fancy little car flitted by you like a bug; you're
aware of that, you experience the car whizzing past, and *that's
all!*

EXPERIENCE

Naturally, this high degree of awareness does not depend
upon some rarefied gymnastics of the mind—everything
that's happening around you must also be *felt*. So not only
must you be aware of all that is going on, but you must at the
same time *experience* all that is happening. By this I mean the
full mind-body sensation of every facet of driving, both
outer and inner. Driving is as much a physical sensation as
it is a mental one.

Be so attuned to the cars around you that you can actually
feel them. Feel them closing in, falling back, boxing you in.
Feel yourself accelerate away from them. Know how the
highway feels, the uneven macadam, the ruts, the smooth
pavement, the wet rainy roads, the hum of the steel bridge.

What feelings does the city's architecture stir? What
smells waft by? What do you hear? The engine? The wind?
The drone of traffic? The blare of a teenager's radio? Experience how your car genuinely feels in your hand: the vibra-
tions and tingle of the steering wheel; the friction of the tires
on the road's surface; the weight and maneuverability of the
car. How quick is it? How sluggish? Feel that turn coming up.
Feel yourself lean into it. Feel your speed. Sense your foot
on the accelerator or brake; feel the car's motion. Feel your
body tighten in the seat belt as you come to a sudden stop;
feel the force of gravity as you leap away from a stop light.

It is this experiential sense, this *being fully there*, nearly
impossible to describe, that makes driving something special, something you can slip into as comfortably as though
the road was custom-made for you.

Continue driving, and meanwhile check in on what's happening in the inner world. Are you late for an appointment? Do you feel anxious? Is traffic so jammed that you feel frustrated? What does the rush of adrenaline feel like when that fellow runs a stop sign just ahead of you? What about anger—are you going to hang on to it? All these feelings, especially anger and fear, have the potential, if indulged, of getting you "out of 'it.' " They take you out of your natural-self (pure awareness/experience). They poke large holes in your Moving Meditation and make driving a chore and not a joy; the road, no longer custom-made, becomes an aggravating obstacle course. So when these intruders pop up, you must snap back. Return to the discipline of Moving Meditation—be aware of, experience, and acknowledge the intruders, then let them go, once again returning your focus to the sights and sensations of driving.

With a degree of faith and trust in the practice of Moving Meditation we reach that level of "full presence participation" where we become our surroundings and are then driving from a new order of things.

16 ❀ The Work of Craft

CARLA NEEDLEMAN

How can a craft teach us to be? What is the craft of being human? The material, myself, that I have to work with constantly changes. It has qualities of clay, glass, metal, wood, wool; it is brittle, flexible, malleable, obdurate. It is as if the study of being human is the ultimate craft and all the crafts reflections of it.

When I began to learn pottery I knew nothing about it as a craft. I came to it, therefore, with a natural attitude of not knowing, and it was possible, with interest and persistence, to learn. I did not have to work for that attitude; it is, so to speak, written into the beginnings of things. After a time, when the technique of the craft had become more or less habitual to my body, knowing replaced not knowing and the mind, always lazy, always seeking self-satisfaction, rested there.

We are all like this, I think; what we do well we enjoy doing again and again for the pleasure of the skill, for the pleasure of competence. I am all the time overshooting the mark. When I am making a circular pot, I think of completing the circle while my hands are working on the base. When I meet a person I could simply take in that impression, but

I immediately begin to think about the person. I am never where I am. I have a territory and am unwilling to give it up, to forsake "knowing" for the unknown with all its uncertainty. "Knowing" is riches and I am unwilling to be poor.

It is a shock to realize this. I need to let that shock in, to allow it really to shock me.

At this point the craftsman has come to a crossroad. At the beginning it is simple ignorance that stands in my way— later on it is "knowing" that blocks me. I need to be where I am. When I'm not, when I'm lost out there somewhere, I am alienated from my life and all my thoughts and feelings take place in dreams. Simply put, if my life is to have meaning, I need to be alive inside my own skin. Craft is a way of working to be alive inside my skin.

A craft appeals at one and the same time to the various parts that make up my disharmonious self, to mind as well as to body, demanding such extraordinary care in the service of craftsmanship that the customary self-involvement of the mind is shaken. Very soon in the study of pottery I realize that my thinking just gets in the way.

The question of my craft is the question of myself—Who am I?—a question the craft can help me to rediscover again and again in those moments when I experience that I don't know. If I try to work honestly at a craft, not turning away when the going gets rough, these moments of myself in question will come. And if this experience occurs often enough, it acts to transform my understanding, chemically and from within.

Craftsmanship begins with disillusion. Disillusion is an extraordinarily interesting state of being, having immediate and far-reaching effects. It is a sacred state, a state that has power. It is an active, not a reactive state, and if the craftsman can bear to stay there, not to turn away, he begins to detect an opening in himself through which he can learn.

Disillusion, the recognition that I am not what I thought I was, that I don't know what I thought I knew, that I can't do what I wish to do, opens us to the creative dialogue. It

renders the craftsman, strains him through a very fine cloth
to rid him of impurities so that he, like the material substance of his craft, can be available to be worked upon.

But, unlike the simpler materials of wood, wool, or clay,
he doesn't remain available. He has feelings that react,
thoughts that explain. He turns away from the experience
into reactions and explanations. He finds himself back where
he started from. Except that something remains, a trace, a
sort of inner tingle, because there, in that special state called
disillusion in which everything is turned inside out, I know
that I'm alive.

Could my experience of disillusion, if more deeply met,
open me to a new energy in myself?

I first approached the work of craft with enthusiasm, with
the desire to learn, the wish to express something real in the
concrete world of objects. As I continue to work at the craft
I become aware of interference, something that comes between me and the object even while I'm working to form it,
a static that prevents the sound from being pure. At first and
for a long time I take this interference as incidental to the
work I'm trying to do, annoying, perhaps even dishearten-
ing, but not truly significant. I try to brush it away as if it
were a buzzing insect, but I somehow never take the time to
look at it more closely. Until I have to. Until it begins to
nibble away at the corners of my self-confidence and I begin
to recognize it, not only from the last hundred times it has
appeared, but more essentially, I begin to recognize it as
being intimately familiar. It is me.

The object I am working on looks like me. It is a mirror,
an accurate reflection. That I took so long to recognize it is
a telling commentary on the fact that I don't know myself.
The way I walk, the way I play cards, my relationships with
other people, the way I weave or carve or throw, express me.
But only in crafts is the result of that expression frozen in
time and space like a still photograph, distinct and separate
from myself, small enough, calling to be seen.

It, the object, contradicts my ideas, my illusions of what

I should be producing and it wounds my self-love to see it. I think it should be better and so I suffer from it. But it is me. I have worked as well as I could, and this object is the only possible truthful representation of that work. Faced with the truth of it, I enter the state of disillusion. I suffer it—which means I allow it to be, I accept the truth of it. I turn toward the object and toward myself, toward the truth, which, although it is bitter, is also, through being true, sweet.

Disillusion is the first appearance in us of a different level of understanding. The experience of disillusion stops thought. And with the screen of associations quieted, only then, the mind is receptive to what lies outside its own closed circle and can experience a moment of more precise knowledge.

Craftsmanship begins with disillusion. And eventually leads to a valuation, a respect, for the state of disillusion. Disillusion begins to be seen as a positive state, having the effect of bringing about in my whole organism a quiet and a seriousness that unite me as nothing else has power to, and I like it.

If I try to bring about quiet in myself, that quiet so subtly important for my well-being, I find that I don't know how to do it. I can't directly quiet myself. I hadn't known that. I am being led, thanks to the craft, thanks to the discoveries about myself that the craft is presenting me with, along a path of self-knowledge without, up to this point, any aspirations that I would call directly spiritual or religious.

Is there a connection between a spiritual way, a Path, and crafts? This question makes me approach my own relationship to my craft with a wider inner perspective. What I am trying to understand through the study of craft has to do with connectedness. What is the connection between me and the world?

Everything is interconnected, one Whole, gorgeously complex and various—huge orchestrated molecules of protein, the circulation of water through the oceans and sky of the planet, the intricate mobile of the planets and sun. In the human body each separate system and organ is so exquisitely well crafted one could write a poem in celebration of the architecture of the foot and another in homage to the kidney. The physical organism in its unified working is—miraculous. And yet, standing under, around, and within this work of art, this creation, I feel left out. I understand least of all things the movement of the energy of mind and know least of all the place of my own mind-self in the total schema.

Yet my efforts in the medium of my craft, my groping efforts toward understanding and expressing something true in the objects I produce, little by little bring about a transformation in myself. This transformation of attitude is itself the channel of connection with the larger world.

Brought by the craft to a condition that brings me into question and shakes my self-security, I turn toward myself in a new way, not knowing what I will find or how to look for it. I turn toward myself not like someone going into his house and shutting the door but like someone in a strange and dangerous new place who does not know what to expect and who has only his awakened senses to rely upon. That is, I turn toward myself not to exclude but to investigate.

The repeated failure at a craft, the failure that comes about because of the lack of correspondence between the truth that I only vaguely feel and the falsity that I express, has an effect. It wears me down, overcomes my resistance, brings me low. But unlike any other experiences of being diminished by life circumstances that I may have had, it does me no harm. I am, if anything, more intact than before. And I find a new strength in myself coming from an unsuspected place, a new and very different sincerity that makes it possible to go on. It feels a bit like the sensation of obedience, although I couldn't say what it is I am beginning to feel obedient to. It may be that what I perceive as obedience is the first thread of real connectedness, of relationship with the movement of energies both within me and in the world.

17 ❈ Working for a Living

JEAN MARTINE

I am at my desk early today, with a moment to sit quietly and listen to the question. Is there a craftsmanlike way of working that is available not only to the worker in his workshop, but to the worker wherever he works, whatever his work is—in a factory or bank, in an executive office or houseful of children; even here in a noisy advertising agency?

Today I want to know for myself if there is still a way of working that would not only support me physically, but would also support this inner hunger that I feel now: a hunger actually to be here at my job, more awake, instead of dreaming at it, swept along from one minor crisis to the next, from paycheck to paycheck.

The New York drama critic Walter Kerr seems to be speaking my thoughts when, in *The Decline of Pleasure*, he writes: "The work we are doing is more or less the work we meant to do in life [but] it does not yield us the feeling of accomplishment we had expected . . . If I were required to put into a single sentence my own explanation of the state of our hearts, heads, and nerves, I would do it this way: we are vaguely wretched because we are leading half-lives, half-heartedly, and with only one-half of our minds actively engaged in making contact with the universe about us.''

This is part of my concern right now: this half-heartedness, half-mindedness with which I live my one and only life. It seems related to the triviality of the work I do, and I would like to place the blame for my dissatisfaction squarely there. I begin to dream about a fulfilling work: in a hospital perhaps; in some use of myself that would satisfy this hunger. Still, what I am doing is the work at hand. It is my livelihood; it needs doing. I would wish to find a way to attend to it more creatively, or at least more carefully, so that it felt more like an exchange: a giving as well as a taking.

I remember the story of two Zen monks, both prodigious smokers. Concerned about the question of smoking during their prayer time, they agreed to consult their superiors. While one received a stern reprimand from his abbot, the other was given a pat of encouragement. The unlucky one, greatly puzzled, asked his friend exactly how he had framed his question. "I asked," the second monk replied, "whether it was permissible to pray while smoking."

Maybe this is the kind of care my work needs. To pray while typing, while answering the phone—would it require a very different way of praying; a way that Zen monks must come to through their training—something like that wordless beseeching one discovers in trying to guide a car along an icy road or in performing any exacting piece of work under all but impossible conditions?

I once looked up the origin of the word "prayer" and found its root is in the Latin precarius—"obtained by entreaty," hence implying uncertainty, risk. The plain truth is that in my usual way of working I feel nothing precarious or risky. Nothing is really at stake. Today, for reasons I don't understand, I feel that something vast and mysterious is at stake, something known only to me, important only to me. I can only call it my being. It's as if my usual way of working serves to sever me from my me-ness, from this new and fragile sense of myself at this typewriter right now.

Before I can go any further with a study of my own work, perhaps I need to ponder the meaning of work in general—in other times as well as in our own—and as I ponder, I sense a kinship between the words "work" and "worship." I begin to suspect that man is physically organized in exactly the way he is, just so that he will need to work in order to live; and it seems possible that the substance required for his own transformation and for the maintenance of the universe is created as a direct result of his work.

"In the sweat of thy face shalt thou eat bread," God told Adam, and if man did not actually *need* to work to feed, shelter, and clothe himself, actually in order to survive, perhaps this essential substance, whatever it is, would never be created. Perhaps, since man was created precisely as he is— exactly this kind of breathing, digesting, thinking, feeling organism—there is a precisely ordered way for him to work and to live in order to serve a universal purpose.

For me this is a fresh thought, this idea that it is man-at-work that serves the universe in a special way; and it sheds new light on the possible meaning of the way of the craftsman. However distracted the cathedral builders must have been, upon occasion, from the spiritual aspect of their work (for surely illness, family problems, all the continuing vagaries of the human condition beset these men as they do us), their inner hunger must have been fed by their way of working, a way indicated by their priests and guild masters who constantly reminded them that they were in the service of something higher, that their work was their means of serving and not an end in itself.

With what heart they must have worked then, entrusting themselves to this higher authority!—this same "heart," perhaps, that set the golden harp (surely a symbol of joy in work) side by side with the tools of gold that were unearthed by archaeologists in the Sumerian city of Ur. The dweller in a golden age or an age of faith seems to have understood that he was living a kind of double life, one in the visible world and one in the invisible. Traditional man was apparently taught from infancy that all that he manifested in his everyday living vibrated invisibly in another dimension and that it was his voluntary attempts to participate in his hidden dimension that set him apart from other living creatures—that made him, in fact, a transformer, a Man.

But today where are such teachers? Where are our priests? Our wise men? I try now to imagine what it would be like to be a member of a guild; to be an apprentice in a workshop at the head of which was a master in the original sense of the word: a man whose craft was truly his own, in his hands and heart and in his bones; a man who could impart the inner as well as the outer element of this craft to those working under him, not just by words and example, but by his very presence.

Guild members, we are told, would begin their day with the master in prayer to the guild's patron saint before turning to the work, and prayers of one kind or another punctuated the whole day. Throughout the day there was the closeness of man to man, the sense of one another's existence, and the exchange between the experienced workers and the novices: the meeting of eyes, the showing and the watching, the speaking and the listening. How different from the usual factories and workplaces of today, where little is "handed" from man to man, where eyes rarely meet, and the human voice cannot always rise above the noise of machinery; where men in their isolation from one another begin to feel a kinship only with their particular machine—a truck driver with his truck, a printer with his press, even a copywriter with her typewriter.

There is an instant now in which I feel the limitation of this kind of kinship, and I wonder how we ever lost touch with one another and with our sacred heritage. How did we become separated from that other dimension in which our forebears felt their common humanity and the common authority for their lives? Our discontent as workers today must stem from this incredible lapse: this mass forgetfulness that we are under any authority higher than that of our boss, whether he be the factory foreman, the president of the company, or oneself.

Oh, for the ordered structure of the guild workshop! The strong clear voice of the master "re-minding" me, in the real sense of that word, to return to the silence. So many of the rituals of the traditional societies must have been created for just this call to inner silence. The beating of drums, the tolling of the Angelus, the sounding of the ram's horn, the repetition of the sacred syllables in whatever language, the ceremonial dances—all these mysterious activities that until this moment have appeared to me like so many quaint customs must have been designed for just this reminding. And at this moment I am shocked to discover the life going on inside me: the breath coming and going; the amazing heartbeat. I am here; the thought is here; and a kind of feeling. I am here in this very ordinary place with a minute, mundane advertisement to write, but it is my work and it requires me.

What I constantly forget is that I always have my place. It is here exactly where I am. Where else could it be? Here is this life that is uniquely mine, one whole unit of creation that is entirely my place and my responsibility.

I feel a great desire not to lose touch with this feeling-thought that is with me this morning. I have felt it before: a wishing for something more for myself or from myself. Is there a master in me to whom I can turn, if—like people in fairy tales—I can wish hard enough? I don't know, but something I have read comes alive for me now: "Wood and stone will teach me what cannot be heard from the master's teaching."

I have no wood or stone, but I have my job; that is my reality for now. "To take what there is and use it," Henry James wrote many years ago, "without waiting forever in vain for the preconceived—to dig deep into the actual and get something out of *that*—this doubtless is the right way to live." A thought from Father Robert Capon's writing stirs vigorously in me. "Adam," he wrote, and he was speaking of twentieth-century Adam, of the likes of you and me, "is the priest of Creation. His truest work is to offer up reality itself, not just a headful of abstractions about it."

It seems as if it could be right here, even in this super-automated, super-franchised, polluted, synthetic age, that I might begin my apprenticeship; right here, now, in this attitude of seeing what is. Perhaps this is the elusive way of working that makes all the difference between the craftsman and the slave—just this reordering of my energies because I want to work this way, because I need to, because I must. The authority is still there. We are not forgotten in spite of our forgetfulness, for natural laws, unlike the ordinances of temporal authority, are never changing. It is the very constancy of these laws that offers us a challenge and a hope. It leaves something up to me; it is for me to seek a way to reconnect with these laws. It is even an obligation, if Simone Weil was right in saying that it is the work of our age to create a civilization "founded upon the spiritual nature of work."

Perhaps it would be just in a daily lifelong attitude of "seeing" that the noisy, chaotic activity I call my job could become a support for my attention instead of a distraction. Perhaps, if I attend to the reality that is in front of me moment by moment—phone, machine, pencil, boss, coffee—constantly failing, accepting to fail and to begin again—this perfectly ordinary work I do might become extraordinary work, might even become my craft.

The phone is ringing now. The first of my co-workers has arrived and is answering it. The question I began with remains:

Is there a way of working that would support this need I feel actually *to be* here at my work?

The answer, I am sure, is not to be found in my head or in any book, but quite simply in an ever-deepening of the question itself.

I confront the outline I left on my desk last Friday, and I get to work.

PART THREE

✿ *Healing and Well-Being*

Whatever pain or problem we have, if it helps us find a quality of presence—where we can open to it, see it, feel it, and find the truth concealed in it—*that* is our healing.

—JOHN WELWOOD

◙ Introduction

What is the source of health? Are physical, mental, and spiritual health different, or is there but one kind of health that takes many different forms? The conventional view is that health is the result of doing the right things, such as eating the right food, exercising, going to church each week, thinking positively, or meditating. However, viewing health as something to achieve gives rise to effort and striving, which create stress. And this can interfere with the natural healing tendencies already present within us.

The meditative traditions see things differently; they regard health as intrinsic to our nature, and thus already fully present within us. The source of health is our buddha-nature, or wakeful awareness, which contains qualities of openness, clarity, vitality, and caring. Tuning into this intelligence at work in us can guide us toward living in a healthy way. In this perspective, dis-ease results from a loss of connection with our intrinsic health, caused by ignorance, distraction, or confusion.

The principles involved in both creativity and healing are much the same. Creative expression arises out of the contact between our open awareness and the vividness of reality—the sound of leaves rustling in the wind, the tenderness we feel toward the one we love, the sudden perception of life's fleeting nature. Similarly, healing arises out of the contact between this awareness—with its intrinsic openness, clarity, and compassion—and our woundedness.

As a psychotherapist I have never seen any deep healing occur without people polishing the mirror of their awareness so that they could clearly see and feel what was going on. When our awareness illuminates what is really happening inside us, something opens up and comes alive inside, our breathing deepens, a new vista is revealed, and we feel an energetic shift in our body. Such moments of ordinary magic are turning points in the healing process.

The healing relationship between two people is simply an outer version of the healing presence we need to cultivate inside ourselves. Our innate wisdom—our ability to see things as they are—is our inner healer because it wakes us up from the distractedness that is literally making us sick. So we need to bring the confused, contracted parts of us into contact with this inner healer, expose our woundedness to awareness, and then listen for inner guidance.

It is not surprising that the terms *healing, whole,* and *holy* all come from the same root. When we meet and honor the inner healer—the source of health within us—we initiate a deeper connectedness with ourselves that makes us whole. And this makes us more sensitive to the sacred quality of life—the ordinary magic, beauty, and power at work in our body, our mind, and in all things.

In the first chapter of this section I describe the heart of the healing process in terms of *unconditional presence.* We all have spontaneous glimpses of this quality of presence in moments of crisis, ecstasy, or surprise—when we first fall in love, when a loved one dies, or when our car goes spinning out of control on an icy highway. Suddenly we are here, senses fully alert, without any other preoccupation. Yet we can also cultivate this kind of presence and bring it to bear on our states of physical and mental distress. Unconditional presence has two main aspects: *letting be*—allowing our experience, giving it space to be there as it is—and *being with*—making contact with what is there, letting it touch us.

Psychotherapist Karen Kissel Wegela explores these two aspects of unconditional presence in terms of "touch" and "go." She speaks of how important it is for a therapist to touch the client's experience, rather than remaining separate from it. The way to do this is by letting the other person's experience affect me. When I feel it inside myself, I have a sense of what things are like for that person. But it is also important not to "stop the mind" at this point, not to get stuck in any fixed reactions or attitudes toward this experience. This is the step of letting go. When I can touch another's experience without holding any fixed attitude toward it, then I can offer a truly helpful response that carries authenticity and weight. This is a guideline for healthy communication in any relationship, including our relationship with ourselves.

Ram Dass and Paul Gorman further explore how to listen in a helpful way, which they call "hearing from the heart." As they point out, this is not just warmth and empathy, but a keen presence of awareness that refuses to buy into someone else's mind games.

Nutritionist Marc David discusses how to practice mindfulness in one of the most unconscious areas of our lives: eating. He points out that the real nourishment we receive from food is not just vitamins and nutrients, but rather the whole process of eating itself. Therefore, if we eat in a more conscious way, our food will provide greater nourishment and well-being. Eating consciously, however, does not just mean buying health food. Oddly enough, many people who take great care shopping for organic food wind up eating it in a mindless, distracted way. Conscious eating means being present with the activity of eating. Here too, "touch"— engaging ourselves in preparing, chewing, tasting food— leads to letting go—not remaining fixated on food.

Writer Stephen Butterfield brings mindful attention to another area of our lives that we would just as soon ignore: illness. He describes how sickness can be a powerful teacher that wakes us from our usual distractions. By prompting us to pay closer attention to our lifestyle, our states of mind, and our relations with others, serious illness quickly helps us distinguish between the essentials of life and superfluous diversions. And by forcing us to slow down, it helps us perceive the simple beauty all around us, the generosity everywhere available, and the kindness all creatures need in order to flourish. Learning to make friends with disease could be important for all of us at some point in our lives.

In the final chapter of this section, Stephen Levine discusses how we can relate more consciously to anger, the most difficult of human emotions. He points out that if we are not on good terms with our anger, we cannot really be kind, because it will leak out unconsciously. The problem with anger is not the feeling itself, but the way we use it to dig ourselves into an oppositional mind-set, vindicating and defending ourselves while blaming and attacking the "other." Levine suggests that we inquisitively examine our anger instead of suppressing it or acting it out. This gives us access to the positive side of aggressive energy. When freed from oppositional mind-sets, the energy of anger can provide fuel, momentum, and stimulus to be straightforward, cut through obstacles, and seize the opportunities that come our way.

18 ❈ The Healing Power of Unconditional Presence

JOHN WELWOOD

> If your everyday practice is to open to all your emotions, to all the people you meet, to all the situations you encounter, without closing down, trusting that you can do that—then that will take you as far as you can go. And then you'll understand all the teachings that anyone has ever taught.
>
> —PEMA CHÖDRÖN

I'd like to discuss the quintessence of the healing process as I've explored it through the practices of psychotherapy and meditation. Before we can talk about healing, however, we need to understand the nature of the dis-ease or distress at the root of our psychological problems. Let us begin with some simple questions, ones that every therapist or healer has probably considered many times. Why is it so

This essay was adapted from a talk presented in Santa Barbara, California, in February, 1989.

difficult simply to open to our experience as it is? Why do we feel so uncomfortable with our feelings? What is this basic dis-ease we feel in relating to our own experience?

THE BASIC DIS-EASE

The nature of our dis-ease or distress is relatively simple, though the forms it takes are often complex: We have all turned away from certain areas of our experience that caused us pain as we were growing up—such as our anger, our need for love, our vulnerability, our will, our sexuality—and withdrawn our awareness from them. As children, when an experience was too much to handle, we would contract our awareness and our body, shutting ourselves down like a circuit breaker, out of fear.

For instance, if our need for love was frustrated, the overwhelming pain of feeling this need caused us to contract. Because we never learned how to open to that pain, our need still feels overwhelming whenever it arises, and so we still contract against it. In this way we become disabled, unable to function in certain areas of our lives. Turning away from our pain also creates a second, more ongoing form of suffering: living in a state of contraction.

CREATING AN IDENTITY BASED ON CONTRACTION

Over time, these contractions form the nucleus of an overall style of avoidance and denial. We develop a whole identity, or view of ourselves, based on rejecting such painful aspects of our experience. If we can't handle anger, for instance, we may try to be "a nice person" instead. Such an identity is always partial and never reflects the whole of who we are. It is based on grasping and identifying with aspects of our experience that we like and rejecting those we dislike. As a result, our identity is skewed, lopsided, incongruent with the totality of our experience.

Because such identities are not really who we are, they require ongoing maintenance. We continually have to prop them up and defend them against the onslaughts of reality that threaten to undermine them. It is as though we are trying to maintain a fragile dike against a restless ocean constantly smashing into it. Life is like the ocean, forever trying to wear away our narrow self-concepts, which compromise its freedom and vastness. The continual need to monitor our experience, in order to screen out feelings that might threaten our identity, creates a third kind of suffering: an ongoing, underlying state of tension and dis-ease.

Thus our psychological distress is composed of at least three elements: the basic pain of feelings that seem threatening and overwhelming; the contracting of awareness to avoid this pain; and the stress of continually having to prop up and defend an identity based on this avoidance and denial.

One of the main ways we try to hold our identity together is by developing an elaborate web of rationalizations—"stories" about the way we are or the way reality is—to justify our denial and avoidance. A story in this sense is a mental interpretation of our experience, a way of organizing our beliefs into an overall view of reality. Such stories may not be entirely conscious. Often they are more like dreams, consisting of sets of pictures or vague imaginings and expectations.

A woman whose father was distant in childhood didn't like to feel her need for emotional contact because it was too painful and frustrating. She justified her rejection of this need by creating a story: "Men are not emotionally available. You can never trust them. I will never let myself need a man." When this woman was in a relationship, she would always contract against her own need. She would hold herself back because she never wanted to be in such a vulnerable position again. As a result, men would always leave her because they couldn't feel connected with her. And this reinforced her story, "You can never count on men to be there."

That is how stories work—they become self-fulfilling prophecies. Our story creates a reality that in turn reinforces the story. In this way, we become more and more locked into a skewed identity. We all do this. We do not unconditionally accept ourselves and our experience. Instead, we live from conditional self-regard—accepting ourselves only when we feel the way we think we should. All psychopathology springs from this failure to value ourselves unconditionally.

Why do we spend so much energy maintaining an identity that keeps us divided and cut off from the fullness of our life? Our self-concept endures because it gives us a sense of solidity, a sense that "this is who I am." Even though it is only a partial identity, incongruent with the whole of who we are, at least it provides an illusion of stability and permanence in the ever-changing flux of existence. Even if my story is "I am nothing, I am nobody," at least *that is something!* In this case, I am something because I am nothing—I know who I am and what I am. I become a known quantity. This provides a certain comfort and security, even though it also completely frustrates me and causes tremendous pain.

UNCONDITIONAL PRESENCE AND HEALING

Yet if we were *totally* one with our identity, it wouldn't create any distress. The pain that our identity causes us arises from our larger intelligence—from our deeper being, which is suffering because we are not living as fully as we could. This more wakeful part of us feels the pain and constriction of being caught in a set of stories and beliefs, scripts and behaviors that cut us off from a rich and expansive openness to life. The nature of our being is an unconditional openness. We are born that way—curious, awake, and completely responsive to our environment—and unless we live that way, we will suffer.

The first and most difficult step in healing is to expose our wound—our disconnectedness from our larger being and the pain that causes. In this pain is our healing. If we turn away from it, we only add another link in the chain of contraction and denial that constitutes our dis-ease. If we attend to it, however, it will put us in contact with those aspects of our experience we have cut off or denied. The first step in healing is to acknowledge our dis-ease.

Yet it is hard to let ourselves feel our pain. Usually we turn away from it or try to cover it up because it threatens our identity. As soon as we start to look at it, a story comes up, a distracting belief, thought, or fantasy. As soon as we ask ourselves, "What is this? Why am I feeling so bad?" our mind steps in and says, "Oh, I know what it is. It's X or Y. It's my hangup with my mother . . . It's my inferiority complex . . . It's the same old thing . . . " Such notions are an obstacle to healing because they keep us in our busy discursive mind and separate us from our real experience.

Thus it is important for psychotherapists to help people discriminate between their stories and their actual felt experience. For example, if I ask a client how he feels and he says, "I feel stupid," I would say, "That's not a feeling. You don't *feel* stupid—that's a story you have about yourself. What's the actual feeling?" Then he might say, "Well, I feel vulnerable or shaky when I have to talk in front of a group." *That's* a feeling. It's very hard to work with someone's story, because it's just a set of thoughts that triggers further thoughts.

To be effective, therapists or healers continually need to sift through their own stories as well as their clients' stories about what is happening. This can be tricky. Therapists like to think that they know what's going on. As professionals, they've been trained for many years and have all this knowledge about what's supposed to be going on with people. Yet when they're actually working with someone, this knowledge in itself is not an agent of healing. It can be useful, it can be an aid. Yet the only way to promote healing is by reversing the condition that has led to our dis-ease.

Since the condition that has created our distress is a biased, narrow, partial view of our experience, we can't heal ourselves or anyone else just by promoting a different view. It might be a wonderful view, it might be the greatest view of reality in the world, but it will not be healing because it's just another set of partial beliefs. It's another frame that will block out some other aspect of our experience. It's another box we will eventually have to outgrow.

Instead of building bigger or fancier boxes, we need to develop the antidote to all our partial views of reality: being present to our experience as it is. We could call this *unconditional presence*. We could also call it *beginner's mind*. As Suzuki Roshi put it, "In the beginner's mind there are many possibilities, in the expert's there are few." We have all become experts at being ourselves, and in so doing we have lost our ability to be present with our experience in a fresh, open-minded way.

Psychotherapists often think of themselves as experts at knowing people. But the truth is that there are no experts in the realm of human experience. That is because the nature of human experience is unbounded—it doesn't come boxed to begin with. If you're an expert, your expertise is based on what you know; and what you know is a set of boxes, a collection of concepts, beliefs, theories, ideas about reality— not reality itself.

To be unconditionally present with our experience is the simplest thing we could possibly do. It means being present to what is, facing it as it is, without relying on any view or concept about it. What could be simpler than that? And yet, what could be more difficult?

How to do this? Actually, we do it all the time, without even knowing it. From moment to moment, our awareness is a simple presence and openness, but we usually don't notice that. What we notice instead are the islands in the stream of consciousness—the islands in this case being our thoughts, the places where our busy mind lands from moment to moment. We only notice where our mind lands, not the spaces through which the mind moves like a bird in flight. We don't notice the gaps between our thoughts, even though they are happening all the time. If I talk very slowly, you . . . will . . . begin . . . to . . . notice . . . the . . . spaces . . . between . . . the . . . words. What is happening in those gaps?

We usually don't notice them because we are so focused on the words, the content of our thought, and what to do with the information we are continually processing. That is our busy, conditioned mind at work. But in the gaps between thoughts a larger background awareness is operating. When we open to this awareness, it becomes unconditional presence—just being with what is, without any agenda.

So we don't have to manufacture unconditional presence; in fact, we cannot, because it is already there, like the sun, when we see through the clouds of our busy mind. That is one of the great discoveries of the meditative traditions, going back thousands of years. Meditation in this sense is a structured way of paying attention to how we work: how the mind works, how perception works, how feeling works, how we construct our whole world from moment to moment.

Our pure awareness, when it is totally present in the moment, is not biased. It's just there, clear and fluid like water. In the midst of this flowing stream of pure awareness, our busy mind is constantly hopping from island to island, from thought to thought, jumping over and through this awareness, which is its ground, without ever noticing it. Meanwhile, our unconditioned awareness keeps on flowing no matter what the busy mind is doing. Pure awareness is never entirely caught or trapped in anything. It is free and open space. We all have access to it. It is our most intimate reality.

Yet we don't recognize it most of the time because we're so busy weaving the strands of our thought together into the familiar fabric of our ego-identity. This identity may appear to be a solid structure, but actually it is full of holes, like Swiss cheese. From ego's point of view, these gaps are scary. They represent the unknown. Experiencing them feels like hanging out in empty space, like a little death. Yet they also contain tremendous aliveness and possibility. If we pay attention to the spaces between our thoughts, we notice an energy there. This is the energy of our unconditioned nature, which we can draw on for healing.

Whenever we open into the unknown, there's a tendency to close that experience down or put it in a box. We may open in a wonderful new way with someone we love, but this may be scary, so the next moment we do something that shuts it down. We're there one moment with a piece of music and the next moment we're distracted. Or we try to recapture that moment—which is another way of shutting it down. Instead of trying not to shut down, all we can do is to notice how we do this, again and again, and see what it feels like. When we bring unconditional presence to the moment of not being present, this brings us back to the present.

Therapists often inadvertently close down their clients' experience in this way as well. Sometimes a client is beginning to open into a deeper dimension of being, but if the therapist cannot allow this opening to take its own course, if the therapist tries to interpret it in some conventional way, the client may quickly fall back into his or her old familiar identity. At other times a client may be feeling something that the therapist has a personal resistance to experiencing. The resulting discomfort makes the therapist pull back from the client, offer a quick fix, or try to steer the client in some other direction. Therapists do that because they can't remain unconditionally present with certain aspects of their own experience.

Therefore the most powerful healers or teachers are those who have access to some quality of unconditional presence in themselves. Developing this ability takes training and practice. Unfortunately, professional psychology training consists mostly of transmitting knowledge and information. The most important thing—the ability to bring a quality of unbiased presence to experience just as it is—is rarely mentioned.

As a practice of simple, basic presence, mindfulness meditation is one of the best trainings for therapists and healers. It teaches us how to settle down with our experience and just be with it as it is. It helps us become more comfortable with those gaps where our identity doesn't exist. We discover that we do not have to hold on to our identity to survive. We find that pain is not solid or overwhelming when we don't contract against it. We see that no states of mind are solid; they only become solid when we weave them into a story. We discover that opening to the vast open space of awareness does not destroy us. We learn to trust in the unknown as a guide to what is most fresh and alive in the moment. With this trust, therapists can begin to let go of their knowledge and let what is needed to help others emerge spontaneously from the strength of their presence.

Unconditional presence is essential for healing because it allows us to *see* or understand our contractedness and *feel* its impact on our body. It is not enough just to see, not enough just to feel. We must *both see and feel*. Of course, it may take months or years to clearly see and feel a pattern we are stuck in. But when this finally happens, we begin to develop the resources necessary to overcome whatever problem we are facing.

Trying to "fix" a problem before we have seen and felt it clearly is like using a drug. Drugs may relieve symptoms, but relieving symptoms does not produce health. What keeps the organism healthy are the immune system and the vital resources of the body. If these are not activated, no amount of symptom relief can ever make us healthy.

Similarly, psychological techniques may relieve symptoms without ever promoting real healing. Our natural healing resources become mobilized only when we see and feel the truth—the untold suffering we cause ourselves and others by rejecting what is. Seeking a remedy or "fix" for our problems does not lead to genuine healing because it keeps us in the same mind-set—wanting our experience to be other than it is—that created our dis-ease in the first place. Only when we slow down and really see and feel our distress can it have an impact on us. Then our pain can begin to awaken our desire and will to live in a new way.

To find out what is really going on inside us, we have to

let go of what we think about it. If I ask you, "How do you feel? What's going on for you right now?" and you look inside yourself, the most honest first answer would probably be, "I don't know." If you know right away what's going on inside you, that's probably just a thought, your mind hopping onto a familiar island in the larger stream of the unknown. Let that go and come back to the question.

When we look inside, we find no single thing to grasp onto, nothing that easily fits into a box. Instead, we discover a multileveled texture of experience. The totality of our present experiencing is much larger and richer than anything we can know or say about it at any one moment. If we want to tap the healing power within us, we first have to let ourselves *not know* so that we can feel this living quality of our experience, beyond any partial beliefs. Then when we speak about it, our words will have real power.

In opening to our experience in this way without holding onto any story about it, we create a compassionate space that allows new parts of ourselves to unfold, and old parts that were cut off to enter the stream of awareness and be included. We can only be healthy and whole when our awareness circulates freely through all aspects of our being. Unconditional presence promotes this kind of circulation, which is the essence of health.

When children are in pain, what they most want is this kind of presence, rather than band-aids or consolations. They want to know we are with them in what they are experiencing. That's what our wounded places most need from us as well—just to be there with them. They don't need us to say, "Things are getting better every day." The full presence of our being is healing in and of itself.

BREAKING THE HEART OPEN

In opening to our experience of life as it is, we often find that it is does not meet our expectations of what it should be. Perhaps we don't fit the picture in our mind of who we should be. Perhaps those we love don't measure up to our ideals. Or we find the state of the world disappointing, even shocking. Reality is continually breaking our heart by not living up to how we would like it to be.

Yet the heart itself cannot actually break, for its very nature is soft and open. What breaks *open* when we see things as they are is the protective shell of ego-identity we have built around ourselves in order to avoid feeling pain. When the heart breaks out of this shell, we feel quite raw and vulnerable. Yet this is also the beginning of feeling real compassion for ourselves and others.

Feeling our "broken-open heart" has a bittersweet quality. Reality never quite fits our fond hopes—that is the bitter taste. The sweetness is that when reality breaks our heart, it is calling on us to soften and open. As we soften and expand, we discover a sweet, raw tenderness toward ourselves and the fragile beauty of life as a whole.

The final step in the healing process is to open our heart to the vicissitudes we are facing in our lives. A friend who was dying of cancer tried every possible treatment she could find. Nothing worked. Finally she realized that the real healing was not in curing the cancer but in coming to terms with it. That was actually a much greater kind of healing. We all need to heal our separation from reality and our struggle with it. The whole world is in need of that.

The greatest difficulties we encounter also offer the greatest opportunities to practice unconditional presence. What is especially helpful in this practice is recognizing again and again that our experience is not as solid as we think. Indeed, nothing is what we think it to be. Meditation lets us recognize this by helping us notice and relate to the gaps or open spaces in our experience, from which real clarity and wisdom arise.

If we take this approach, our old wounds from the past can reveal buried treasure. In the places where we have contracted and turned away from our experience we can begin to uncover genuine qualities of our being that have been lost.

In the most painful corners of our experience something alive always wants to come forth, as the poet Rilke suggests:

> Perhaps all the dragons in our lives are princesses who are only waiting to see us act just once, with beauty and courage. Perhaps everything that frightens us is, in its deepest essence, something helpless that needs our love.[1]

So whatever pain or problem we have, if it helps us find a quality of presence—where we can open to it, see it, feel it, include it, and find the truth concealed in it—*that* is our healing.

---

1. *Letters to a Young Poet*, translated by Stephen Mitchell (New York: Random House, 1984), p. 92.

19 ❀ *Touch and Go*

KAREN KISSEL WEGELA

> We could use the phrase *touch and go*. You are in contact, you're touching the experience of being there, actually being there, and then you let go. That applies to awareness of your breath and also to your day-to-day living awareness. The point of *touch and go* is that there is a sense of feel.
>
> —CHÖGYAM TRUNGPA

*H*ealing involves reconnecting with our intrinsic health. This is not the same as curing symptoms. To say that health is intrinsic means that it is in us already. From the Buddhist perspective, each person possesses what is known as buddha-nature—a core of unconditional openness and wakefulness. This nature is our intrinsic health and sanity. It is who we are. The activity of the healer, then, is not to infuse health into the client, but rather to help uncover the already existing health that is the client's birthright.

A therapist, to be truly effective, must also be concerned with uncovering his or her own intrinsic healthiness. Thus both client and therapist are co-travelers on the same journey. In this way, therapy becomes mindful practice for both participants.

In the Buddhist tradition the practice of sitting meditation is considered to be the most effective way to reconnect with one's intrinsic health and sanity. The practice of sitting down with oneself brings forth qualities of intrinsic health such as spaciousness, clarity, and warmth. The guidelines are to include whatever arises; thoughts of eating cookies are regarded as no more or less important than thoughts of killing your dearest friend. Any thought, any emotion, any bodily sensation is simply noticed and not pushed away. This is the quality of "touch." One allows oneself to experience fully whatever arises. If jealousy arises, one lets oneself feel that fully for a moment. One does not hold back. One touches the jealousy completely. This is not a lengthy examination process, but rather a momentary "touch." One can touch completely and at the same time momentarily.

Then, in accordance with the technique of mindfulness meditation, one lets the experience go. One identifies with the outbreath. As the breath dissolves into space, whatever attention one has put on the breath dissolves along with it. Whatever one has touched, one lets go. This is the quality of "go." It is relaxing one's hold, so to speak.

There is a rhythm of touching and going, touching and going. It is like the process of natural or unself-conscious breathing itself. One does not push one's breath out; one does not hold one's breath.

Often one discovers a tendency to touch and grasp. Instead of simply touching an experience, one hangs onto it and thinks it over. One makes up stories about it and gets completely caught up to the point of forgetting where one is. This is getting lost in discursive thought. Thoughts proliferate and then emotions connected with the thoughts come up. One can find oneself spending many minutes completely lost in this way before one realizes where one is. Mindfulness/awareness sitting practice provides training in noticing the moments when one has "come back," and in exerting some effort in not jumping onto the next thought-train leaving the depot.

On the other hand, one may discover that one's tendency is to "go" and not to touch very much. For example, rather than really allowing oneself to feel the pain of heartbreak, the feeling of longing and sadness, one quickly tells oneself that this is just thinking and goes out with the breath. This, too, is a way of getting "lost." Mindfulness/awareness also trains us to stay with our experience: with our broken-heart, our boredom, whatever it is in any one moment.

This technique, then, is directly concerned with cultivating openness, clarity, and friendliness to our experience—the qualities of health and sanity.

TOUCH AND GO IN PSYCHOTHERAPY

The technique of touch and go can be brought into psychotherapeutic work as well, helping the therapist to lay the ground of a healing relationship. The use of touch and go can provide the opportunity, again and again, to return to the fundamental ground of experience. Here there is no aggression or manipulation. Skillful action and speech can arise only from this openminded, nonaggressive ground. Laying this ground is not the whole of what therapy is about, but it is an essential basis for the therapeutic journey.

By practicing touch and go, the therapist can help provide occasions when the client may also begin to practice touching and letting go on the spot. Here it is not a question of sitting quietly in the meditation posture and going out with the breath, but rather of touching the experience one has in the moment and letting it go. This may mean touching one's "internal" experience, noticing that one's mind is getting speedy, or that one's hands are trembling. One does not then analyze these "symptoms," but rather notices them fully in the moment, lets them go, and moves on to what happens next. This may mean noting what is going on with the client. Perhaps he is talking rapidly, his voice is growing louder, he is talking about how angry he is feeling about his boss. Again, the therapist feels that completely. She may discover that she is experiencing anger herself. Again, the point is not to analyze, but to touch and to go. One does not try to figure out if the anger is "one's own" or the "client's," if this is transference, countertransference or anything else. One remains open to whatever comes next.

I find that this approach directs my attention to the touch quality in an interesting way. I am more likely when I am practicing "touch and go" to notice the textures and emotional tones of an interaction. I might find myself appreciating the energetic quality of a client, or feeling the sadness connected with his loss of a valued friend. At the same time that there is a heightened sense of touch, I am less likely to become tangled up in the story that accompanies that feeling or texture. I can experience someone's pain and feel myself moved by it, feel that pain myself, and not have to "buy" my client's view that he is terrible, or that his life is bad and the best thing to do is kill himself.

My practice is to touch whatever is arising, and then to let it go. Neither half of the practice is regarded as more important than the other. It is not the point to go without touching. Touch and go is not a gimmick for escaping from the intimacy of pain.

I was once sitting with the husband of one of my clients. He had come in, with her permission, to tell me "his side of things." He sat in my office, telling a list of her faults. "She doesn't wash her hands above the wrist. She doesn't take good care of things. She's dirty. I don't want her preparing my food." As I listened to him, I noticed that I was starting to shake. I was not aware of regarding him as dangerous, and yet I was growing increasingly nervous. I let myself really feel that feeling. I was extremely shaky in my body and my mind was growing more agitated, jumping from topic to topic. I had been asking him questions to draw out what was on his mind, and at this point, I stopped. I let go of any agenda. I noticed that he became more quiet as well. There was a moment of simple contact between us. The conversation shifted, and he began to speak of his own fear.

What occurred in this situation, when I began to feel nervous, is a kind of "exchange." This is a phenomenon that is common to all relationships, and is particularly well-known to therapists. When we let ourselves be open, and often even when we do not, we find that we "catch" what our clients are feeling. Sometimes we regard this as a problem and tell ourselves that we have poor boundaries. Yet it is simply our openness and warmth that allows us to be touched by another's experience. The problem is what we do with that. We may identify with it, grab on to it, and make it something solid. We may not realize the extent to which we may have "bought" the client's storyline. Then we have become "stuck in the exchange."

Imagine, if you will, being with a client whose mind is very speedy. He jumps from one thought to the next, talking without a stop. Let me describe one such man with whom I worked. He is tall, very well-filled out, in his mid-forties. He often runs his hand through his hair, pushing the hair back from his face. He is wearing jeans and a flannel shirt. He has very large hands and feet. He is wearing dirty work boots because he has been working outside. He looks weathered. He has a warm face: he smiles often, looks at me with a direct gaze, but not in a challenging way. He has large lips, sensuous. His mouth is moving most of the time. The only way to get him to listen to me is to interrupt him. Sometimes I have to wave my arms to get his attention. This makes him laugh, and he admits freely that he gets caught up in what he is saying and loses track of where he is. Other times his voice is loud and he is talking about how angry he is. He cannot keep track of what he is doing long enough to get it done. He blames the anti-psychotic drugs he was given ten or more years ago.

Now he is describing how difficult it has been for him to try to make a decision about what to do next in his life. He starts to list all the alternatives. Maybe he should go back to school again and study to be a teacher. "Teaching would be a good job to have since it has the summer off and it has lots of structure and, you know, structure is really helpful to me. When I don't have structure then I get caught up in all kinds of things. You know, I can be working on the house and then I forget what I had just figured out. I can't figure out how to fix the floor because I can't keep the numbers in my head. If I keep the numbers in my head then I can't remember what the numbers are for. I can't really do math anymore. I used to be really good at that."

My mind is starting to race. I want to ask him if he really thinks he would like teaching. Wouldn't it make him feel crazy, trying to keep up with a roomful of speedy children? I want to offer him advice. I want to help him sort through the pros and cons of teaching. And could he really manage at school? I think I remember when he described his last schooling experience to me that it was really hard for him to study. He could do it, but he took a very long time to get things accomplished, and he found that frustrating.

". . . the plumbing. And then I had to ask the guy next door to help me."

Where am I? I lost track of what he was saying. What was that? I'd better try to catch up.

"But then, if I do that I will lose all of the insurance support that I have. I'm not sure I want to do that, especially if there isn't any chance of getting this other thing to work out. I can't sort this out. They all seem the same [speeding up more]. If I can't get this figured out, then I am going to just keep on as I am, and I'm getting really sick of this. I am sick of it. I have been sick of it for a long time. If I go to visit my sister she will give me the ticket. Maybe I'll just do that. But we don't really get along all that well and I probably should try to do something for my mother."

His mother? He is interested in doing something for her. That is the first time he's said he would like to do something for someone else. Or is it? I'm not sure if I'm remembering this right.

" . . . because I have a ride there. Isn't that a ridiculous reason to do something?" [His voice is louder.]

Whoops. I missed him again. Ride? Where?

This kind of thing is likely to happen again and again. I cannot be said to have "touched" my experience yet. At some point I notice my own experience. (Perhaps a few minutes have gone by. Perhaps a lot longer. Sometimes a whole session could get eaten up.) I am feeling speedy. My mind is jammed with thoughts and solutions to offer to his many problems. I cannot keep up with his thoughts or my own thoughts. I am feeling tense in my upper arms and shoulders. My stomach is tight. My jaw is tight. My brow is a bit furrowed. I feel as though I am working very hard, but I don't know at what. I feel much the same way now, writing about the experience. I am feeling rushed, as though I have to catch each thought before it gets away from me.

As I let this experience be here, it is just this, just this moment. If you have come along, you might be feeling some kind of speediness of mind too. So, the technique at this point is simply to touch, simply to feel this moment. No big thing, no analysis. Just this.

Let it go. Breathe again. Look. Here is my client. He looks back at me. He starts up, or maybe continues again. For a moment I am not trying to take away his speed, to take away his pain. I am available to whatever happens next.

Times in which one "comes back" to the moment at hand happen quite naturally. According to Buddhist teaching such naturally occurring openings can assist us in developing mindfulness. The practice of meditation, in particular, works with this tendency of mind to return to what is going on now. Through meditation we can train ourselves to notice when we have come back, to acknowledge (touch) that we were "gone," and to let go even of this discovery.

When such moments arise for the therapist, she can practice touch and go. Then there is no particular action to be taken. One might or might not do or say something. The point is that one is practicing the dropping of any preconceptions, any preconceived strategies, and returning to this very situation.

With this particular client, sometimes I have said nothing. Other times, I have simply said what I am experiencing. "I feel my mind speeding. It's pretty uncomfortable. I can't keep up with you."

Sometimes he does not seem to hear me, but just keeps going. One time he stopped for a moment and looked at me and said, "Yes. That's it." It was nothing profound, but there was a moment of mutual touch. A moment of shared acknowledgment of pain. Then, there was a moment of shared laughter. Just a short time in which nothing was complicated, a simple moment.

Discovery of Common Ground

Touch and go is a simple, though sometimes difficult technique. The practice of mindfulness/awareness meditation can provide powerful training in recognizing when one is or is not touching one's experience. It also trains one to let go.

When one practices touching and going in working with others, one discovers over and over again the common ground of intrinsic health that we all share. The therapist's practice of touch and go provides many occasions to return to what is happening in the relationship in the moment. When the therapist can touch her experience in this way, there is a greater chance of touching the client's real experience as well. In this way a path of healing can be shared.

Such a path begins with the acknowledgment of pain. By practicing in this way, the pain is not just the client's pain or the therapist's pain. How each of them learns to relate to that pain is the path they share together.

Sometimes one can touch simply. Other times one gets "stuck in the exchange." That is to say, one grasps the experience, identifies with it. Sometimes this grasping is a kind of holding back from touching something new. Often when one is holding back in this way one feels "overwhelmed." When one truly lets go there is nothing that can be overwhelmed. If one touches this experience completely, the grasping can relax for a moment. It may seem paradoxical, but when one goes toward one's pain, one relaxes. If one fully opens to the experience of being stuck, of being confused, of being whatever one is, one touches completely. Such complete touching is already letting go. On the other hand, completely letting go allows one to touch fully in the next moment.

In such moments of really touching and fully letting go, there is the possibility of genuine contact. Such meeting between two people, free from aggression, contains intrinsic health. Communication of this kind cannot be captured in words, yet it cannot be doubted when it occurs.

20 ❂ *The Listening Mind*

RAM DASS AND
PAUL GORMAN

Much of our capacity to help another person depends upon our state of mind. Sometimes our minds are so scattered, confused, depressed, or agitated, we can hardly get out of bed. At other times we're clear, alert, and receptive; we feel ready, even eager, to respond generously to the needs of others. Most of the time it's really not one extreme or the other.

Because the mind's capacity to think is so brilliant, we tend to be dazzled by it and fail to notice other attributes and functions. There is more to the mind than reason alone. There is *awareness itself* and what we sometimes think of as the deeper *qualities* of mind. Most of us know how supportive it is merely to be in the presence of a mind that is open, quiet, playful, receptive, or reflective. These attributes are *themselves* helpful. Moreover, there is something we frequently experience—perhaps we can call it intuitive awareness—that links us most intimately to the universe and, in allegiance with the heart, binds us together in generosity and compassion. Often it leaps to vision and knowledge instantaneously. "My understanding of the fundamental laws of the universe," said Albert Einstein, "did not come out of my rational mind."

This resource of awareness can give us access to deeper power, power to help and heal.

•

I had been meditating for a number of years. My progress, in terms of increased concentration and a more peaceful, quiet quality in my mind, was noticeable, though not dramatic. In the ancient texts I'd read accounts of monks who through meditation had gained great powers, and I kept wondering if the stories were true.

Then I visited the wife of the former American ambassador in Thailand, and she told me about a monk who had built a monastery in which heroin and opium addicts were cured in ten days . . . for fifteen dollars. These kinds of statistics are unheard of in the West. Possibly this was one of those monks with the meditation powers. I prevailed on her to take me to meet him.

The monk had previously been a Thai "narc" . . . something like our federal drug enforcement agency. He had an aunt who I was told was a Buddhist saint, whatever that means. One day she apparently said to him, while he was still a narc, "What are you doing? If you don't watch out you're going to end up killing people in this job. Why don't you help these people instead of hurting them?" He said that he didn't know how. She apparently told him to clean up his act and she'd show him.

So he left government service and became a monk. Now the Buddhist monks in Thailand are part of the Theravadin tradition which requires very severe renunciation in order to purify your mind so that you can do deep meditation. There are some two hundred and eighteen prohibitions, all of which he adopted. Then he even added ten more on his own, such as never driving in automobiles. This meant that when he had business in Bangkok, about a hundred and fifty miles away, he'd just pick up his walking stick and start walking.

This rigorous training prepared him to do very intensive

meditation practice which allowed him to tune in to the deeper and more powerful parts of his mind. When his aunt felt he was ready, she instructed him in the preparation of an herbal diuretic which she instructed him to give to the addicts, and he started his monastery.

When we met him, my most immediate reaction was that I was shaking hands with an oak tree. His presence was immensely powerful and solid. He had us shown through the monastery where some three hundred addicts were undergoing treatment.

You could really see who was which. The first-day arrivals all looked like strung-out junkies. They were in one room. Then, further on, by the time they had been there for four days you could really see a change. And by eight days they seemed cheerful, were bumming cigarettes from me, and seemed really friendly—not particularly like addicts at all. And then after ten days they were gone. And their statistics showed seventy percent remained free of addiction afterwards. Amazing.

When I interviewed the monk, I asked him, "How do you do it?" He said, "Well, it's simple. I tell them that they can only come for ten days and they may never come again, and that the cure will work." I asked him if a lot of religious indoctrination was included in the ten-day program. "No," he said, "none of that. These people aren't suitable for that."

I had heard that many drug experts, media people, and even some congressmen had come from the West, but that none of them could figure out why what he did worked. The herbal brew clearly wasn't the whole ballgame. As I hung out with him longer I began to realize that his mind was so centered and one-pointed that his being was stronger than their addiction. Somehow he conveyed to those addicts a sense of their non-addiction that was stronger than their addiction. And I saw that his commitment was so total that he wasn't just someone using a skill. He had died into his work. He *was* the cure.

This was the example I had been looking for. Just being

with him I could feel the extraordinary quality of his mind. Meeting him reassured me that the ancient stories were probably true. I returned to meditation with renewed vigor.

•

Most of us are not really ready to become renunciates in order to develop the concentration and quality of awareness necessary to help others at such an extraordinary level. But if we are prepared to investigate our minds even a little bit, we start a process that can improve our effectiveness in life, and therefore in helping as well. If we are willing to examine the agitation of our own minds and look just beyond it, we quite readily find entry into rooms that hold surprising possibilities: a greater inner calm, sharper concentration, deeper intuitive understanding, and an enhanced ability to hear one another's heart. Such an inquiry turns out to be critical in the work of helping others.

The phone rings. We turn from the checkbook we were balancing to answer. It's someone seeking counsel. Even as the person begins to speak, our minds are conflicted. We don't quite want to leave that column of figures unadded, and yet we know that we have to let go of our bookkeeping to listen carefully to the problem.

The voice on the other end tries to find words to describe suffering: "I'm just feeling so . . . it's like I . . . I really don't know, but . . . " Painstaking work. But sometimes even as it starts, our mind may begin to wander. "This is going to be a tough one . . . Am I up to this? . . . What about dinner? . . . I'd better circle that place where I think the bank screwed up."

At a certain stage, personal judgments may start competing for attention. "He's really romanticizing it a lot . . . He ought to be done with this one by now . . . He's not hearing what I mean." We may get a little lost in evaluating—"Is it working? Am I helping?" Or we could as easily turn the evaluation on ourselves—"I don't care that much. I really don't like him."

Sometimes we catch ourselves in distraction and rejoin the person on the other end of the phone. Now it's better. Something's beginning to happen. Then we take an intentionally audible in-breath—we've got something helpful to say—but the signal goes by; he keeps right on talking. Off goes the mind to utterly unrelated topics: "Call Dad . . . That picture on the wall is crooked . . . I'm tired . . . I have to feed the cat."

This mental chatter goes on and off. Sometimes we really get lost, and by the time we're back, we realize we've missed a key point, and it's too late to ask for it to be repeated. At other times we can take quick note of our reactions and still stay with it. Perhaps we just let it all run off; it's not something we even notice—it fades into the background like film-score music we're hardly aware is there.

Then the call is over. The voice on the other end says "Thank you." We reply "You're welcome." But how welcome was he? How much room did the mind give him? How much did we really hear? How much did he *feel* heard? Maybe we sit back in the chair and reflect on that for a moment. Or perhaps we get up, walk to the kitchen, and savor the "thank you" along with a sandwich. Perhaps we simply turn back to the checkbook.

Reckoning, judging, evaluating, leaping in, taking it personally, being bored—the helping act has any number of invitations to reactiveness and distraction. Partly we are agitated because we so intensely want to help. After all, someone's in pain. We care. So part of the time we are listening, but we may also be using our minds to try to solve the problem. There's a pull to be efficient, to look for some kind of resolution. We reach for certain familiar models or approaches. In order to be helpful, our analytic mind must stay on top of it all.

So we jump between listening and judging. But in our zeal to help, we may increase the distance between the person and our own consciousness. We find ourselves primarily in our own thoughts, not *with* another person. Not only are we listening less, but the concepts our mind is coming up with start to act as a screen that preselects information. One thought rules out another.

One of the results of all this mental activity is that there's less room to meet, less room for a new truth to emerge, less room to let things simply be revealed in "their own good time." The mind tries to do too many things at once. It's difficult to know which mental vectors are useful and which are distractions, static on the line, bad connections.

This agitation and reactiveness should be no surprise to most of us. We have come to expect and accept this state except in rare situations. Yet it need not be that way.

If we continue to observe our mind over some time, we notice that it's not always distracted and busy. For all of us, there are times when our minds become concentrated, sharp and clear.

Many times the needs of others are what bring us to a state of sharp concentration. Whether it's because we feel very secure with those we're with or because we are functioning under conditions of extreme crisis, we find that in this state of intense concentration helpful insights arise on their own, as a function of our one-pointedness. In these experiences we meet a resource of remarkable potential. While we may be frustrated in not having access to it all the time, these experiences lead us to inquire whether there might be something we could do more regularly and formally to quiet the mind, strengthen its concentration, make available the deeper insights that often result, and bring them into closer attunement with the empathy and compassion of our heart. How immeasurably this might enhance our ability to help others!

Traditionally, one such way to begin this investigation is through meditation, systematically observing the mind itself and becoming more familiar with the ways in which we are denied the experience of full concentration. When we do this, with even a simple exercise like focusing our attention on our breath, we begin to see that there is a continuous stream of thoughts going on all the time. Meditation may be frustrating if we think we can stop this process right away. We can't. But by penetrating and observing it, we can free ourselves from being carried away by our thoughts.

Our thoughts are always happening. Much like leaves floating down a stream or clouds crossing the sky, they just keep on coming. They arise in the form of sensations, feelings, memories, anticipations, and speculations. And they are all constantly calling for attention: "Think of me." "Notice me." "Attend to me." As each thought passes, either we attend to it or we don't. While we can't stop the thoughts themselves, we can stop our awareness from being snared by each one. If you are standing by a river and a leaf floats by, you have your choice of following the leaf with your eye or keeping your attention fixed in front of you. The leaf floats out of your line of vision. Another leaf enters . . . and floats by.

But as we stand on the bank of the river and the leaves float by, there is no confusion as to whether or not we *are* the leaves. Similarly, it turns out that there is a place in our minds from which we can watch our own mental images go by. We aren't our thoughts any more than we are the leaves.

If we imagine that our mind is like the blue sky, and that across it pass thoughts as clouds, we can get a feel for that part of it which is other than our thoughts. The sky is always present; it contains the clouds and yet is not contained by them. So with our awareness. It is present and encompasses all our thoughts, feelings, and sensations; yet it is not the same as them. To recognize and acknowledge this awareness, with its spacious, peaceful quality, is to find a very useful resource within. We see that we need not identify with each thought just because it happens to occur. We can remain quiet and choose which thought we wish to attend to. And we can remain aware *behind* all these thoughts, in a state that offers an entirely new level of openness and insight.

There are systematic exercises that can help to establish us in the skylike awareness that encompasses thought. One of these meditation exercises is called "Letting Go." It very quickly can show us through direct personal experience that our awareness is separate from our thoughts. You may want to read it through until you understand it, and then, if you choose, try it.

LETTING GO

Find a position in which you can comfortably remain for ten minutes with your back straight but not rigid. This time, instead of picking an object of focus such as the breath, just observe thought itself. Simply let things happen as they do. Just watch. Be aware, as thoughts arise, that the thoughts are there, without getting involved in the content of the thoughts. Let all images, thoughts, and sensations arise and pass away without being bothered, without reacting, without judging, without clinging, without identifying with them. Just keep letting go of one thing after another.

The thoughts that arise are not obstacles or hindrances. They are just the objects of our observation. Keep the mind sharply aware, moment to moment, of what is happening, what the mind is attending to. If you feel tense from trying to watch your mind, relax. The sky doesn't get all tense trying to see the clouds. Everything is just as it is.

Keep in mind the idea of letting go. As thoughts or sensations, images, memories, whatever, rise into your awareness, notice them, witness them, and then let them go. Keep letting go again and again. And of course, once you are really comfortable and at home in pure awareness, then you can let go of the thought of letting go as well.

In skillful helping action, when our awareness remains quiet and clear, there's breadth to our perspective. It's aerial, wide-screen, panoramic, and yet able to focus quickly. With all of this, we are not only thinker-participants but observers of our thinking and participation as well. The quiet mind makes possible an overall awareness of the total situation, including ourselves. It's sometimes called an awareness of the Gestalt—in which separate elements of consciousness are so integrated that they function as a unity.

•

There's a guy up on the roof, right at the edge, with his infant son in his arms; he's threatening to throw him off and then jump himself. Homicide-suicide—happens a lot with children. He's been having trouble with his wife—mother interfering, they lock him out, he's sleeping in the hallway, and it's gone to the edge. That's where he is, and I'm up there with him. I'm the final guy in the hostage recovery system we set up in New York City, which I've been working in for eight years and heading up for the last two. We haven't lost anybody in all that time.

Now, if you're not able to see the whole picture—how he's reacting, where and who your backup forces are, what's on the street, how long it's been going on, your own past experience, the chance that this is a new kind, and certainly what's going on inside *you* from moment to moment—if you can't hold on to all of that and still be there listening to this guy in a way he can feel . . . chances are he's gonna go over the edge. Someone is going to be killed. We've learned that.

And he's in this very intense, complex public situation. Several of us are up there—a net in the street below, a lot going on all around. To say nothing of what's going on in him: this lack of self-esteem and manliness, feeling pushed around by his family, no work. But I also can recognize this overriding love he has for his child, who he's convinced would be better off dead than with those two. Sounds crazy, but it was real to him. So there's a lot for all of us to take in.

So I'm helping him get a sense, an awareness of everything that's happening, just so he has the picture of it all. And the more he does, the more he is opening up to me. Turns out what concerns him most is that there be a hearing at family court to work out fair custody. He wants a hearing. But he won't accept a promise from me, or a signed note. He tells us we got to get a lawyer and have it on legal paper—which we send out a car and find a local lawyer and get for him. When he feels he's got support from the system, he hands us the child. At that point we have to jump him, because we know that's the crucial moment to prevent the suicide. He gets pissed at me, because we were talking together and now this. And I have to give him this look of "That's how it all is, kid." Some part of him understands.

Funny thing is, I can't remember much of what I've been saying to people at the end of these episodes. I'm running very much on intuition from moment to moment. I've had special training, of course, but that becomes a part of you, and it's only a part of what you're calling on.

You have to be steady and quiet inside. You have to have a foundation of belief in the absolute value and beauty of life. You can't get too caught up in it all. You step back, get as much of the picture as possible, and you play it moment to moment. That's what I've learned from hundreds of these situations.

•

In the clarity of a quiet mind, there is room for all that is actually happening and whatever else might also be possible. Though we may be mindful of myriad details, our attention never wavers from the specific situation or person in need. The intimacy of our attention becomes a heart-to-heart life-line made firm and fast; no one need fall from the edge. The quiet appreciation of the total situation and its inherent possibilities steadily move things toward resolution.

Such feats might seem to be the result of crisis. Many of us have experienced rising to the occasion under such conditions. The intensity of the situation keeps the mind from wandering. For most of us, fortunately or unfortunately, our helping work doesn't entail the intensity that brings forth these heightened faculties. But whatever the circumstances, and however extensive the training and experience, it's important to recognize that the faculties of awareness being called into play are exactly those we have been cultivating and discovering in the practice of meditation and the investi-

gation of awareness. General laws are operating under particular circumstances.

Why, for example, if one was tightly attentive to a single
object—a man on the edge of a roof—wouldn't everything
else disappear from awareness? Because, as we've discovered,
it is possible to notice a single thought, sensation, or situation arise, but not get totally lost in identifying with it. We
observe the cloud but remain focused on the sky, see the leaf
but hold in vision the river. We are that which is aware of
the totality. And our skills develop with practice. First, we
have to appreciate the value of such qualities of mind and
desire to develop them. Next, we have to have faith in the
possibility that we can indeed make progress. Finally, we
have to explore and practice appropriate techniques. Twenty
minutes a day of such practice can lead to results and the
incentive to go deeper still. Continuous practice brings
about great transformation of mind and leads to a new quality of service.

When we function from this place of spacious awareness
rather than from our analytic mind, we are often surprised
to find solutions to problems without our having "figured
them out." It's as if out of the reservoir of our minds which
contains everything we know and everything we are sensing
at the moment, all that could be useful rises to the surface
and presents itself for appropriate action. Sudden flashes of
memory, past experience, or understanding seem to get expressed: "I can't explain it." "It just came to me." "It all
suddenly became clear." "I forgot I even knew that."

We often call this quality of mind "intuition" but often
we don't trust or honor it. Unlike our thinking mind, which
arrives at solutions through a linear process of analysis
which we can follow, the intuitive mind seems to leap to a
solution. Perhaps the process is going on outside the range
of our consciousness; perhaps we are delving into regions of
the mind where thinking, in the conventional sense, is not
necessary.

Ultimately, this kind of listening to the intuitive mind is a kind of surrender based on trust. It's playing it by ear, listening for the voice within. We trust that it's possible to hear into a greater *totality* which offers insight and guidance. Ultimately, but really ultimately, we trust that when we are fully quiet, aware, and attentive, boundaries created by the mind simply blur and dissolve, and we begin to merge into All That Is. And All That Is, by definition, includes answers as well as questions, solutions as well as dilemmas.

When we have been used to knowing where we stand at every moment, the experience of resting in awareness without any specific thoughts to hold onto and trusting our intuition turns out to be a refreshing and exciting adventure. In this choiceless spacious awareness, we don't necessarily know from moment to moment how everything is going to come out. Nor do we have a clear idea of what is expected of us. Our stance is just one of listening . . . of fine tuning . . . trusting that all will become apparent at the proper time.

To rest in awareness also means to stand free of the prejudices of mind that come from identifying with cherished attitudes and opinions. We can listen without being busy planning, analyzing, theorizing . . . and especially judging. We can open into the moment fully in order to hear it all.

As we learn to listen with a quiet mind, there is so much we hear. Inside ourselves we can begin to hear that "still small voice within," as the Quakers call it, the voice of our intuitive heart which has so long been drowned out by the noisy thinking mind. We hear our skills and needs, our subtle intentionalities, our limits, our innate generosity.

In other people we hear what help they really require, what license they are actually giving us to help, what potential there is for change. We can hear their strengths and their pain. We hear what support is available, what obstacles must be reckoned with.

In most helping situations "I hear you" reflects a much deeper message: "I understand. I'm with you." Such a message can be immensely reassuring for a person who has felt isolated or alone in their pain and suffering. The reassurance does not come from the words themselves, of course, but from what the words represent. It comes if the person indeed *feels* heard. It may not be that a particular story from one's life is so important. But sharing it is a way of being to-gether—heart to heart.

To reach its full potential, however, this hearing from the heart requires that we remain alert to entrapments of the mind. Seeking to help others, we may start out open and receptive, but after a short time being with them seems to bring us down rather than lift them up. Somehow their suffering, self-pity, despair, fear, or neediness begins to get to us. It's a little like trying to pull someone out of quicksand and feeling ourself suddenly starting to sink. As reassuring as it may be for one depressed person to be heard by another depressed person, the relationship doesn't really open the door to escape from depression. Empathy is not enough.

Here, once again, our ability to remain alert to our own thoughts as they come and go serves us in our relations with others. We hear into their pain . . . they feel heard . . . we meet together inside the confusion. And yet we ourselves are able to note, perhaps even to *anticipate*, that moment when another's entrapment of mind might be starting to suck us in. We are as alert to what is happening within *us* as we are to what is happening in *them*.

The ability to avoid being entrapped by one another's mind is one of the great gifts we can offer each other. With this compassionate and spacious awareness, and the listening it makes possible, we can offer those we are with a standing invitation to come out from wherever they are caught, if they are ready and wish to do so. It is as if we are in the room of experience with them, but also standing in the doorway, offering our hand, ready to walk out together.

•

A woman came to see me who was suffering greatly because of her daughter. She told me her daughter was real bad trouble. "She's run away to live with my other daughter down in Tennessee, and now she's forged a check with her sister's name on it, and she's gotten pregnant and she's only sixteen. I've been a seamstress all my life, supporting the kids and myself since my husband ran out when the youngest was still in the womb. Now she's run away, and you can't imagine what it's like . . . "

I'm shortening the story. It actually took about fifteen minutes to run it all down. I just listened as openly as I could. I could feel her pain and discouragement and felt my heart hurt at the hard life she had had. At the same moment I felt very quiet inside, figuring maybe all I had to offer was to be with her. A little bit I felt she was wearing the albatross of this story, like the Ancient Mariner, and I was just another in a long line of people who had heard it. So when she finished I said, "Right."

She sensed I wasn't getting caught, and her immediate reaction was "No, you don't understand." And she recited the whole thing one more time, fifteen more minutes. And when she'd finished the second time, I said again, "Right."

This time she stopped for a moment. She'd heard me. She paused, and then said with a kind of wry smile, "You know, I was kind of a hellion when I was a kid, too." She just let it go.

•

For someone deeply trapped in a prison of thought, how good it can feel to meet a mind that hears, a heart that reassures. It's as if a listening mind is, in and of itself, an invitation to another mind to listen too. How much it can mean when we accept the invitation and hear the world anew.

Much, then, can be accomplished in the work of compassion by exploring the activity of the mind. Through concentration, we are able to establish a more intimate contact with one another. Through spacious awareness we can sense the totality of situations and allow insight to come into play. More and more we are a vehicle for service. All of this may seem as if we are acquiring something new, but that is not so. Rather, we are clearing away obstacles that have prevented us from using our natural abilities. We regain what Suzuki Roshi, a Zen master, called "beginner's mind"—one that is open to the freshness of many possibilities.

To dissolve agitations and attachments of the mind is to remove the veils from our heart. It allows us to meet one another in the purity of love.

21 ❁ On Being Unable to Breathe

STEPHEN BUTTERFIELD

Something was drastically wrong with my lungs: every night, they made sounds like a basketful of squealing kittens. I was always coughing, had pains under the sternum, and could not push a car or even run up a flight of stairs without gasping like an old melodeon full of holes. This condition came on slowly; no single daily or weekly change was ever big enough to scare me out of my habits.

I decided to look into the problem after a long period of meditation practice, at a time when I was looking into my whole life: marriage, livelihood, everything. I gazed at the chest X-ray as though it belonged to someone else: thick white clouds in the center, where I felt the pain, and swirls, like mares' tails, reaching deep down into the bottom lobes. Air capacity for a man my age and size should be 5.5 liters; I had 2.8.

According to the medical profession, the cause of sarcoidosis is unknown; my doctor is not convinced that it is a direct result of inhaling smoke. He thinks it is hereditary, actualized by environmental insult of some kind.

Sarcoidosis is a progressive inflammatory swelling of the alveolar membranes, gradually scarring the tissue so that it no longer exchanges gas. Oxygen will not pass into the body through a scar. The only method of treatment known to Western science is prednisone, a cortico-steroid drug which suppresses the inflammation; the drug does nothing, however, about the cause, which is still not understood. The side effects of prednisone are, alas, unpleasant: leg pains, weight gain, craving for sugar, dizziness, cataracts, liver spots, adrenal imbalances, possible weakening of the immune system, and worse, depending upon the dose. But if it is a question of being able to breathe, you take the medicine. It buys time.

How much time? More than if you had cancer, typically. I could wheeze out a sigh of partial relief and say, "I'm glad it's not lung cancer." Approximately one third of the cases get better, one third stay the same, and one third get worse. Even with treatment, it can get worse. I have lived with it for about seven years.

Being a buddhist, I accept that nothing lasts, and that impermanence, suffering, and absence of solid reality are the three marks of existence. Saying this is one thing; living it is another. The actual presence of a chronic, disabling, possibly life-threatening disease is a relentless and vivid reminder of death. It wonderfully accelerates your spiritual journey.

We would like to avoid that kind of acceleration. Armies of joggers and physical fitness buffs are out there right now, trying to strengthen their cardiovascular systems and increase their lung capacities to ward off the message delivered by the Buddha that day in the Deer Park of Benares 2,500 years ago. Plenty of my readers could probably give me good advice on the diet and holistic treatments I should try in order to cure myself and prolong my life. I would listen to this kind of advice, but what interests me the most is whether I can make use of the disease. Magazines are full of articles about this or that public figure who carried on a "battle for life" against cancer, AIDS, emphysema, kidney failure, or some other agent of transformation. The articles usually imply that these people are heart-rending models of quiet heroism in the never-ending struggle not to go gentle into that good night. Illness and death are assumed to be very bad news, perhaps a punishment of some kind, bogeymen in the dark closet of deep, dark fears.

I would rather not make a knee-jerk reflex toward "battle." There is a message in my body; do I have to go to war about it? Paraphrasing the words of Dylan Thomas, do I have to burn and rave and rage? Can I make another kind of response? What is this message all about, where does it come from, what does it say? I don't mean purely in a medical or scientific sense, although medicine and science are not to be lightly disregarded. Disease is experienced, and perhaps originates, primarily in the mind. What is it doing *there?*

Let us begin by examining the effects, without pity or hope. Being unable to breathe introduces challenging modifications to your daily schedule.

In one of their movies, Sally Field wraps her arms around Burt Reynolds's neck, and her legs around his hips; he carries her that way into the bedroom. It is a sweet and tender scene. To be able to walk around screwing your lover against walls and doors, or to bounce her on the bed while imagining that you are very powerful, taking charge—to play that scene requires air. Oxygen must be taken in through the alveoli and pumped to the muscles. Otherwise Burt and Sally (especially Burt, since he is doing most of the work) would gradually deflate, crumple, and fold up on the floor, and their faces might as well be painted on the surfaces of withering balloons. In terms of life passages, I am entering the withered balloon stage.

Singing is punctuated with interesting silences at times, depending on the duration of the line to be sung. If the line is much over ten syllables, my voice simply disappears. "Whoops," the lungs wheeze. "Sorry, we are having technical difficulties."

Household projects are scaled down drastically. I would like to dig flowerbeds and build an addition onto the living room. "Too bad," says the body. "Be grateful you can still walk across the yard." Ten years ago I swore that I would never own a rider lawnmower. Now I bless the person who invented it.

When somebody's car gets stuck in the snow, there is not much I can do. Pushing or shoveling are out of the question. I become sharply mindful during bad weather, driving fully present, right on the dot all the time. I like that; going over the mountain to the store in January is almost an adventure.

But giving yourself space and time is also giving yourself kindness; no pressure, no speed. Do I really need that trip up the stairs? When I am there, what am I forgetting, what can I take down with me so that I won't have to come back in two minutes? If my car is stuck on the ice, how can I handle it to avoid physical expenditure? Take it easy. Look around.

Sitting calmly and looking around, I notice the lavender ripples of light on the snow in a field, and the stubble of dead weeds coming up through the crust. The snow makes a separate system of rings around each stalk; no two systems are alike, but they all show the direction and patterns of the wind. How important is it that I go anywhere? The light on a group of stones—that is a masterpiece of art, made in the roadside ditch by nobody at all.

Once, when I was stuck in a snowbank, the rear wheels buried up to the bumper, I had to measure each and every shovelful of snow, like an ant moving a mountain, one grain at a time. It was a pleasant surprise to find that, in such a situation, even with a serious lung disease, I was not entirely helpless. There was plenty of time to see the tracks of the car, how they slid into the brook, how I had turned the wheel trying to bounce out of the rut and did not quite have the forward momentum to regain the road. What a precise reflection of my state of mind.

I walked slowly to a house. There was a bag of salt on the porch and a four-wheel-drive truck in the yard. The owner of the truck was doing carpentry upstairs. We talked about carpentry. He was glad to be of service and pulled out my car with a tow chain. The world is full of generosity. By having to ask for help, I tune into that inexhaustible bank of kindness that is all-pervasive and unconditional, and feels so good when it comes through us to someone else. Because of my need, his routine changed; maybe he took another step on the path.

We have little choice about anything, moving around as we do in a sleepy, anxious cloud of habit and conditioned response. When we slow down, that cloud settles, finally, and the details hidden within it begin to emerge with startling precision. I hold the kettle to the faucet; hear the water swirl in the bottom; place it on the stove, the little drops sizzling away from the hot grill; stare out the window at the vortex of snow down in the valley, swirling over the trees. Finally, the steam whistles through the spout and I pour a cup of tea. My thoughts flutter and swirl like water, like the snow. Having to slow down begins to seem less like a disability and more and more like a precious gift.

But I cannot delude myself that this is some kind of accomplishment, for I would dearly love to leap, like my cat, from the stairs to the floor; I would love to dance, run like a horse across the yard, play football, go out for a pass. The fact that slowing down is *choiceless* becomes part of the gift: taking credit for things just keeps stirring up that cloud. Since I cannot take credit, what really matters is the scent of the tea. The only choice we have anyway is to wake up.

A year before my mother died, she asked me what was wrong with my chest. She was the one person in the world who would want to hear whatever I had to say about it. As I narrated the details, she passed her hand over her face and named an old friend of hers who had died of my ailment. "I hope you don't croak before I do," she said. "It wouldn't be right."

I felt as though at long last I had graduated to her level. The generation gap vanished; I had finally grown up. I had something more serious to reveal to her than mumps and divorce. It was as though I now possessed an admission ticket to some kind of secret society—the society of those who have made friends with Yama, the Lord of Death. We could call this the Order of the Black Monk. The requirement for admission would be terminal or disabling sickness, battle experience, prolonged imprisonment and torture, waiting for execution, or working with the dead and dying on a regular basis. Attempted suicide would not qualify, since this act implies continued attachment to the illusion that you can escape.

While I had health, youth, food, friends, and comforts, I would hear about disasters and think, "I'm glad that did not happen to me." Then I would play the "what-if" game: what if I were trapped in the plane going down; what would I do if I had six months to live; what if I had six minutes? . . . But during this game there was always the separation between me and those who were "less fortunate"; I think that the purpose of the game was to maintain that separation. The initiation rite into the Order of the Black Monk is realizing that you are it; there is no separation anymore; you have been tagged.

In such an order, I am still a mere novice, for my mind remains cluttered with the detritus of hope and fear. But some kind of flip has taken place: from the viewpoint of the Order, hope is irrelevant; fear is fulfilled and consequently dissolved. There is no need to maintain any kind of class system between less and more fortunate, happy and miserable; each experience has its own texture, and absolutely everything is path. If a disease brings this kind of realization, then in what sense does it continue to be "disease"?

We think of disease as infirmity, disability, and tragedy, or reify it as "enemy" and project our aggression onto it, as though flesh could ever be preserved from decay. In looking at how great spiritual masters handle disease, other possibilities begin to appear. His Holiness the Sixteenth Gyalwang Karmapa, Tibetan buddhist of the Kagyu lineage who visited America twice, died of cancer in 1981. Right up to the final moments, he never uttered a word of complaint and was totally concerned for the welfare of those who waited on him. In a real sense, the cancer was not "his" cancer, any more than life itself was "his" life; because he was on this planet for us, whatever he suffered was part of that gift.

The late Chögyam Trungpa Rinpoche, my root guru and student of the Karmapa, was paralyzed on one side of his body throughout most of his teaching career in America. He limped, wore a special elevated shoe, spoke (and sang, comically) with one vocal cord, used a wheelchair, and endured intense pain without pity, hope, apology, or false heroics of any kind. His response to anyone in pain was not "quit your whining and be like me," but limitless compassion and sense of humor. Affliction was his principal teaching tool. He transformed it into dignity and presence simply by the way he took his seat on the *vajra* throne. The concept of "disability" melts before such an example like a shadow in the sun.

The ignorance which results in karma is a kind of localized or attenuated intelligence, falling away from the luminous emptiness which is the ground of our being, into identification with structures of *this* and *that*. The unconscious components of personality are formed out of whatever we ignore. Having invented ourselves, for example, we forget that we have done that, and then we generate a story-line to maintain our invention: other people become characters in our own melodrama; we define them as "good guys" or "bad guys" according to how they fit the labels and preconceptions of the story, and project mental systems of aggression or seduction onto them, which might be interpreted as "relationships." Then we forget that we have a story-line, or a labeling system that keeps it going. The projections appear to us as an external "reality." Our emotional responses are shaped in terms of these ignored and forgotten systems; eventually our illnesses begin to be shaped by them as well. In this way, our physical and mental functioning becomes determined by skeins of psychic energy that we have frozen, from the very beginning, by diminishing luminous-emptiness-without-boundary into ego-form.

According to buddhist teaching, from ignorance we create

neurotic tendencies in our stream of being that will ripen at some future date into painful results. The ripening process is karma. A painful result always removes the particular cause of the karma, although we can renew the cause by our failure to understand it.

My case is a clear demonstration of this process. Begin with a weakness in the lungs, which itself is a karmic result of some kind, carried in the chromosomes perhaps, or in what biologist Rupert Sheldrake would call the *morphogenetic field*—a good Western synonym for the buddhist concept of a being-stream. Add now the attenuation of intelligence, which creates the belief in *me* and *that*, which is the beginning of the neurosis characterized by grasping pleasure and avoiding pain. Viewing the source of pleasure as outside of myself, but somehow necessary for the well-being of *me*, I begin to smoke. By smoking I induce euphoria and dispel boredom and fear. At this stage a full-blown conditioning process is under way: behavior, reinforcement, strengthened behavior. It is part of an addiction to pleasure. Additional psychic factors might be a general holding back, holding in, a tendency toward intellectual fixation and brutal self-criticism which is let go only by more smoking, and which slowly begins to manifest as a swelling of lung tissue leading toward complete suffocation.

The ultimate purpose of it all is to maintain ignorance— that is, to confirm ego. How does this happen? Boredom, loneliness, and fear unconfirm the notion of self: they are the first re-assertion of luminous emptiness manifesting as a gap, a space with nothing to do, nowhere to stand, nothing to hope for. That experience brings on fundamental uncertainty; from ego's point of view, it is a living death. You could go mad in such a space; you could shuffle from room to room haunted by guilt and failure. We call it "the pits," "the black hole," showing by our choice of terms that we know perfectly well it is a gap; it is open space, no boundaries, no definitions, no beliefs. Trying to avoid the gap, I set into motion the chain of causes leading to physical infirmity.

I do it to myself as an individual; we do it collectively to each other as a social system.

My first step toward self-healing may seem almost masochistic to a non-buddhist, but it makes good sense and has very far-reaching effects: I allow the disease to be there and make friends with it.

Tai Situ Rinpoche, in *Way To Go*, writes that we can be *grateful* for affliction, once we have understood that it is the ripening of karma and that its appearance removes the cause. This traditional buddhist doctrine resembles the view that fever is the body's healthy response to the intrusion of harmful microbes; by means of the fever, the microbes are processed out. The buddhist approach is not merely physical, but comprehends our totality over unlimited vistas of time. Affliction inspires wakefulness, which in turn removes ignorance, which is the ultimate cause of suffering.

It is important to distinguish between this approach and "positive thought." Both agree that illness is strongly connected with mind.

The notion that illness begins in the mind has gained widespread credence in our culture, but what that means is still not properly understood. "Positive thinkers" generally perceive that sickness originates in, or is in some way supported by, negative mental attitudes—such as the desire to be punished or taken care of in a dependent role—and the suggested treatment might include looking in the mirror and telling yourself how wonderful you are, pacifying your anxiety with soothing cassette tapes, lying in a circle with a support group for mutual strokes, or forcing yourself to continue performing difficult physical tasks of self-help even while your strength is ebbing away.

But something is lacking in this kind of technique. There is still an underlying assumption that death is *terrible* and that we can talk ourselves out of it. What shall we do with patients who refuse to be "positive"—lecture them on their inadequacy? Or do we simply write them off, saying they cannot—will not—be helped? Negativity is real; it does not fade away because I listen to ocean waves and tell myself jokes.

For the most part, we want to understand disease only in order to get rid of it as quickly as possible, just like we want to get rid of the inconvenient tasks of caring for the old and the homeless, and disposing of the dead; as though we could thereby reach some dreamland of health and happiness, where people never get sick and die. Hearing that disease is caused by improper diet or unhealthy attitude, we might become health-food fanatics and search aggressively for the mental hang-ups that make us fat or cause our skin to break out in a rash. But our desire to reject negativity and cling to pleasure has been the problem from the very beginning.

As long as our goal is to hang on to something, or get rid of our own mortality, then we are still only suppressing symptoms. "Healing" could become one more ambitious project by which we try to ignore the message of luminous emptiness: that there is no place to stand in the endless cascade. We thought that we had a cozy little observation balcony, but it is all Niagara Falls no matter where we turn. Even the parking lot is being swept away. On the other hand, it might be fire, too; we are on fire every moment, dying and being born all the time, spreading out everywhere. The work of ego is a mode of experiencing the heat and the color; within that mode, enlightenment is the ash.

Making friends with the disease leads to discoveries of the sort that I have described earlier: slowing down, shedding excess baggage, observing without struggle, deepening mindfulness, letting go of attachment to pleasure, feeling the texture of discomfort and pain, finding the roots of fear. Slowly the ground of ignorance is dispelled, like beginning to recognize a landscape in the very early dawn.

Ignorance is the environment of the whole karmic chain. If there is no ignorance, then the concept of "disease" becomes superfluous, as do the other "dis-" categories: discomfort, discontinuity, disillusion, disability, dissonance, disappointment, disbelief. Some buddhist masters wake themselves up further with a practice in which they invite all the demons of chaos and disaster to visit them. My little self says, "I am not at that point," but a braver, more expansive self answers, "Maybe that is what I have already done."

But whether I am brave or not, the "dis-ease" is here, however it is defined. By using it as path, and as a means to inspire someone else, I am hanging out with the masters. That is not such a bad result. If it means that I can hang out with the likes of Trungpa Rinpoche and His Holiness the Karmapa, then bring on the demons; they can sit on my shoulders while I type. (The mouse, getting drunk, bangs his tankard on the bar and declaims, "Bring on the cat!")

Another method to reject luminous emptiness and cling to the ground of ignorance is to make affliction *mean* something: to say, for example, that it ennobles the human spirit, toughens our courage to endure, takes away our sins—or even that we are being punished for our sins.

The second of the four stages of dying outlined by Elisabeth Kubler-Ross, in her classic study of the death process, is *bargaining*—the attempt to hang on to some kind of ground by giving up something else: "I will give all my money to the church if only I can get well." (The four stages are denial, bargaining, anger, and acceptance. These stages are all from ego's point of view, and they are encountered also in meditation practice as we slowly give in to the experience of egolessness.)

Interpreting pain and loss as meaningful in a philosophical or religious context is another form of bargaining, a consolation prize: "My legs are gone, I have been tortured, my children went to a concentration camp, my tumor is inoperable, but there is a reason for everything: it is to test my faith; it is all for the greater glory of God or the Party; it brings humankind to a realization of existential despair; even from the jaws of defeat we can salvage a mustard seed of victory, we shall rise from the ashes, we shall be changed." Explanation is still the game of hope and fear: "If I submit to suffering, then maybe I will gain a higher truth."

The pressure of affliction tends to blow these answers away like chaff. A political prisoner being drowned in a bucket of floating sewage is interested in only one thing: the next breath. Sarcoidosis is not quite as severe, but the concern is the same. Beyond that, I want to open completely, without disguises, consolations, or illusions of any kind. By refusing to assign *meaning* to it, we stay with the *emptiness* of suffering, and thus begin to live in a reality that is luminous, limitless, unconditional, and immediate.

The cheerfulness that results from this renunciation of meaning cannot be destroyed, because it does not deny anything, and it does not have to be maintained. Misery and death are included, and allowed. It is not "my" cheerfulness; it does not come from anywhere. You can let go of it and laugh. You could drink from skull cups and make trumpets from human bones.

Remaining with emptiness is also a gift of compassion—to myself, and perhaps, to others; instead of giving the arrogance of Job's comfort, we can offer the witness of silence, and the example of path. It may be a more generous and intimate experience, for both parties, to wait on someone who is disabled than to preach a sermon on self-reliance. Where action is called for, it comes best from an empty mind.

The basic terror of nihilistic despair seems to arise from sensing the truth of emptiness, and yet not living it. Can we open that final closet door? With the best intentions, our comforters say, "No—keep it closed."

Even if all the pain in the world means absolutely nothing, can we admit that and live? Can we still wake up? The answer is yes—with a smile. But not until we give in to that "nothing," and know it in our bones.

22 ❂ Conscious Eating

MARC DAVID

During a particularly stressful time in my life I was looking for the right vacation spot to help me unwind and feel more relaxed about life. A friend had recently returned from a ten-day meditation retreat in the country and was clearly a changed man. He explained that from four-thirty in the morning till nine in the evening, all the participants did was sit in silence and meditate. There were short breaks for meals, walks, and the bathroom. Otherwise, it was pure silence for ten days. No socializing, no talking, no music, no videos, and no external distractions. It helped him calm down and gave him a very positive outlook on life. He suggested I give it a try. It sounded like the last situation I would put myself in, but a few weeks later I decided to try it.

After the initial "excitement" of meditating eleven hours a day wore off, there was not much to look forward to when waking up each morning. Because all possible distractions and diversions were eliminated, there was only one thing to grab onto—food. Each day 160 meditators eagerly waited for the breakfast, lunch, and dinner bells to ring. Once in the dining hall, people would pile their plates with a surprisingly large amount of food. It was certainly not because they were exercising all day and needed more calories than usual. It was because the process of meditation can bring up boredom, anxiety, tension, and a host of negative emotions, and food was the only available source of immediate gratification. Many people would eat so much so fast that they would fall asleep during the meditation session. Here they were attempting to observe and "control" their minds during eleven hours of meditation each day, yet at mealtimes they ate recklessly, shoveling down their food with little attention.

I was observing the way everyone else ate and noting the extent of their emotional eating, but by about the fourth day I realized that I was behaving no differently. Not only was I using food as an emotional crutch, eating in an unconscious trance without any awareness of my food, I realized that I always ate that way. I could not remember ever eating with a quiet mind, focusing attention on my food, and really tasting the full experience of eating.

This insight swept over me just as I was about to take my first bite of lunch, and the impact of this *aha* experience sent me into uncontrollable laughter. There I was, sitting in the dining hall with 160 meditators who had been silent for four days, and I was laughing at the top of my lungs, unable to stop myself. When I finally took a bite of my food, it felt like the first bite in the universe. I now knew what it meant to "savor" food, to experience whole body eating.

WHOLE BODY EATING

If you eat, you owe it to yourself to experience what you eat. "Whole body eating" is a simple practice of eating with awareness that can be done with minimal effort and maximal results.

Step 1: *Make a Conscious Choice to Eat.*

Chances are good that you eat at least three times a day with some snacking in between. How often, though, do you question yourself to see if eating is what you really want to do?

Many of us eat on automatic pilot. We are driven by habit to eat when we are not hungry or not to eat when we are hungry. In the first step of whole body eating we perform the most basic act of the eating process. We look within to see what we are hungering for. We make the conscious choice of whether or not to eat.

Step 2: Ask Your Body What It Wants.
Once you have decided to eat, consciously choose *what* to eat. In fact, go to an authority for advice: your body. The body has an intuitive wisdom that goes beyond words and explanations. Dancers, healers, yogis, athletes, and others know this. You know it too: You just may not know that you know it.

If you are concerned about asking your body and getting the "wrong" answers, remember that choosing the "right" foods is less important than eating whatever you choose *wholeheartedly*. We eat what we eat regardless of whether we tune into our body wisdom or not, so why not just enjoy it? It is perfectly fine to draw on somatic information and make mistakes. The more we practice the better we become.

Step 3: Eat with Awareness.
This is the heart of whole body eating: Be there when you eat. Achieve the fullest experience of your food. Taste it. Savor it. Pay attention to it. Rejoice in it. See how it makes your body feel. Take in all the sensations.

But don't just eat the food. Eat the ambiance. Eat the colors. Eat the aromas. Eat the conversation. Eat the company sitting next to you. Eat the entire experience.

Have you ever really eaten? Many of us haven't had a "pure" experience of food. We eat but are "out to lunch." We are busy with something else or drifting off in fantasyland. This fundamental inattention to the meal leaves us starving for more. We may eat a nutritionally complete meal yet still remain undernourished.

We don't just hunger for food alone. We hunger for the experience of it—the tasting, the chewing, the sensuousness, the enjoyment, the textures, the sounds, and the satisfaction. If we continually miss these experiences, we will naturally want to eat again and again, but will remain unfulfilled.

Exercise
Find a time when you feel unhurried and can put your obligations aside. Be alone. Cook yourself a meal that you will enjoy eating. Then take the food to a comfortable room where you can be undistracted. Sit with your back straight. Let your eyes close. Take three or four deep breaths. When you are relaxed, allow your eyes to open and look at your food. Sense your hunger for it. Smell it. Wonder about it. And then eat it.

Notice all the sensations in your body. Feel the food in your mouth and on your tongue. Listen to the sounds of chewing. Follow the food as it goes down your throat. At what point does it disappear from your awareness? Can you feel the moment-to-moment changes from excitement to relaxation to anticipation as you consume your meal? Eat slowly and deliberately. Do nothing else for twenty minutes but immerse yourself in eating. Don't go off to Jupiter, become president of the United States, or digest more newsprint than food. No distractions of any kind. Issues and emotions are bound to emerge as you eat—fear, excitement, longing, confusion, boredom. As you watch these come up, allow them to go by. Return to the food. Surrender yourself to a 100-percent experience of eating.

People who practice this experiment often report that they feel as if they are tasting food for the first time. One woman could not believe she had spent a whole lifetime without noticing her food. Eating with awareness helps us use the bodily sensations experienced during a meal as an anchor for the restless mind, a mind that can't wait to eat yet refuses to pay attention once it *is* eating. When we are relaxed, receptive, attentive, and without self-rejection, doubt, expectations, or judgments, we are in the most appropriate condition for the digestive system to function at its optimal level.

Eating with awareness increases the nutrient assimilation of a meal as well as the assimilation of the entire sensory experience. Obviously you cannot eat this way all the time, but you can incorporate the essence of "conscious eating" into any eating situation. Try devoting at least a few minutes of each meal to conscious eating. You may also wish to set aside several meals during the week for conscious, silent dining.

Eating with awareness is the most important and powerful tool to transform your relationship to food and the body. Once you begin to practice it, it becomes a lifelong habit. There is no goal or ideal to strive for. All there is to do is eat, observe, and accept. No matter what kind of food you eat or nutritional system you follow, eating with awareness is the key to diet.

Step 4: Listen for Feedback.
Now that you have eaten your meal, take a few minutes to relax. Learn from the meal by reflecting upon *what* you have eaten and *how* you have eaten it. Did you pay attention to the meal? Did the food satisfy you? Would you eat differently next time? Slower, faster? Consume more food, less food, different food? Do you feel heavy? Are you still hungry?

Take whatever information that comes to you and simply note it. If you are unhappy with how you feel or how you have eaten, try not to punish yourself. Relax. Use the experience as a teacher, as a method to improve the way you eat next time.

Step 5: Release the Meal.
Once you have finished your food, let it go. Forget about eating for a while. Forget about health, weight, and anything that looks, smells, or tastes like food. Go on to the next thing at hand. Live your life.

This is the last step in whole body eating and perhaps the most difficult. The inability to release food is at the root of our most challenging eating habits. Even though we have finished a meal, the eating has not really ended. The mind may continue to munch on thoughts of food, dieting, body image, or optimum nutrition. Do you realize the tremendous amount of energy spent by holding on to these things?

Perhaps the biggest obstacle to releasing food is our inability to "assimilate" it. Many of us finish a meal without any integration time. We eat and run, fall asleep from overeating, or become a couch vegetable. The experience of eating remains undigested like morsels of food in an upset stomach.

Once you have listened for feedback about the meal, take time to just be with it. Listen to music, talk to friends, stare out the window, read a book, or just breathe.

True Nourishment

What nourishes? What is it that truly feeds us and provides the satisfaction we seek? We believe that good nutrition nourishes us, and it does, yet it is easy to lose sight of all that nourishes and focus on nutrition alone. There is a wonderful scene in Woody Allen's movie *Sleeper* where he wakes up after two centuries of suspended animation. The scientists who have brought him out of this long sleep explain his plight, and one of the first questions he asks is, "Where are all my friends?" He is told that his friends are dead, to which he replies with his classic forlorn and quizzical look, "I don't understand it; they all ate organic rice."

The question of what nourishes is often difficult to answer because our dietary notions change constantly. What we thought was good to eat yesterday is not always what we think is good today.

Most nutritional assertions that originate from authoritative sources have a brief shelf life. Our nutritional information is not based on what is ultimately good to eat, but what we *believe* is good to eat at the time. Within this unstable state of affairs, one thing does remain constant—the connection between our relationship to food and our inner world. How we eat is a reflection of how we live. Our hurrying through life is reflected in hurrying through meals. Our fear of emotional emptiness is seen in our overeating. Our need for certainty and control is mirrored in strict dietary rules. Our looking for love in all the wrong places is symbolized in our use of food as a substitute for love.

The more we are aware of these connections, the greater the potential for our personal unfolding and inner satisfaction. For in changing the way we eat, we change the way we live. By focusing attention while eating, we learn to focus attention in any situation. By enjoying food, we begin to enjoy nourishment in all its forms. By loosening dietary restrictions, we learn to open up to life. By accepting our body as it is, we learn to love ourselves for who we are. And by eating with dignity, we learn to live with dignity.

23 ✿ *Being with Anger*

STEPHEN LEVINE

Before one thinks of "doing good," one must seriously contemplate removing oneself from doing harm. Before we can play with the angels of our compassion, we need to take tea with the "demons" of our holding. To meet these hobgoblins like Milarepa we approach open-handedly, offering sweets to the tricksters, watching them regress, curled childlike by the fire, sucking at the breast of loving kindness.

Most people are basically kind and gentle but haven't yet cured themselves of the reactive, injurious quality of their anger. Few have taken tea with their outrage or confusion. Most try to push it away, causing it to explode unconsciously into a world already overflowing with violence and reactivity. Few, in order to cultivate the quality of harmlessness in their lives, have taken responsibility for their anger. To take responsibility for our anger means to relate *to* it instead of *from* it. To be responsible to our anger is to bring it within the realm of the voluntary. To react to it leaves life frozen in the mechanical action of old mind. Responsibility enters the moment anew. Reactivity is the same old thing.

To react to our anger is to roll the boulders of fear and

distrust into the mouth of our cave. To respond to it is to invite it in for tea, to meet it eye to eye in the light that streams through the wide entrance to our cavern. It is seldom we meet our anger so completely. We are usually quite unfamiliar with its presence until we become enraged. We seldom meet anger in its infancy because we have a tendency to deny it and judge it as "bad." And so we don't notice its subtler quality on first arisal. This shadowy comprehension of our anger is a byproduct of our having pulled back too often from the unpleasant, from becoming angry at ourselves for becoming angry.

Everyone has anger because everyone has desires. It comes with the territory. Desire leads to anger. As desire moves toward its fulfillment, if something arises to block it, frustration occurs.

Relating directly to anger, we explore its roots. Examining the momentum of desire, one comes to understand deeply the push and pull of the mind, the nature of frustration itself, the feeling of not having, of more wanting, a denseness, a tightening, a nausea. Watching frustration closely, one explores the point where it flicks over into anger. It is very important that we explore our anger so we are not perpetually reacting to the vicissitudes of the world, leaving the debris of unfinished business in our wake.

Anger unexplored breeds anger. Anger explored leads to harmony. Exploring anger, we discover how isolated we feel when angry. When we are angry, everything in the world is an "other." In anger we are already in so much pain we can hardly stand it, yet the merciless reactive mind thinks we deserve further punishment. In fact, what would be a greater curse than if someone were to say, "May you be angry the rest of your life!" We would see and smell and taste nothing. Our life would shrivel to a fearful defense of imagined safe territory. We would not even be able to touch the world because anger acts as a film across the senses. It blocks reception. Indeed, as we watch frustration closely, we see that anger arises uninvited and has a life of its own, a momentum from all the previous moments of identifying with anger, becoming angry and separate. But meeting frustration in "don't know," nothing tightens down on the content to obscure the natural unfolding of its process as we learn to respond to it instead of reacting angrily. Reacting to anger creates the violence, the abuse, the separation which pains us so.

As mercy develops, we see how painful it is to be in anger and we are reminded to soften, to look gently on it as it arises. And we realize that we don't have to hellishly react, impulsively putting ourselves and the whole world out of our heart. Sensing the power of non-injury, we begin to respond to ourselves as we would to a frightened child, with a deeper kindness and care.

We have been taught that there were only two things we could do with our anger. One was to reactively suppress it. The other was to reactively spit it out. But both are forms of attachment to anger. One is a condemning, the other a clinging. What is ironic is that when we examine anger, we notice that no matter how much we have emoted this feeling, we have never felt rid of it for long. We become exhausted before we can get it all out. The involuntary emoting of anger just creates more of the same.

There are, at this time, some very skillful means of working with suppressed anger that involve bringing it to the surface. For those who have difficulty making contact with their anger there are ways of stimulating it, such as beating on a mattress or screaming, which therapists have skillfully employed. Because nothing which is not accepted can be healed, some people need to bring up anger to have direct access to it. This is a technique that must be used in a very balanced manner so that anger brought to the surface can be investigated without being identified with as self. It takes the most balanced of therapists to help one uncover anger without trapping one in identification with its dynamics.

Exploring its nature, we discover how unskillful it can be to suppress anger. Pushing it down, it accumulates beyond the reach of our ordinary awareness. It has access to you, but you no longer have access to it. It drives you, it motivates you, it makes choices for you, but you can't see "who" has the reins in their hands because it is suppressed below the level of awareness. And just as we can see that we can't get it all out, we notice that we can't suppress it quite completely either. We are always ready to explode or implode.

Thus we come to recognize a third alternative with anger and other heavy states. Rather than pushing them down or spitting them out, we can let them come gently into awareness. We can start to give them space, to get a sense of their texture, of their voice, of their inclination. We begin to investigate the nature of *the* anger instead of getting lost in *my* anger. Indeed, to give anger space takes courage. It takes acceptance, which, interestingly enough, is the exact opposite of anger. Anger and fear are both strong aversion reactions. Acceptance is a welcoming response. The very act of accepting anger begins to melt it and gives access to subtler and subtler levels of holding. Acceptance takes the mask off anger and lets you look it straight in the eye. It allows anger to come and allows it to go. I have seen people sitting in meditation, their clothes drenched with perspiration having come upon the deep magma of their impotent rage, just trying to stay with the moment a breath at a time. If that underground fire is brought to the surface, it might light our way.

When we see that anger is not a single state of mind and begin to experience it in its unfolding—frustration flipping over into intense wanting, flipping over into feelings of abandonment, into not having, into self-pity, into righteousness, into pride, into aggression, into confusion, back into self-pity and pride again—one can come to ask oneself, "Which of these states is anger?" As we relate *to* it instead of *from* it, we see that anger is a process.

We notice in our investigation of frustration a certain quality of stress that permeates the mind/body. Some react to stress with anger, others with fear. Seeing clearly each state as it momentarily predominates allows us to break mind's automatic chain of events. We are able to reside a bit more in being itself, the space in which anger is unfolding, without getting lost in its content. Not suffering from the mistaken identity that we are the anger, we instead recognize in space the tightness passing through. Anger or fear are the inevitable momentum of old mind, which, deeply observed, begins to lose its power. Recognizing the well-forged and deeply imprinted links in this chain of action and reaction, we recognize how natural it is to have anger. As natural as the underlying frustration, the underlying desire. But when we understand the naturalness of anger, when we no longer back away in shock, we see that each moment of its arisal is an opportunity for practice, for awareness and mercy. Recognizing, for instance, that we may be angry ten thousand more times, the next time the anger arises, we meet it as Milarepa met the ogres at the mouth of his cave, and invite it in for closer inspection. "Take tea. Make yourself comfortable. Warm yourself by the fire." Then anger can begin to float. And instead of 10,001 more times of anger there may be only 9,999. Each moment of responding to it mindfully instead of reacting to it compulsively lessens the momentum of old mind. Each time we relate to anger, instead of from it, lessens its seductive quality, its mechanical, compulsive reactivity, which has so often propelled action.

I remember once looking at the "Ten Rules of Practice" on a wall of a monastery. One of the rules was "Don't be angry." And I thought, "No one is going to get enlightened in this place." For how is one going to get liberated if one excludes anything from investigation? When someone says to you, "Don't be angry," that means don't be. To allow anger to come into being without becoming it takes a very delicate balance, but to react to anger with fear is just more of the same old thing. Until anger, like boredom or restlessness, is equally invited into the heart of mindfulness, one will always be thrown off kilter by its momentary arisal. We have been very strongly conditioned not to be angry, usually by someone who was angry at the time. We cultivate a mercilessness with ourselves, and our judgment meets anger in an angry way. The hardness tightens; we become the object and subject of abuse.

Anger, like all heavy states, even pain, is workable when we approach it with a merciful awareness. In fact, anger can be quite fascinating to watch. We begin to see anger's grade B script, its shadowboxing and interior monologue. "They should have done this." "They ought to be like that." "If it was up to me, I'd do this." We watch it run out its game, and if we stay with it long enough we notice, quite to our chagrin, that it begins the same old story line all over again. We start to see the tape-loop quality, the impersonal process, which repeats over and over again what it has already said. Listening mercifully to the repeating images, the all-too-familiar insistence that we are right, the pride, the sense of rejection, the feeling of not being loved enough, we begin to have compassion for our anger and bring it a cup of tea. We begin to have mercy on that poor painful state of mind, that compulsive violence to itself, that closedness, that hard living. Then anger reminds us to soften the belly and that no one is an object, but all are a living suchness, baby flesh, ourselves.

The exploration of such a state becomes a very interesting endeavor. You explore it, listen to it, feel it, come to know it. What is anger in the body? What is its voice in the mind? What is its tone of voice? What is the script it reads out? Are there other accompanying states of mind? What precedes it? What follows? The process unfolding in vast space.

As our anger comes within the circle of responsibility, we get a sense of what it means to be fully alive. And that circle widens to allow more and more of our states of mind, and the states of mind of our loved ones, to come within the deep stillness of a choiceless investigation, a willingness to be. We no longer hide in the dark forest of reactivity, constantly ambushed by our feelings, frightened and hardened to the world. Instead, we go deep within and notice that if we add love to any situation we are angry about, the cause of anger dissolves. Staying with the changing qualities of anger in the mind/body, the words in the mind, the images, the denseness in the body, we discover under all this anger a deep sadness. Omitting nothing, the investigation continues into the sadness, all the moments of not having, all the frustrated griefs of a lifetime, and beneath that sadness we discover an ocean of love beyond our wildest dreams.

So the investigation of anger becomes an end of injury in the world and leads us directly to the love beneath, to our underlying nature. When we bring anger into the area where we can respond to it, where we can investigate it, where we can embrace it, it emerges into the light of our wholeness. Then even anger does not close our heart. Then anger is no longer a hindrance but a profound teacher, a reminder to go deeper, to discover what is real.

The Tibetan Buddhist tradition speaks of taking anger and turning it around to motivate practice because in anger are qualities like straightforwardness and resoluteness which can be turned into commitment. It can be the anger of "I am not going to let my heart be closed a moment longer— enough is enough!" It is not a destructive anger, it is the creative urge to get on with our work. In anger's tendency toward reaction can be discovered an energy which can be redirected toward entering the moment wholeheartedly. Anger too has the quality of an unwillingness to allow things to remain as they are. Separated from its aggression, that quality of discontent can motivate us to take the path of healing. It is alchemy. We take the dross and turn it into gold. Then we see that anger has not been the problem. Our manner of relating to it has been the main problem.

Having taken tea so many times with our anger, we are no longer frustrated or surprised by its deep tendency to draw identification, but mercifully acknowledge that the nature of the mind is to grasp, to think about itself, and instead of tightening in just more identification, more repulsion toward mind, toward the seat of pain, we learn to have mercy. We learn to let the mind be in the heart. We learn to love ourselves.

Then we see how the nature of anger is resentment, an integral part of the armoring about the heart. And we see that anger is a form of grief. It is a response to loss. It is a response to not getting what we want. We recognize that anything we are angry about we are actually grieving over. And so our relating to anger becomes the grief work that calls on our heart for mercy and healing. In seeing what closes us, we can stay awake a millisecond longer the next time.

In making this much room in our heart for anger, we acknowledge that at times our anger is so great that we have very little room for it. The thoughts are so seductive that identification automatically adheres and pride nurses it into flame. But that is only the beginning. We see that the mind, in its long personal history, feels every right to be angry, and we do not block that either, for we know that without permission to be angry we don't have consent to be alive. So we allow anger to come wholeheartedly into the mind, instead of getting lost in the old way of trying to squeeze it into some manageable shape.

When anger becomes so intense, so identified with that there is no space in the mind in which to investigate, you can come into the body and start to examine anger as sensation. Because often you can stay mindful of anger longer as sensation than you can as thought. It may be very difficult to examine fear in the frightened mind, but it is always accessible to exploration in the body—its denseness, its rapidity of change, its tension quite noticeable in the gut, the throat, the lower back. Every state of mind has an accompanying, a concomitant state of body. By directing awareness into the body again and again to rediscover the body pattern of anger, the mind does not get sucked into reinforcing it. So that you can start to see some of its empty quality, so that some aspect of it at least can be touched with mercy and awareness. Theoretically, if we had no mind to be angry, still anger would be recognizable by the contractions and patterns it left in the body. Indeed, we could tell whether we were joyous or frightened, doubtful or expectant, by the bodily echo of these states. When we can't stay with the mind of anger, we always have access to the body of investigation. And there we can find at least one more millisecond of not being angry, but being with anger. One more opportunity for freedom from the old.

When we relate wholeheartedly to emotions, we can let go of trying to be rational about emotion. To be rational about emotion is to try to fit a square peg in a round hole. Emotions have their own nature, just as thoughts have theirs. They are not the same. They are two separate levels of the mind. To try to be rational about emotions is to go crazy. The back wards are filled with people who are trying to think their feelings rather than experience them as they are.

To attempt to make emotions rational is to cause great conflict within. But to simply watch how the mind emotes, how it smiles and frowns in reaction to the world, can give some insight into its natural unfoldings.

Exploring the hindrances deeply, we attempt to make nothing other than it is. Just to see its nature as it plays itself out. No longer angry at anger. When there is anger, there is just anger. When there is fear, there is just fear. And when there is joy, there is just joy. We have room for it all. We take life as a blessing instead of a curse.

PART
FOUR

✺ *Community*

First, awaken on your own.
Then, see someone else.

—Zen Master Keizan

At a time like this, when there's so much chaos and
suffering in the world, individuals who are willing to
wake up and make friends with themselves are actually needed, because they can work with others, they
can hear what people are saying to them, they can
come from the heart and be of use.

—Pema Chödrön

✿ Introduction

Meditation and spiritual practice are often thought of as rarefied activities divorced from "real life"— from family, relationships, and social concerns. The final section of this book is designed to help lay that notion to rest. Although spirituality often *has* been kept separate from social concerns, it does not need to be. Indeed, the more dysfunctional our culture becomes, the more it becomes clear that we need above all a large-scale spiritual renewal where people start to bring a new kind of sensitivity and awareness into family and work relationships, into social action, and into their dealings with each other at every level.

The relevant archetype here is that of the bodhisattva, someone whose life is dedicated to helping all beings. To aspire to be a bodhisattva means to develop an intention to live in a way that benefits others, that enhances the whole of life. Yet how do we go about finding sanity in an insane world, and how do we bring that sanity to bear on this world?

Can we dedicate ourselves to others' well-being if we cannot find the source of well-being inside ourselves? Can we help others if we don't know how to help ourselves? Can we be peacemakers if we have no real inner peace? The Christian contemplative Thomas Merton suggests that we cannot:

He who attempts to act and do things for others and for the world without deepening his own self-understanding, freedom, integrity, and capacity to love, will not have anything to give to others. He will communicate to them only the contagion of his own obsessions, his aggressiveness, his ego-centered ambitions, his delusions about ends and means, and his doctrinaire prejudices and ideas.[1]

Thus it seems that inner and outer work are two sides of the same undertaking. The inner work we do to become more wakeful and present can only benefit our relations with others, just as our relationships cannot help but show us where we have more work to do on ourselves.

This section opens with some of Thich Nhat Hanh's most beautiful writing on the relation between working on ourselves and working for others. Mindful awareness helps us discover how we can put an end to war—inside ourselves, first of all. When we mindfully enjoy drinking a cup of tea, we are sowing the seeds of peace and well-being not just for ourselves, but for everyone. "If we are not able to smile, then the world will not have peace."

We should not interpret what Thich Nhat Hanh is saying here simplistically. He is not saying that all we have to do is to find inner peace, and then everything will be all right. Rather, he is stressing that some measure of inner peace and awareness is a necessary prerequisite for truly effective and compassionate action in the world. Recognizing that social policies are dictated by a people's way of life, he suggests that we change our life, from the inside out. The conventional social action perspective claims that we must change the world because our society is causing so much suffering. In another passage from his writings, Thich Nhat Hanh acknowledges this, yet he suggests that creating a wholesome life for ourselves also starts to change the world:

The explosion of bombs, the burning of napalm, the violent deaths of our neighbors and relatives, the pressure of time,

---

1. Thomas Merton, *New Seeds of Contemplation* (New York: New Directions, 1972).

noise, and pollution, the lonely crowds—these have all been
created by the disruptive course of our economic growth. They
are all sources of mental illness, and they must be ended. Anything we can do to end them is preventive medicine. [Yet]
political activities are not the only means . . . Many of us cannot
see things [clearly] because we are not wholly ourselves. Wholly
ourselves, we can see how one person by his or her way of living
can demonstrate that life is possible, that a future for the world
is possible.[2]

Mindfulness practice shows us how we are not at one with
ourselves, how we are driven by our thoughts and feelings,
which in turn have been conditioned by our life circumstances. Understanding the nature of this conditioning allows us to feel greater compassion and kinship with others:
If we had grown up in the rapist's circumstances, we too
could have become a rapist. This understanding cuts
through the "us" and "them" mentality, leaving us no high
ground on which to stand and condemn anyone. Thich Nhat
Hanh also suggests that by helping to root us in our own
being, meditation provides a ground of sanity from which we
can relate to our rootless society. Thus "meditation is not an
escape from society."

We often hear about the importance of finding inner
peace, but rarely do we come across such a graphic account
of what this entails as Deena Metzger's description of her
own inner peacemaking process. She uses the metaphor of
herself as a country with two antagonistic populations, the
Suns and the Shades. All her life she has been ruled by the
Suns' dictatorial regime, which has mercilessly repressed and
exploited the more life-affirming Shade majority. Who of us,
if we look deep enough into the structure of our inner life,
cannot find our own version of this inner repression and
warfare? It is common in our culture to repress the juicy,

2. "The Individual, Society, and Nature," in *The Path of Compassion*,
edited by Fred Eppsteiner (Berkeley, Calif.: Parallax Press, 1988), p. 45.

sensitive parts of ourselves because they seem to be threatening or unproductive. Our tyrannical superego—that part of
us that wants to censor and control our experience—often
sacrifices or enslaves the life-loving parts of us because they
seem to resist its decrees.

Yet fighting against this inner tyranny is not the key to
genuine peace or well-being. That would be just another
form of self-aggression. Our inner tyranny is a distorted
form of a more basic and genuine impulse: the need to take
care of ourselves. So instead of struggling with the supergo,
we need to uncover and cultivate the genuine impulse contained within it.

Taking care of ourselves in a more life-affirming way
means renouncing aggression as an instrument of both domestic and foreign policy. We need to withdraw our support
both from the superego's dictatorship, with its whole defense establishment, and from our guerilla rebellion against
it. And we need to set up a neutral peacekeeping force (i.e.,
the presence of awareness) to watch over these warring fac-
tions. We can start to establish genuine inner peace and
well-being only by paying attention to all the different needs
and concerns within us. As Deena Metzger describes this
discovery: "A lost function of government was being restored: to nurture, sustain, and protect the entire population
. . . Rather than being militaristic or aggressive, protection
began to feel maternal or paternal in the sweetest way. It was
characterized by tenderness."

In this chapter, Deena Metzger describes some of the most
important work that any of us can do—ending the inner war,
healing the split between self and other inside us, and overcoming our penchant for creating enemies and then arming
ourselves against them. This kind of inner work has obvious,
direct consequences for how we relate to our world and to
all beings.

Activist Joanna Macy explores how our beliefs about self
and other affect our ability to be agents of positive social
change. She argues that "a sense of profound inter-connect-

edness with all life" is the only basis for effective social action. This approach suggests a new direction for political activism, one that could take us beyond the stale intrigues of interest-group politics, where vested interests fight for their own agendas against those with different interests. When we realize that this earth *is* our body, that the rain forest is our lungs, that it is impossible to find genuine happiness by ignoring the collective suffering around us, that all human beings share the need for a healthy society and a clean environment, our focus can shift to the common welfare of our planet and all its inhabitants. We can start to act for the good of the whole, rather than for some narrow self-interest.

Yet understanding the interconnectedness of all beings as an intellectual belief is not as effective as knowing it more deeply, in our body and bones. By showing us that we cannot separate what goes on inside us from what goes on outside, mindfulness practice provides direct experience of what Thich Nhat Hanh calls interbeing. Once we see how we create our own pollution and strife every day in the ways we think, speak, and act, we can no longer target some enemy "out there" to blame for the world's ills—whether it is welfare recipients, corporate polluters, the Pentagon, or a policeman who is trying to do his job. By acknowledging how we each contribute to the problems the world is facing, we are already moving toward real solutions. If practiced widely, this approach could lead to a more meaningful kind of social change than the endless cycle of revolutions that lead to new tyrannies, which in turn spawn further revolts.

Meditation teacher Jack Kornfield also regards the principle of interconnectedness as an essential foundation for compassionate action and service. Yet he recognizes that it is often difficult to know just what to do about the overwhelming problems in our world. The starting-point is to open our eyes and our heart and simply become more aware of what is happening. Never before have humans had to face the real possibility that their activity could doom the very existence of life on this planet. This prospect often seems too frightening and overwhelming to face, so we turn away, narrow our awareness, and live in a state of denial, trying to eke out a little personal happiness amid the gathering storm. Yet the more we avert our gaze from what is going on, the more likely the planetary disaster we most fear becomes. Even if we cannot be a Gandhi or a Mother Teresa, each of us can discover how best to serve life on this planet by listening to our heart and following the guidance that comes from deep within. Service does not have to take the form of charity or social work. Living with attention and concern, being mindful of how our every action affects others, is also an important kind of service.

In exploring the specifics of mindful social action, activist Ken Jones also stresses the importance of not creating an enemy. This is particularly important in social action, where unjust and immoral activities must often be firmly opposed. Mindfulness practice can help us maintain our wits in such stressful situations and cut through our tendency to be self-righteous as well. Because our personal and collective fates have become so inextricably linked, Jones argues, social action provides a particularly useful way to work on oneself while serving others at the same time.

In his short but powerful piece, the Tibetan teacher Chagdud Tulku suggests that becoming a peacemaker can be a spiritual path in itself, for it requires us to overcome our tendency to be consumed by egotistical and aggressive emotions. The most essential difference between peacemakers and warmakers is that the former are working on their own egotism and aggression, while the latter are posioning the world with it. If we can confront the warmakers of the world without being consumed by anger, then perhaps we can, as Chagdud says, "penetrate the terrible delusion that causes war and all its hellish sufferings." Chagdud is not suggesting that we suppress our anger, but that we learn to work with it and tame it so that we can be "awakened warriors."

In the next chapter Chögyam Trungpa brings this discussion closer to home and builds another bridge between personal awareness and social action. He points out that it is hypocritical to try to change society if our own living situation is a mess. Creating a healthy society can only begin at home. It requires an appreciation of what Trungpa calls "nowness." Our materialistic society can abuse and pollute the world so heedlessly only because it is numb to the freshness of the present moment and addicted to the feverish pursuit of some "great big beautiful tomorrow." We cannot create a sane society unless we appreciate nowness, which allows us to apprehend the sacred quality of our life. In Trungpa's words, "Appreciating sacredness begins very simply by taking an interest in all the details of your life."

One of the most important details we need to pay attention to in our domestic situation is our relationship with our intimate partner. As the *I Ching* suggests, the health of society depends on the well-being of the family, and the well-being of the family depends on healthy relations between husband and wife. Yet now that family and society no longer define, support, and enforce the relations between intimate partners, we need a whole new approach to relationships. It no longer works to treat them solely as a vehicle for pleasure or security. As I suggest in the next chapter, relationships need to reflect and promote our true nature if they are to flourish in these times. We need to realize that intimacy is, more than anything, a path, a series of opportunities for realizing more deeply who we really are. Intimate relationship is an awareness practice that can be as powerful, in its own way, as meditation. It wakes us up by mirroring back to us our weak spots and calling on us to develop our inner strengths.

Monica Furlong also explores the relevance of contemplative practice for intimate relationship. Awareness practice is humbling, for it shows us just how unaware we are most of the time. Yet it also helps us come to terms with ourselves as ordinary, imperfect beings and teaches us that it is all right just to be ourselves. This is excellent training for relationships, since the gift of who we are is, after all, the best that we can give someone we love. Contemplative practice and intimate relationship are mutually enhancing because they both help us make friends with our humanity, with all its beauty and its flaws.

In discussing how family life and child-rearing can also be part of one's spiritual path, Zen student Fran Tribe describes how her children have been her greatest teachers. Her frank discussion of her doubts and discoveries about the spiritual value of motherhood is refreshing. And her discovery of domestic life as an important practice in itself helps cut through the conventional dichotomy between family and spiritual life.

Having explored how we can work with many different aspects of our lives as both spiritual practice and path, we end this book with some reflections on how we can also connect with death in the same way. Although the questions Stephen Levine considers—"Your practice is fit for calm, but is it fit for disturbance?" and "Can you keep your heart open in Hell?"—are also relevant for relationships and family life, he considers them here in the context of a hospital ward for the terminally ill. Levine's description of being there with those who are dying, not separating himself from their pain and fear, provides a graphic picture of what it is like to put spiritual understanding into practice. Here, once again, we see that the most important thing we can do for others is simply to be present with them, without forcing our reality on them. Compassion in this context is not telling people things to make them feel better, but helping them be there with what they are experiencing. If working with the dying has meaning, it is one that goes beyond our usual concerns and can never entirely be put into words.

The late Zen master Katagiri Roshi also speaks of the unspeakable quality of facing death. When we are present with someone who is dying, we also feel our own death. Katagiri Roshi regards this as a wonderful practice. He reminds us that giving up our concepts about dying can help us open into a much vaster realm of awareness—the realm of totality where all things are connected. In the moment when we glimpse the larger totality that our life is part of, we "return to the silent source of life and stand up there." In this vivid moment of nowness, we share with all beings the essence of what it is to be here on this earth.

24 ❀ Being Peace

THICH NHAT HANH

Meditation is not to get out of society, to escape from society, but to prepare for a reentry into society. We call this "engaged Buddhism." When we go to a meditation center, we may have the impression that we leave everything behind—family, society, and all the complications involved in them—and come as an individual in order to practice and to search for peace. This is already an illusion, because in Buddhism there is no such thing as an individual.

Just as a piece of paper is the fruit, the combination of many elements that can be called non-paper elements, the individual is made of non-individual elements. If you are a poet, you will see clearly that there is a cloud floating in this sheet of paper. Without a cloud there will be no water; without water, the trees cannot grow; and without trees, you cannot make paper. So the cloud is in here. The existence of this page is dependent on the existence of a cloud. Paper and cloud are so close. Let us think of other things, like sunshine. Sunshine is very important because the forest cannot grow without sunshine, and we humans cannot grow without sunshine. So the logger needs sunshine in order to cut the tree, and the tree needs sunshine in order to be a tree. Therefore you can see sunshine in this sheet of paper. And if you look more deeply, with the eyes of a bodhisattva, with the eyes of those who are awake, you see not only the cloud and the sunshine in it, but that everything is here: the wheat that became the bread for the logger to eat, the logger's father— everything is in this sheet of paper.

The *Avatamsaka Sutra* tells us that you cannot point to one thing that does not have a relationship with this sheet of paper. So we say, "A sheet of paper is made of non-paper elements." A cloud is a non-paper element. The forest is a non-paper element. Sunshine is a non-paper element. The paper is made of all the non-paper elements to the extent that if we return the non-paper elements to their sources, the cloud to the sky, the sunshine to the sun, the logger to his father, the paper is empty. Empty of what? Empty of a sepa-rate self. It has been made by all the non-self elements, non-paper elements, and if all these non-paper elements are taken out, it is truly empty, empty of an independent self. Empty, in this sense, means that the paper is full of every-thing, the entire cosmos. The presence of this tiny sheet of paper proves the presence of the whole cosmos.

In the same way, the individual is made of non-individual elements. How do you expect to leave everything behind when you enter a meditation center? The kind of suffering that you carry in your heart, that is society itself. You bring that with you, you bring society with you. You bring all of us with you. When you meditate, it is not just for yourself, you do it for the whole society. You seek solutions to your problems not only for yourself, but for all of us.

Leaves are usually looked upon as the children of the tree. Yes, they are children of the tree, born from the tree, but they are also mothers of the tree. The leaves combine raw sap, water, and minerals, with sunshine and gas, and convert it into a variegated sap that can nourish the tree. In this way, the leaves become the mother of the tree. We are all children of society, but we are also mothers. We have to nourish society. If we are uprooted from society, we cannot trans-form it into a more livable place for us and for our children.

The leaves are linked to the tree by a stem. The stem is very important.

I have been gardening in our community for many years, and I know that sometimes it is difficult to transplant cuttings. Some plants do not transplant easily, so we use a kind of vegetable hormone to help them be rooted in the soil more easily. I wonder whether there is a kind of powder, something that may be found in meditation practice that can help people who are uprooted be rooted again in society. Meditation is not an escape from society. Meditation is to equip oneself with the capacity to reintegrate into society, in order for the leaf to nourish the tree.

I think that our society is a difficult place to live. If we are not careful, we can become uprooted, and once uprooted, we cannot help change society to make it more livable. Meditation is a way of helping us stay in society. This is very important. We have seen people who are alienated from society and cannot be reintegrated into society. We know that this can happen to us if we are not careful.

I have learned that many of the Buddhist practitioners in America are young and intellectual, and have come to Buddhism not by the door of faith, but by the door of psychology. I know people in the Western world suffer a great deal psychologically, and that is why many have become Buddhists, practicing meditation in order to solve psychological problems. Many are still in society, but some have been uprooted. Having lived for quite some time in this society, I myself feel that I cannot get along with this society very well. There are so many things that make me want to withdraw, to go back to myself. But my practice helps me remain in society, because I am aware that if I leave society, I will not be able to help change it. I hope that those who are practicing Buddhism succeed in keeping their feet on earth, staying in society. That is our hope for peace.

Life is filled with suffering, but it is also filled with many wonders, like the blue sky, the sunshine, the eyes of a baby.

To suffer is not enough. We must also be in touch with the wonders of life. They are within us and all around us, everywhere, any time.

If we are not happy, if we are not peaceful, we cannot share peace and happiness with others, even those we love, those who live under the same roof. If we are peaceful, if we are happy, we can smile and blossom like a flower, and everyone in our family, our entire society, will benefit from our peace. Do we need to make a special effort to enjoy the beauty of the blue sky? Do we have to practice to be able to enjoy it? No, we just enjoy it. Each second, each minute of our lives can be like this. Wherever we are, any time, we have the capacity to enjoy the sunshine, the presence of each other, even the sensation of our breathing. We don't need to go to China to enjoy the blue sky. We don't have to travel into the future to enjoy our breathing. We can be in touch with these things right now. It would be a pity if we are only aware of suffering.

We are so busy we hardly have time to look at the people we love, even in our own household, and to look at ourselves. Society is organized in a way that even when we have some leisure time, we don't know how to use it to get back in touch with ourselves. We have millions of ways to lose this precious time—we turn on the TV or pick up the telephone, or start the car and go somewhere. We are not used to being with ourselves, and we act as if we don't like ourselves and are trying to escape from ourselves.

Meditation is to be aware of what is going on—in our bodies, in our feelings, in our minds, and in the world. Each day 40,000 children die of hunger. The superpowers now have more than 50,000 nuclear warheads, enough to destroy our planet many times. Yet the sunrise is beautiful, and the rose that bloomed this morning along the wall is a miracle. Life is both dreadful and wonderful. To practice meditation is to be in touch with both aspects. Please do not think we must be solemn in order to meditate. In fact, to meditate well, we have to smile a lot.

Recently I was sitting with a group of children, and a boy named Tim was smiling beautifully. I said, "Tim, you have a very beautiful smile," and he said, "Thank you." I told him, "You don't have to thank me, I have to thank you. Because of your smile, you make life more beautiful. Instead of saying, 'Thank you,' you should say 'You're welcome.' "

If a child smiles, if an adult smiles, that is very important. If in our daily life we can smile, if we can be peaceful and happy, not only we, but everyone will profit from it. This is the most basic kind of peace work. When I see Tim smiling, I am so happy. If he is aware that he is making other people happy, he can say, "You are welcome."

Even though life is hard, even though it is sometimes difficult to smile, we have to try. Just as when we wish each other, "Good morning," it must be a real "Good morning." Recently, one friend asked me, "How can I force myself to smile when I am filled with sorrow? It isn't natural." I told her she must be able to smile to her sorrow, because we are more than our sorrow. A human being is like a television set with millions of channels. If we turn the Buddha on, we are the Buddha. If we turn sorrow on, we are sorrow. If we turn a smile on, we really are the smile. We cannot let just one channel dominate us. We have the seed of everything in us, and we have to seize the situation in our hand, to recover our own sovereignty.

When we sit down peacefully, breathing and smiling, with awareness, we are our true selves, we have sovereignty over ourselves. When we open ourselves up to a TV program, we let ourselves be invaded by the program. Sometimes it is a good program, but often it is just noisy. Because we want to have something other than ourselves enter us, we sit there and let a noisy television program invade us, assail us, destroy us. Even if our nervous system suffers, we don't have the courage to stand up and turn it off, because if we do that, we will have to return to our self.

Meditation is the opposite. It helps us return to our true

self. Practicing meditation in this kind of society is very difficult. Everything seems to work in concert to try to take us away from our true self. We have thousands of things, like video tapes and music, which help us be away from ourselves. Practicing meditation is to be aware, to smile, to breathe. These are on the opposite side. We go back to ourselves in order to see what is going on, because to meditate means to be aware of what is going on. What is going on is very important.

Suppose you are expecting a child. You need to breathe and smile for him or her. Please don't wait until your baby is born before beginning to take care of him or her. You can take care of your baby right now, or even sooner. If you cannot smile, that is very serious. You might think, "I am too sad. Smiling is just not the correct thing to do." Maybe crying or shouting would be correct, but your baby will get it—anything you are, anything you do, is for your baby.

Even if you do not have a baby in your womb, the seed is already there. Even if you are not married, even if you are a man, you should be aware that a baby is already there, the seeds of future generations are already there. Please don't wait until the doctors tell you that you are going to have a baby to begin to take care of it. It is already there. Whatever you are, whatever you do, your baby will get it. Anything you eat, any worries that are on your mind will be for him or her. Can you tell me that you cannot smile? Think of the baby, and smile for him, for her, for the future generations. Please don't tell me that a smile and your sorrow just don't go together. It's your sorrow, but what about your baby? It's not his sorrow, it's not her sorrow.

Children understand very well that in each woman, in each man, there is a capacity of waking up, of understanding, and of loving. Many children have told me that they cannot show me anyone who does not have this capacity. Some people allow it to develop, and some do not, but everyone has it. This capacity of waking up, of being aware of what is going on in your feelings, in your body, in your perceptions, in the world, is called Buddha nature, the capacity of understanding and loving. Since the baby of that Buddha is in us, we should give him or her a chance. Smiling is very important. If we are not able to smile, then the world will not have peace. It is not by going out for a demonstration against nuclear missiles that we can bring about peace. It is with our capacity of smiling, breathing, and being peace that we can make peace.

How can we bring meditation out of the meditation hall and into the kitchen, and the office? How can the sitting influence the non-sitting time? If a doctor gives you an injection, not only your arm but your whole body benefits from it. If you practice one hour of sitting a day, that hour should be all 24 hours, and not just for that hour. One smile, one breath should be for the benefit of the whole day, not just for that moment. We must practice in a way that removes the barrier between practice and non-practice.

When we walk in the meditation hall, we make careful steps, very slowly. But when we go to the airport, we are quite another person. We walk very differently, less mindfully. How can we practice at the airport and in the market? That is engaged Buddhism. Engaged Buddhism does not only mean to use Buddhism to solve social and political problems, protesting against the bombs, and protesting against social injustice. First of all we have to bring Buddhism into our daily lives. I have a friend who breathes between telephone calls, and it helps her very much. Another friend does walking meditation between business appointments, walking mindfully between buildings in downtown Denver. Passersby smile at him, and his meetings, even with difficult persons, often turn out to be very pleasant, and very successful.

We should be able to bring the practice from the meditation hall into our daily lives. How can we practice to penetrate our feelings, our perceptions during daily life? We don't deal with our perceptions and our feelings only during sitting practice. We have to deal with them all the time. We need to discuss among ourselves how to do it. Do you practice breathing between phone calls? Do you practice smiling while cutting carrots?

In Plum Village in France, we receive many letters from the refugee camps in Singapore, Malaysia, Indonesia, Thailand, and the Philippines, hundreds each week. It is very painful to read them, but we have to do it, we have to be in contact. We try our best to help, but the suffering is enormous, and sometimes we are discouraged. It is said that half the boat people die in the ocean; only half arrive at the shores in Southeast Asia.

There are many young girls, boat people, who are raped by sea pirates. Even though the United Nations and many countries try to help the government of Thailand prevent that kind of piracy, sea pirates continue to inflict much suffering on the refugees. One day we received a letter telling us about a young girl on a small boat who was raped by a Thai pirate. She was only twelve, and she jumped into the ocean and drowned herself.

When you first learn of something like that, you get angry at the pirate. You naturally take the side of the girl. As you look more deeply you will see it differently. If you take the side of the little girl, then it is easy. You only have to take a gun and shoot the pirate. But we cannot do that. In my meditation I saw that if I had been born in the village of the pirate and raised in the same conditions as he was, I am now the pirate. There is a great likelihood that I would become a pirate. I cannot condemn myself so easily. In my meditation, I saw that many babies are born along the Gulf of Siam, hundreds every day, and if we educators, social workers, politicians, and others do not do something about the situation, in 25 years a number of them will become sea pirates. That is certain. If you or I were born today in those fishing villages, we might become sea pirates in 25 years. If you take a gun and shoot the pirate, you shoot all of us, because all of us are to some extent responsible for this state of affairs.

After a long meditation, I wrote this poem. In it, there are three people: the twelve-year-old girl, the pirate, and me. Can we look at each other and recognize ourselves in each other? The title of the poem is *Please Call Me by My True Names*, because I have so many names. When I hear one of these names, I have to say, "Yes."

> Do not say that I'll depart tomorrow
> because even today I still arrive.
>
> Look deeply: I arrive in every second
> to be a bud on a spring branch,
> to be a tiny bird, with wings still fragile,
>   learning to sing in my new nest,
> to be a caterpillar in the heart of flower,
> to be a jewel hiding itself in a stone.
>
> I still arrive, in order to laugh and to cry,
>   in order to fear and to hope,
> the rhythm of my heart is the birth and
>   death of all that are alive.
>
> I am the mayfly metamorphosing on the
>   surface of the river,
> and I am the bird which, when spring comes,
>   arrives in time to eat the mayfly.
>
> I am the frog swimming happily in the
>   clear water of a pond,
> and I am also the grass-snake who,
>   approaching in silence, feeds itself on the frog.
>
> I am the child in Uganda, all skin and bones,
>   my legs as thin as bamboo sticks,
> and I am the arms merchant, selling deadly
>   weapons to Uganda.
>
> I am the 12-year-old girl, refugee
>   on a small boat,

who throws herself into the ocean after
    being raped by a sea pirate,
and I am the pirate, my heart not yet capable
    of seeing and loving.

I am a member of the politburo, with
    plenty of power in my hands,
and I am the man who has to pay his
    "debt of blood" to my people,
dying slowly in a forced labor camp.

My joy is like spring, so warm it makes
    flowers bloom in all walks of life.
My pain is like a river of tears, so full it
    fills up the four oceans.

Please call me by my true names,
so I can hear all my cries and my laughs
    at once,
so I can see that my joy and pain are one.

Please call me by my true names,
    so I can wake up,
and so the door of my heart can be left open,
the door of compassion.

We have to look deeply at things in order to see. When a swimmer enjoys the clear water of the river, he or she should also be able to *be* the river. One day I was having lunch at Boston University with some friends, and I looked down at the Charles River. I had been away from home for quite a long time, and seeing the river, I found it very beautiful. So I left my friends and went down to wash my face and dip my feet in the water, as we used to do in our country. When I returned, a professor said, "That's a very dangerous thing to do. Did you rinse your mouth in the river?" When I told him, "Yes," he said, "You should see a doctor and get a shot."

I was shocked. I didn't know that the rivers here are so

polluted. You may call them dead rivers. In our country the rivers get very muddy sometimes, but not that kind of dirt. Someone told me that there are so many chemicals in the Rhine River in Germany that it is possible to develop photographs in it. We can be good swimmers, but can we be a river and experience the fears and hopes of a river? If we cannot, then we do not have the chance for peace. If all the rivers are dead, then the joy of swimming in the river will no longer exist.

If you are a mountain climber or someone who enjoys the countryside, or the green forest, you know that the forests are our lungs outside of our bodies. Yet we have been acting in a way that has allowed two million square miles of forest land to be destroyed by acid rain. We are imprisoned in our small selves, thinking only of the comfortable conditions for this small self, while we destroy our large self. One day I suddenly saw that the sun is my heart, my heart outside of this body. If my body's heart ceases to function I cannot survive; but if the sun, my other heart, ceases to function, I will also die immediately. We should be able to be our true self. That means we should be able to be the river, we should be able to be the forest, we should be able to be a Russian citizen. We must do this to understand, and to have hope for the future. That is the non-dualistic way of seeing.

During the war in Vietnam we young Buddhists organized ourselves to help victims of the war rebuild villages that had been destroyed by the bombs. Many of us died during service, not only because of the bombs and the bullets, but because of the people who suspected us of being on the other side. We were able to understand the suffering of both sides, the Communists and the anti-Communists. We tried to be open to both, to understand this side and to understand that side, to be one with them. That is why we did not take a side, even though the whole world took sides. We tried to tell people our perception of the situation: that we wanted to stop the fighting, but the bombs were so loud. Sometimes we had to burn ourselves alive to get the message across, but even then the world could not hear us. They thought we were supporting a kind of political act. They didn't know that it was a purely human action to be heard, to be understood. We wanted reconciliation, we did not want a victory. Working to help people in a circumstance like that is very dangerous, and many of us got killed. The Communists killed us because they suspected that we were working with the Americans, and the anti-Communists killed us because they thought that we were with the Communists. But we did not want to give up and take one side.

The situation of the world is still like this. People completely identify with one side, one ideology. To understand the suffering and the fear of a citizen of an enemy nation, we have to become one with him or her. To do so is dangerous—we will be suspected by both sides. But if we don't do it, if we align ourselves with one side or the other, we will lose our chance to work for peace. Reconciliation is to understand both sides, to go to one side and describe the suffering being endured by the other side, and then to go to the other side and describe the suffering being endured by the first side. Doing only that will be a great help for peace.

During a retreat at the Providence Zen Center, I asked someone to express himself as a swimmer in a river, and then after 15 minutes of breathing, to express himself as the river. He had to become the river to be able to express himself in the language and feelings of the river. After that a woman who had been in Russia was asked to express herself as an American, and after some breathing and meditation, as a Russian citizen, with all her fears and her hope for peace. She did it wonderfully. These are exercises of meditation related to non-duality.

To practice meditation is to be aware of the existence of suffering. The first Dharma Talk that the Buddha gave was about suffering, and the way out of suffering. In South Africa, the black people suffer enormously, but the white people also suffer. If we take one side, we cannot fulfill our task of reconciliation in order to bring about peace.

Are there people who can be in touch with both the black community and the white community in South Africa? If there are not many of them, the situation is bad. There must be people who can get in touch with both sides, understanding the suffering of each, and telling each side about the other. Are there people doing that kind of understanding and mediation and reconciliation between the two major political blocs on the earth? Can you be more than Americans? Can you be people who understand deeply the suffering of both sides? Can you bring the message of reconciliation?

You may not be aware that your country has been manufacturing a lot of conventional weapons to sell to Third World countries for their people to kill each other. You know very well that children and adults in these countries need food more than these deadly weapons. Yet no one has the time to organize a national debate to look at the problem of manufacturing and selling these deadly things. Everyone is too busy. Conventional weapons have been killing in the last 30, 40, 50 years, very much. If we only think of the nuclear bombs that may explode in the future and do not pay attention to the bombs that are exploding in the present moment, we commit some kind of error. I believe President Reagan said that the U.S. should continue to make conventional weapons to sell because if you don't, someone else will and the U.S. will lose its interest. This is not a good thing to say. It is off course. This statement is just an excuse, but there are real factors that push him and push the whole nation to continue to manufacture conventional weapons to sell. For instance, many people will lose their jobs if they stop. Have we thought about the kind of work that will help these people if the weapons industry stops?

Not many Americans are aware that these weapons are killing people in the Third World every day. The Congress has not debated this issue seriously. We have not taken the time to see this situation clearly, so we have not been able to change our government's policy. We are not strong enough to pressure the government. The foreign policy of a government is largely dictated by its people and their way of life. We have a large responsibility as citizens. We think that the government is free to make policy, but that freedom depends on our daily life. If we make it possible for them to change policies, they will do it. Now it is not possible yet. Maybe you think that if you get into government and obtain power, you can do anything you want, but that is not true. If you become President, you will be confronted by this hard fact. You will probably do just the same thing, a little better or a little worse.

Therefore we have to see the real truth, the real situation. Our daily lives, the way we drink, what we eat, has to do with the world's political situation. Meditation is to see deeply into things, to see how we can change, how we can transform our situation. To transform our situation is also to transform our minds. To transform our minds is also to transform our situation, because the situation is mind, and mind is situation. Awakening is important. The nature of the bombs, the nature of injustice, the nature of the weapons, and the nature of our own beings are the same. This is the real meaning of engaged Buddhism.

In the peace movement there is a lot of anger, frustration, and misunderstanding. The peace movement can write very good protest letters, but they are not yet able to write a love letter. We need to learn to write a letter to the Congress or to the President of the United States that they will want to read, and not just throw away. The way you speak, the kind of understanding, the kind of language you use should not turn people off. The President is a person like any of us.

Can the peace movement talk in loving speech, showing the way for peace? I think that will depend on whether the people in the peace movement can be peace. Because without being peace, we cannot do anything for peace. If we cannot smile, we cannot help other people to smile. If we are not peaceful, then we cannot contribute to the peace movement.

I hope we can bring a new dimension to the peace movement. The peace movement is filled with anger and hatred. It cannot fulfill the path we expect from them. A fresh way of being peace, of doing peace is needed. That is why it is so important for us to practice meditation, to acquire the capacity to look, to see, and to understand. It would be wonderful if we could bring to the peace movement our contribution, our way of looking at things, that will diminish aggression and hatred. Peace work means, first of all, being peace. Meditation is meditation for all of us. We rely on each other. Our children are relying on us in order for them to have a future.

25 ✺ *Personal Disarmament*

DEENA METZGER

In a small, segregated country, called Zebra, the Sun minority has relegated the Shade majority to reservations far from the cities and the centers of power. The government is a dictatorship.

The dictator, as well as the majority, knows nothing of the culture, mores, values, or spiritual inclinations of the Shades; nevertheless, fear and control of the Shades is behind every governmental decision. It is fully believed that if the Shades came near prominence or power, the entire way of being of the country would be altered. The minority does not fear for its lives; it fears for its way of life. To change this would be worse than death. One day there is a serious power outage. The power lines have been cut. Up to this point, energy has been the major export of this country. The country is paralyzed. The Shades do not deny they cut the lines, but assert that the power has always belonged to them. . . .

This scenario could describe conditions in any one of numerous countries. In fact, it is a description of my own inner state of being, a political description of the nation-state of my own psyche. I have come to understand that an individual is also a country, that one contains multiple selves who are governed as nations are governed, and that the problems and issues that afflict nations also afflict individuals. For most of my life, I have been completely unconscious of the real mode of government and the status of the beings within my territory.

A few years ago, confronted by an inner coup in the making, I realized that, despite my politics and activities, I was not identifying with the Shades, the oppressed and disenfranchised majority within, notwithstanding the rumors of their vitality, spiritual development, and artistic skills. To my horror, I was identifying completely with the dictator, the official church, and the empowered. Unthinkingly, I was supporting the status quo, order for its own sake, separatist minority tradition, efficiency, production, export, and growth, and I was acting in loyalty to priests who had long forgotten the true meaning of a spiritual life. Forced to consider negotiating with the Shades, I was overcome with terror and despair. I knew nothing of the Shades, whom I distrusted and denigrated. I co-opted their cultural resources while forcing them to work as slaves. I believed that the Shades were irrational, incompetent, irrelevant people. I ridiculed the preposterous assertion that they could govern themselves, let alone the entire country, and take their chances in the modern world.

Until then, Zebra had been developing into one of the largest, most valuable and respected energy exporters in the region. Now the lines were cut, the energy sources occupied, and the army and police without energy were totally immobilized. Against my will, I had to learn to negotiate with these "barbarian" and threatening forces.

Feeling the demand to arbitrate from this position of extreme fear and distrust, I learned invaluable political lessons as real politics—personal politics—became real life. There was no choice; my country—that is, my life—was at stake. Having once had a life-threatening disease whose underlying causes in the psyche I'd come to understand, I knew the gravity of the situation.

When I began to think about myself as a country, as well as an individual, I was struck by what seemed an overwhelming truth. While nations suffer the delusions that they can destroy one segment of their populations and remain intact or thrive, a nation-state such as I was, like a physical body, cannot hack off one limb or cut out one vital organ, and remain intact. I had managed to suppress some selves up to this time, but I suspected, and even the Suns and later the Shades came to know, that extermination of the opposition meant death. Therefore, albeit unwillingly, slowly, and painstakingly, I began to dismantle the minority supremacist government. I did this although the Suns insisted this meant the end of progress and growth, that it meant disaster.

Attentive to the alien feelings and ideas of the Shades inside myself, it occurred to me that this new empathy could serve me later in political activities in the world at large.

I found it most difficult to give priority to the needs and demands of the Shade people when these challenged the "national" goals of production, export, and defense. The internal Sun police continued working out of habit and desperation, and, although they no longer had authority, they remained eerily competent. The Shades, still being repressed, remained mysterious and frightening.

Terrorism existed on both sides. Time and again, I was deprived of sufficient energy to do work while, in response, books and other creative projects were burned; there were many other atrocities. Censorship and spying still flourished. I fell into the pattern of punitive, relentless, even mindless work, followed by periods of utter collapse. The work was insisted upon by the deposed Suns while the collapse was the retaliation of the not-yet-enfranchised Shades.

But while this desperate cycle continued, something new was occurring. There was someone in me watching it, some interim government or peacekeeping force that managed to hold another vision and to continue the careful process of change. Somehow, against inner public opinion, I made a decision to forego violent revolution or a new military coup and was not drawn into either alternative, despite provocations against each other and against the interim regime itself.

I don't know what finally changed the balance of power and led to the development of a new government and a new country. Perhaps it came from empowering a group of international advisors and observers, or from instituting an interim regime. Certainly it derived from the inner realization that all-out war was untenable—the equivalent of a global nuclear holocaust. For whatever reason, slowly, very slowly things began to shift.

The real crises of conscience occurred after I regained a more natural affiliation with the Shades. Within the reality of my own psyche, I learned that the former brutality and ethnocentricity of the Suns came from enormous trauma, grief, and pain in their ancient and forgotten history. Despite loathing, I was forced to a position of compassion. Sometime in the past, Zebra had suffered a series of crises that threatened the existence of the nation. At that point, the Suns came to power through certain naive but necessary decisions. Later these emergency procedures were codified as holy law. The culture of the Suns followed from this, developing out of the real need to protect the country. This ancient grief did not mitigate the contemporary suffering of the Shades but it had to be acknowledged. Just as I was finally reunited with the Shades, I had to recognize the value of the Suns. It became clear that if the Suns were massacred or imprisoned, the entire country would become demoralized and disoriented. Energies would be diverted endlessly and unproductively toward defense and armaments, and the cycle would begin again in the other direction. I had to find a way to allow the Shades to govern with the Suns, despite the Shades' history of persecution and the Suns' connection with power.

This was not metaphor. Each time something interfered with the process of change in government, I could feel it in my body. I experienced on the inner plane the risks, dangers, violence, and terrorism that characterize contemporary political life.

Soon it became clear that a lost function of government was being restored: to nurture, sustain, and protect the entire population, to support distinction, and to provide dynamic communication between the disparate elements.

Protection took on an entirely different tone. It did not have to do with police, prisons, armies, walls, or armaments. It meant providing for diverse needs. Fortunately, then, intelligence work took on a different emphasis. Sleuthing the inner needs, motivations, and practices that had long been disguised and hidden became an honorable and essential activity. This time the intent was not to eradicate them but to support them adequately. Rather than being militaristic or aggressive, protection began to feel maternal or paternal in the sweetest way. It was characterized by tenderness.

In the recovery period foreign travel was curtailed; there had been so much of it. Emphasis was put upon domestic travel (inner exploration). Publishing increased. But this emphasis upon communication was also potentially dangerous. How could this level of contact, these modern systems, be introduced without destroying the Shades? After all, their culture was based upon the occult; to expose this might have dire consequences. Also, the Shades needed time to solidify their own culture, and find the means to protect their ways and oral traditions against corruption and co-option, for their own sake as well as the nation's. So when Suns came to the Shades' territory, they had to live exactly like Shades. The government had to provide without interfering in their way of life so the Shade culture once more became the living vibrant source of meaning in Zebra.

Now I was ready to attempt the most difficult work of all. Having achieved some harmony within my own nation, having begun to dismantle the inner police force and the system and values upon which it depended, I turned to the outer world and foreign relations (friends, family, community, and career). I had come to the realization that the inner enemy had been the heroic substance of my domestic life for eons, and that I had been dependent upon it as a source of identity and control. The concept of enemy had been a false and dangerous premise, wasting my resources and diverting my nature. I hadn't known how severely I'd been deprived by being alienated from half of myself. Now I was ready to examine my system of defenses and armaments vis à vis the public world.

I began to identify my external so-called enemies and drop the distinction of self and other in this sphere. I had to learn how I could maintain my own diversity and sense of self while yielding to the values of others, even those who seemed so contrary to myself. I had to see how we could coexist. Perhaps instead of declaring war, we could write treaties asking for help in protecting our differences. I had to examine the weapon arsenals I had created. Secret information, hidden even from myself, had to be exposed, so that I knew the number and nature of every weapon I had.

Finally, I wanted to bring myself at least to a single, sincere act of unilateral, personal disarmament as a sign, primarily to myself, of sincere desire to trust, sincere abdication of the notion of enemy, sincere interest in peace.

I did begin this process of disarmament. It is slow, difficult work.

I began for my own sake to seek out each instance where I created or reinforced the idea of an enemy, in order to deconstruct it. I sought out the information on every munitions factory and began to dismantle them. I began to take down the unnecessary walls. I did this not because I thought it was safe outside, but because I lived better within the concept of the possibility of safety. I lived better—even if it were a temporary condition—as if I could be safe. I began to live as best as I could, looking for points of reconciliation, without creating the concept of an enemy, without the backup of a military system.

I would not have been able to believe that a country could

eschew past occurrences, could return to less lethal, if less powerful, forms, if this were not my own personal experience. I would not have been able to believe that a country could turn away from weaponry and war if this were not my own personal experience. But I am learning it in the only place I can know it thoroughly: in my own psyche, my own body, and my own life.

I realized that I was beginning to experience a complete, and comparatively bloodless, revolution in the spheres of the political, social, military, cultural, and spiritual. There was a change in government, in every aspect of my way of life. This tentative success, while living "in this world," led me to hope that it may be possible to achieve democracy, disarmament, and peace in the world at large. I was gaining a political understanding that no courses in political science and history could duplicate. At the same time, I was healing a serious emotional condition and saving my life.

Long before I could begin to enact these changes, I came to understand that the system of government that controlled me internally was similar to the systems of government in the world. It took a long while to admit that this was so—in part, because I was always projecting into the world the systems by which I was living. It was heartbreaking to realize that all the work I'd done in the world was undermined by the constant seepage of contrary values from my inner being. I could not be a democrat in the world or promote democracy while I was a tyrant within. I had tried it. I had devoted my life to it. It looked good in terms of paper and deeds, but I had to admit that my efforts were fundamentally ineffective. Each day of my life, I had unwittingly reinforced and reseeded the world with what threatened it, myself, and everyone I knew: tyranny, slavery, militarism. I couldn't hope to accomplish change in the outside world until I changed the inner one.

This filled me with despair at first. There was so much to be done. I asked how was it possible to make any change if almost everyone had to change themselves internally. Underneath that despair was another more hidden despair. I didn't think I could make such overwhelming changes myself. I didn't know how. Gradually despair was replaced by hope and confidence. I began to make some changes. I saw it was possible.

I began to see that the despair so many of us feel when confronting world conditions might also be alleviated. Those who feel that there is nothing they can do to affect such a monster can come to see that there is something they can do, that only they can do, that can be effective, a real and substantial contribution. They can at the very least (which might turn out to be the very most) institute a government in their inner world that has integrity with their ideas and ideals. And in the very mundane living out of that system, they can project into the outer world some of the ways they hold dear—democracy, equality, equal access, respect for indigenous peoples, environmental protection, disarmament, and peaceful coexistence.

This new way of thinking was very humbling. I had to lay aside all glorious ambitions to save the world either by myself or in concert with a special cadre of beings. The task of change, the ant work of only one individual, was tedious, overwhelmingly absorbing, and took all my energy. Each individual had to do it for himself or herself. I could not be a hero though I must confess the difficulty of doing it even for myself did at times make me feel heroic. Still I persisted, humbled and doggedly devoted. Why? Because I discovered I really cared for this little nation and for the world, and I did not want to continue to do them harm.

This is the story of a journey from within the journey. I knew before I started that we all live in an armed camp. But I didn't know that I was also one of the architects. I didn't realize how thoroughly I had introjected the realities of the outside world, had unconsciously internalized the hostile systems that surround us, had absorbed so many variations on duality, division, repression, suppression, hierarchy, superiority, intolerance, and violence, until the world I con-

structed was a kaleidoscopic image of the horrors and deva-
stations of planet earth in the twentieth century.

I didn't realize how thoroughly I was living the way
women have been living in Western culture, thrice colonized, so to speak: first, by living under actual foreign (patri-
archal) rule in the world; second, by living under foreign rule
within themselves; and third, by being given the task of
socializing their children according to the dictates of this
foreign domination. It had long seemed to me that the forms
women create reveal cooperative, noncompetitive, non-
hierarchical, and intimate patterns that incline toward trust,
interrelationship, and peacemaking; but women are social-
ized and then socialize others into paranoia, conflict, and
war. I didn't realize that I was living this way and that, in fact,
it was not only the way of women, but also of men. We are
all living this way.

So even the distinctions between women and men fell
away from me. Because the inner world is an unconscious
introjection of the outer world, it cannot be selective about
the forms that influence it; there is no filter to keep out one
system while absorbing another. Each of us breathes in all
the tyrannies and dictatorships, all the enslavements and
tortures. China, Africa, Latin America, the United States,
Europe, Asia, the Middle East—all come to us democrati-
cally in one breath. We are each other. Even as we run from
each other, try to destroy each other, we are each other. The
entire universal, global armed camp in all its manifestations,
all the variations on militarism, terrorism, imperialism, and
expansionism, are in each of us. Different uniforms, the
same organism. All of us, all people, all men and all women
are living in an armed camp, are similarly colonized, similarly socializing ourselves and others, no matter how unwittingly, and similarly reprojecting the forms into the world.

Once again, this realization caused me despair and then
hope. Because I was beginning to hope there was a way out
for me, I thought it might be a way out for some others.
It seemed to me these changes were in our collective self-
interest.

I began to develop a series of questions that I continue to pose to myself as rigorously as I can. I return to them again and again. Posing the questions, trying to understand the answers, and keeping the dynamics of Zebra in my awareness has been a way of clawing my way toward change. I try to be aware of the constant need to accord the inner reality of Zebra with my principles. I don't believe that because I've started this process it is automatically maintained. I do try to be vigilant. These are some of the questions I ask:

What is the form of my internal government? Is it tyrannical, a dictatorship, an oligarchy? Is it a military government? Is it a police state? Is it a false theocracy?

Whom do I identify as the enemies within? The enemies without?

What are my defense systems? What are the natures of my police force and armies?

What weapons are in my arsenal? Do I stockpile? Am I in an arms race?

What is the equivalent of my nuclear bomb?

Will I sign a no-first-strike treaty?

Do I have slaves?

Whom do I imprison?

Do I torture?

Do I have an internal FBI and CIA, a secret police?

What is the nature of my own propaganda and disinformation bureau?

What territories do I seal off? Do people need passports or visas?

Who are disadvantaged, exploited, oppressed, or disenfranchised in my country?

Do I exploit, invade, colonize, or imperialize other countries?

Do I pollute?

Am I run by ideologues?

Am I racist?

Can I learn to tolerate and then praise diversity?

Am I willing to disarm? To sign disarmament treaties? Am I willing to allow inspection? Am I willing to trust and be trustworthy?

Do I really want peace? Can I teach peace to my inner populations?

Once, in a personal disarmament workshop, a man who'd been a peace activist had to confront the extremity of his distrust of others. Gently, I raised the analogy to the disarmament table. I suggested that the officials who sat at that table trying to reach agreements were as distrustful, suspicious, and injured as he was. He was broken by this realization and confessed that he couldn't in their place conscientiously advocate weakening the defense system; yet he had advocated disarmament all his life. Admittedly, if he were in their position, feeling the way he did, he would have to say, "More bombs." For a while, he lived with rage and humiliation. Then he began looking in himself for whatever was possible to allow him to trust. He found inner defenses that were not aggressive. He began to validate inner security so that he could come to the negotiating table in a wholehearted manner. When he returned to the ranks of peace activists, he had a new authority. He had found a way to test the sincerity of his political positions as well as a way to reconstruct his inner world so that it accorded with his principles. He was creating a dialogue between the two worlds.

In another personal disarmament class, a woman recounted that her house had just been broken into and her roommates raped at knife point. This woman had been raped and physically injured by a stranger on two other separate occasions and had herself been abused as a child. She was agonized about the effect of all this upon her adolescent daughter. Yet, as she spoke about her response to the incident, all of us were moved away from despair. As awful as the break-in had been, her courageous refusal to create an enemy and live in fear gave us enormous hope.

At the peace tent at the Non-Governmental Organizations–United Nations Conference on Women in Nairobi in July 1985, I asked an audience of African, American, and European women who it was that ruled their inner countries. The majority painfully acknowledged that they were ruled by tyrants. They agreed that nothing could change in the world until they also altered their inner conditions. The women had been saying similar things about foreign policy, that nothing would change internationally until domestic changes were instituted. Perhaps through the talk we'd managed to move the definition of the domestic closer to the heart and hearth. It wasn't that we thought we needed to stop efforts in the public world, but that there was other urgent work, also on the inner plane, which had to be pursued simultaneously. I didn't realize how much consensus we'd reached until I was approached later by the head of the Soviet women's delegation. There were tears in her eyes. She said, "We have been working so very hard, so very, very hard for peace, we didn't even begin to think how urgent it was to attend to ourselves. We didn't even consider that we have personal selves who need to be attended. Now the Soviet women have to begin this inner work." Yes, I thought, for all our sakes.

26 ❀ The Greening of the Self

JOANNA MACY

Something important is happening in our world that you are not going to read about in the newspapers. I consider it the most fascinating and hopeful development of our time, and it is one of the reasons I am so glad to be alive today. It has to do with what is occurring to the notion of the *self*.

The self is the metaphoric construct of identity and agency, the hypothetical piece of turf on which we construct our strategies for survival, the notion around which we focus our instincts for self-preservation, our needs for self-approval, and the boundaries of our self-interest. Something is happening to the self!

The conventional notion of the self with which we have been raised and to which we have been conditioned by mainstream culture is being undermined. What Alan Watts called "the skin-encapsulated ego" and Gregory Bateson referred to as "the epistemological error of Occidental civilization" is being unhinged, peeled off. It is being replaced by wider constructs of identity and self-interest—by what you might call the ecological self or the eco-self, co-extensive with other beings and the life of our planet. It is what I will call "the greening of the self."

At a recent lecture on a college campus, I gave the students examples of activities which are currently being undertaken in defense of life on Earth—actions in which people risk their comfort and even their lives to protect other species. In the Chipko, or tree-hugging, movement in north India, for example, villagers fight the deforestation of their remaining woodlands. On the open seas, Greenpeace activists are intervening to protect marine mammals from slaughter. After that talk, I received a letter from a student I'll call Michael. He wrote:

> I think of the tree-huggers hugging my trunk, blocking the chainsaws with their bodies. I feel their fingers digging into my bark to stop the steel and let me breathe. I hear the bodhisattvas in their rubber boats as they put themselves between the harpoons and me, so I can escape to the depths of the sea. I give thanks for your life and mine, and for life itself. I give thanks for realizing that I too have the powers of the tree-huggers and the bodhisattvas.

What is striking about Michael's words is the shift in identification. Michael is able to extend his sense of self to encompass the self of the tree and of the whale. Tree and whale are no longer removed, separate, disposable objects pertaining to a world "out there;" they are intrinsic to his own vitality. Through the power of his caring, his experience of self is expanded far beyond that skin-encapsulated ego. I quote Michael's words not because they are unusual, but to the contrary, because they express a desire and a capacity that is being released from the prison-cell of old constructs of self. This desire and capacity are arising in more and more people today as, out of deep concern for what is happening to our world, they begin to speak and act on its behalf.

Among those who are shedding these old constructs of self, like old skin or a confining shell, is John Seed, director

of the Rainforest Information Center in Australia. One day
we were walking through the rainforest in New South Wales,
where he has his office, and I asked him, "You talk about the
struggle against the lumbering interests and politicians to
save the remaining rainforest in Australia. How do you deal
with the despair?"

He replied, "I try to remember that it's not me, John Seed,
trying to protect the rainforest. Rather I'm part of the rainforest protecting myself. I am that part of the rainforest
recently emerged into human thinking." This is what I mean
by the greening of the self. It involves a combining of the
mystical with the practical and the pragmatic, transcending
separateness, alienation, and fragmentation. It is a shift that
Seed himself calls "a spiritual change," generating a sense of
profound interconnectedness with all life.

This is hardly new to our species. In the past poets and
mystics have been speaking and writing about these ideas,
but not people on the barricades agitating for social change.
Now the sense of an encompassing self, that deep identity
with the wider reaches of life, is a motivation for action. It
is a source of courage that helps us stand up to the powers
that are still, through force of inertia, working for the destruction of our world. I am convinced that this expanded
sense of self is the *only* basis for adequate and effective
action.

When you look at what is happening to our world—and
it is hard to look at what's happening to our water, our air,
our trees, our fellow species—it becomes clear that unless
you have some roots in a spiritual practice that holds life
sacred and encourages joyful communion with all your fellow beings, facing the enormous challenges ahead becomes
nearly impossible.

Robert Bellah's book *Habits of the Heart* is not a place
where you are going to read about the greening of the self.
But it is where you will read *why* there has to be a greening
of the self, because it describes the cramp that our society
has gotten itself into with its rampant, indeed pathological,

individualism. Bellah points out that the individualism that sprang from the Romantic movement of the eighteenth and nineteenth centuries (the seeds of which were planted even earlier than that) is accelerating and causing great suffering, alienation, and fragmentation in our century. Bellah calls for a moral ecology which he defines as a moral connectedness or interdependence. He says, "We have to treat others as part of who we are, rather than as a 'them' with whom we are in constant competition."

To Robert Bellah, I respond, "It is happening." It is happening in the arising of the ecological self. And it is happening because of three converging developments. First, the conventional small self, or ego-self, is being impinged upon by the psychological and spiritual effects we are suffering from facing the dangers of mass annihilation. The second thing working to dismantle the ego-self is a way of seeing that has arisen out of science itself. It is called the systems view, cybernetics, or new paradigm science. From this perspective, life is seen as dynamically composed of self-organizing systems, patterns that are sustained in and by their relationships. The third force is the resurgence in our time of nondualistic spiritualities. Here I am speaking from my own experience with Buddhism, but it is also happening in other faith-systems and religions, such as "creation spirituality" in Christianity. These developments are impinging on the self in ways that are undermining it, or helping it to break out of its boundaries and old definitions. Instead of ego-self, we witness the emergence of an eco-self!

The move to a wider ecological sense of self is in large part a function of the dangers that are threatening to overwhelm us. Given nuclear proliferation and the progressive destruction of our biosphere, polls show that people today are aware that the world, as they know it, may come to an end. I am convinced that this loss of certainty that there will be a future is the pivotal psychological reality of our time. The fact that it is not talked about very much makes it all the more pivotal, because nothing is more preoccupying or energy-draining than that which we repress.

Why do I claim that this erodes the old sense of self? Because once we stop denying the crises of our time and let ourselves experience the depth of our own responses to the pain of our world—whether it is the burning of the Amazon rainforest, the famines of Africa, or the homeless in our own cities—the grief or anger or fear we experience cannot be reduced to concerns for our own individual skin. It can never be the same.

When we mourn over the destruction of our biosphere, it is categorically distinct from mourning over our own death. We suffer with our world—that is the literal meaning of compassion. It isn't some private craziness. Yet, when I was weeping over the napalming of villages in Vietnam twenty years ago, I was told that I was suffering from a hangover of Puritan guilt. When I expressed myself against President Reagan, they said I had unresolved problems regarding my own father. How often have you had your concerns for political and ecological realities subjected to reductionistic pop-therapy? How often have you heard, "What are you running away from in your life that you are letting yourself get so concerned about those homeless people? Perhaps you have some unresolved issues? Maybe you're sexually unfulfilled?" It can go on and on. But increasingly it is being recognized that a compassionate response is neither craziness nor a dodge. It is the opposite; it is a signal of our own evolution, a measure of our humanity. We are capable of suffering with our world, and that is the true meaning of compassion. It enables us to recognize our profound interconnectedness with all beings. Don't ever apologize for crying for the trees burning in the Amazon or over the waters polluted from mines in the Rockies. Don't apologize for the sorrow, grief, and rage you feel. It is a measure of your humanity and your maturity. It is a measure of your open heart, and as your heart breaks open there will be room for the world to heal. That is what is happening as we see people honestly confronting the sorrows of our time. And it is an adaptive response.

The crisis that threatens our planet, whether seen from its military, ecological, or social aspect, derives from a dysfunctional and pathological notion of the self. It derives from a mistake about our place in the order of things. It is a delusion that the self is so separate and fragile that we must delineate and defend its boundaries, that it is so small and so needy that we must endlessly acquire and endlessly consume, and that it is so aloof that as individuals, corporations, nation-states, or species, we can be immune to what we do to other beings.

This view of human nature is not new, of course. Many have felt the imperative to extend self-interest to embrace the whole. What is notable in our situation is that this extension of identity can come not through an effort to be noble or good or altruistic, but simply to be present and own our pain. And that is why this shift in the sense of self is credible to people. As the poet Theodore Roethke said, "I believe my pain."

This "despair and empowerment" work derives from two other forces I mentioned earlier: systems theory, or cybernetics, and nondualistic spirituality, particularly Buddhism. I will now turn to what we could call the cybernetics of the self.

The findings of twentieth-century science undermine the notion of a separate self distinct from the world it observes and acts upon. Einstein showed that the self's perceptions are shaped by its changing position in relation to other phenomena. And Heisenberg, in his uncertainty principle, demonstrated that the very act of observation changes what is observed.

Contemporary science, and systems science in particular, goes farther in challenging old assumptions about a distinct, separate, continuous self, by showing that there is no logical or scientific basis for construing one part of the experienced world as "me" and the rest as "other." That is so because as open, self-organizing systems, our very breathing, acting, and thinking arise in interaction with our shared world through the currents of matter, energy, and information that move through us and sustain us. In the web of relationships that sustain these activities there is no clear line demarcating a separate, continuous self.

As postmodern systems theorists say, "There is no categorical 'I' set over against a categorical 'you' or 'it.' " One of the clearer expositions of this is found in the teachings and writings of Gregory Bateson, whom I earlier quoted as saying that the abstraction of a separate "I" is the epistemological fallacy of Western civilization. He says that the process that decides and acts cannot be neatly identified with the isolated subjectivity of the individual or located within the confines of the skin. He contends that "the total self-corrective unit that processes information is a system whose boundaries do not at all coincide with the boundaries either of the body or what is popularly called 'self' or 'consciousness.' " He goes on to say, "The self is ordinarily understood as only a small part of a much larger trial-and-error system which does the thinking, acting, and deciding." Bateson offers two helpful examples. One is the woodcutter, about to fell a tree. His hands grip the handle of the axe, there is the head of the axe, the trunk of the tree. Whump, he makes a cut, and then whump, another cut. What is the feedback circuit, where is the information that is guiding that cutting down of the tree? It is a whole circle; you can begin at any point. It moves from the eye of the woodcutter, to the hand, to the axe, and back to the cut in the tree. That is the self-correcting unit, that is what is doing the chopping down of the tree.

In another illustration, a blind person with a cane is walking along the sidewalk. Tap, tap, whoops, there's a fire hydrant, there's a curb. What is doing the walking? Where is the self then of the blind person? What is doing the perceiving and deciding? That self-corrective feedback circuit is the arm, the hand, the cane, the curb, the ear. At that moment that is the self that is walking. Bateson's point is that the self is a false reification of an improperly delimited part of a much larger field of interlocking processes. And he goes on to maintain that this false reification of the self is basic to the planetary ecological crisis in which we find ourselves. We have imagined that we are a unit of survival and we have to see to our own survival, and we imagine that the unit of survival is the separate individual or a separate species, whereas in reality through the history of evolution, it is the individual plus the environment, the species plus the environment, for they are essentially symbiotic.

The self is a metaphor. We can decide to limit it to our skin, our person, our family, our organization, or our species. We can select its boundaries in objective reality. As the systems theorists see it, our consciousness illuminates a small arc in the wider currents and loops of knowing that interconnect us. It is just as plausible to conceive of mind as coexistent with these larger circuits, the entire "pattern that connects," as Bateson said.

Do not think that to broaden the construct of self this way involves an eclipse of one's distinctiveness. Do not think that you will lose your identity like a drop in the ocean merging into the oneness of Brahman. From the systems perspective this interaction, creating larger wholes and patterns, allows for and even requires diversity. You become more yourself. Integration and differentiation go hand in hand.

The third factor that is aiding in the dismantling of the ego-self and the creation of the eco-self is the resurgence of nondualistic spiritualities. Buddhism is distinctive in the clarity and sophistication with which it deals with the constructs and the dynamics of self. In much the same way as systems theory does, Buddhism undermines categorical distinctions between self and other and belies the concept of a continuous, self-existent entity. It then goes farther than systems theory in showing the pathogenic character of any reifications of the self. It goes farther still in offering methods for transcending these difficulties and healing this suffering. What the Buddha woke up to under the Bodhi tree was the *paticca samuppada*, the co-arising of phenomena, in which you cannot isolate a separate, continuous self.

We think, "What do we do with the self, this clamorous 'I,' always wanting attention, always wanting its goodies? Do we crucify it, sacrifice it, mortify it, punish it, or do we make it noble?" Upon awaking we realize, "Oh, it just isn't there." It's a convention, just a convenient convention. When you take it too seriously, when you suppose that it is something enduring which you have to defend and promote, it becomes the foundation of delusion, the motive behind our attachments and our aversions.

Oh, the sweetness of being able to realize: I am my experience. I am this breathing. I am this moment, and it is changing, continually arising in the fountain of life. We do not need to be doomed to the perpetual rat-race. The vicious circle can be broken by the wisdom, *prajna*, that arises when we see that "self" is just an idea; by the practice of meditation, *dhyana*; and by the practice of morality, *sila*, where attention to our experience and to our actions reveals that they do not need to be in bondage to a separate self.

Far from the nihilism and escapism that is often imputed to the Buddhist path, this liberation, this awakening puts one *into* the world with a livelier, more caring sense of social engagement. The sense of interconnectedness that can then arise, is imagined—one of the most beautiful images coming out of the Mahayana—as the jeweled net of Indra. It is a vision of reality structured very much like the holographic view of the universe, so that each being is at each node of the net, each jewel reflects all the others, reflecting back and catching the reflection, just as systems theory sees that the part contains the whole.

The awakening to our true self is the awakening to that entirety, breaking out of the prison-self of separate ego. The one who perceives this is the bodhisattva—and we are all bodhisattvas because we are all capable of experiencing that—it is our true nature. We are profoundly interconnected and therefore we are all able to recognize and act upon our deep, intricate, and intimate inter-existence with each other and all beings. That true nature of ours is already present in our pain for the world.

When we turn our eyes away from that homeless figure, are we indifferent or is the pain of seeing him or her too great? Do not be easily duped about the apparent indifference of those around you. What looks like apathy is really the fear of suffering. But the bodhisattva knows that to experience the pain of all beings is necessary to experience their joy. It says in the *Lotus Sutra* that the bodhisattva hears the music of the spheres, and understands the language of the birds, while hearing the cries in the deepest levels of hell.

One of the things I like best about the green self, the ecological self that is arising in our time, is that it is making moral exhortation irrelevant. Sermonizing is both boring and ineffective. This is pointed out by Arne Naess, the Norwegian philosopher who coined the phrase *deep ecology*. This great systems view of the world helps us recognize our embeddedness in nature, overcomes our alienation from the rest of creation, and changes the way we can experience our self through an ever-widening process of identification.

Naess calls this self-realization, a progression "where the self to be realized extends further and further beyond the separate ego and includes more and more of the phenomenal world." And he says,

> In this process, notions such as altruism and moral duty are left behind. It is tacitly based on the Latin term 'ego' which has as its opposite the 'alter.' Altruism implies that the ego sacrifices its interests in favor of the other, the alter. The motivation is primarily that of duty. It is said we *ought* to love others as strongly as we love our self. There are, however, very limited numbers among humanity capable of loving from mere duty or from moral exhortation.

Unfortunately, the extensive moralizing within the ecological movement has given the public the false impression that they are being asked to make a sacrifice—to show more responsibility, more concern, and a nicer moral standard. But all of that would flow naturally and easily if the self were widened and deepened so that the protection of nature was felt and perceived as protection of our very selves.

Please note this important point: virtue is *not* required for the greening of the self or the emergence of the ecological self. The shift in identification at this point in our history is required precisely *because* moral exhortation doesn't work, and because sermons seldom hinder us from following our self-interest as we conceive it.

The obvious choice, then, is to extend our notions of self-interest. For example, it would not occur to me to plead with you, "Oh, don't saw off your leg. That would be an act of violence." It wouldn't occur to me because your leg is part of your body. Well, so are the trees in the Amazon rain basin. They are our external lungs. And we are beginning to realize that the world is our body.

This ecological self, like any notion of selfhood, is a metaphoric construct and a dynamic one. It involves choice; choices can be made to identify at different moments, with different dimensions or aspects of our systemically interrelated existence—be they hunted whales or homeless humans or the planet itself. In doing this the extended self brings into play wider resources—courage, endurance, ingenuity—like a nerve cell in a neural net opening to the charge of the other neurons.

There is the sense of being acted through and sustained by those very beings on whose behalf one acts. This is very close to the religious concept of grace. In systems language we can talk about it as a synergy. But with this extension, this greening of the self, we can find a sense of buoyancy and resilience that comes from letting flow through us strengths and resources that come to us with continuous surprise and sense of blessing.

We know that we are not limited by the accident of our birth or the timing of it, and we recognize the truth that we have always been around. We can reinhabit time and own our story as a species. We were present back there in the fireball and the rains that streamed down on this still molten planet, and in the primordial seas. We remember that in our mother's womb, where we wear vestigial gills and tail and fins for hands. We remember that. That information is in us and there is a deep, deep kinship in us, beneath the outer layers of our neocortex or what we learned in school. There is a deep wisdom, a bondedness with our creation, and an ingenuity far beyond what we think we have. And when we expand our notions of what we are to include in this story, we will have a wonderful time and we will survive.

27 ❖ The Path of Service

JACK KORNFIELD

*T*rue spirituality is not a removal or escape from life. It is an opening, a seeing of the world with a deeper vision that is less self-centered, a vision that sees through dualistic views to the underlying interconnectedness of all life. Liberation is the discovery of freedom in the very midst of our bodies and minds. A Zen master recently gave a simple talk on this teaching of nonseparation at an international peace conference. He explained it by making his two hands into two different people. One he called Gertrude and the other Harry. He enacted a conversation between Gertrude and Harry about what they liked and what they didn't like. Everyone started to laugh. He went on and on about it. He said, "That's what we do. Somehow we actually believe we are Harry or Gertrude, separate from one another." This sense of separation creates all the sorrow and suffering in the world. In pursuing our spiritual practice we must learn how to put them all together, to bring the whole world into our heart. When we undertake this practice in a genuine way, we become what is called a bodhisattva, a being *(sattva)* committed to liberation *(bodhi)*. Suzuki-roshi says, "Even if the sun should rise in the west, the bodhisattva has only one way."

In the worst circumstances, even if our world turns upside down, the bodhisattva has only one way—to continue to express compassion and wisdom there too.

Once while in India I spoke with a meditation master named Vimala Thakar about the question of meditation and activity in the world. Vimala had worked for many years with the followers of Gandhi in Indian rural development and land redistribution projects. She was then asked by Krishnamurti, of whom she had been a long-time student, to teach meditation. After devoting years to teaching meditation, she has in recent years returned to development work and helping the hungry and homeless, teaching much less than before. I asked her why she decided to go back to the type of work she had been involved with years before. Did she find meditation too limited and feel a need for more direct action? In responding to the question, Vimala resisted any attempt to separate the two parts of her life. She replied, "Sir, I am a lover of life, and as a lover of life, I cannot keep out of any activity of life. If there are people who are hungry for food, my response is to help feed them. If there are people who are hungry for truth, my response is to help them discover it. I make no distinction."

The Sufis have a saying, "Praise Allah, and tie your camel to the post." This brings together both parts of practice: pray, yes, but also make sure you do what is necessary in the world. Have a life of meditation and genuine spiritual experience and, at the same time, discover how to manifest that here and now. Realization brings a balance between understanding emptiness and having a sense of compassion and impeccability guide our lives. Seeing emptiness means seeing that all of life is like a bubble in a rushing stream, a play of light and shadow, a dream. It means seeing that this tiny blue-green planet hangs in the immensity of space amid billions of stars and galaxies, that all of human history is like one second compared with the aeons of the earth's history, and that it will all be over very soon. This context helps us to let go amid the seeming seriousness of our problems, to discover what Don Juan calls our controlled folly and to enter life with a sense of lightness and ease.

On the other hand, the quality of impeccability entails realizing how precious life is, even though it is transient, and how each of our actions and words does count, affecting all beings around us in a profound way. There is nothing inconsequential in this universe, and we need to personally respect this fact and act in accordance with it. Even if a person meditates in a cave somewhere far away, it has a power and a value far beyond what we ordinarily assume, because what each part of this whole does affects the rest. We are not ultimately separate.

How can we actually bring together these two sides of practice—the development of compassionate and caring attention with the fleeting and empty nature of life? Taken separately, each point of view is compelling. One could make a very convincing case for just concentrating on meditation and nothing else, and then make another convincing argument for devoting oneself entirely to service in the world. Let's look at it from the first vantage point. Does the world need more medicine and energy and buildings and food? No. There is enough food and medicine, there are enough resources for all. There is starvation and poverty and widespread disease because of human ignorance, prejudice, and fear. Out of greed and hatred we hoard materials; we create wars over imaginary geographic boundaries and act as if one group of people is truly different from another group somewhere else on the planet. Although political and economic change is important, it alone can never be sufficient because the ongoing source of war and poverty is the power of these forces in the human heart. What the world needs is not more oil, but more love and generosity, more kindness and understanding. The most fundamental thing we can do to help this war-torn and suffering world is to genuinely free ourselves from the greed and fear and divisive views in our own minds and then help others to do the same. If we cannot do that, how can we expect it from others? Spiritual practice and transforming the heart are the most important task in our life. From this point of view spiritual life is not a privilege; it is our basic responsibility.

The other side of this question is also compelling. We have only to consider the horror of Cambodia, the violence in Central America, the starvation in Central Africa—situations in which the enormity of suffering is almost beyond comprehension. In India alone 360 million people live in poverty, where one day's work can mean that night's meal. I once met a man in Calcutta who was sixty-four years old and still pulled a rickshaw for a living. He had been doing it for forty years and had ten people dependent upon him for income. He had gotten sick the year before for ten days, and after a week the family ran out of money and had nothing to eat. How can we possibly let this happen? As you read this, forty children per minute will die from starvation while $15 million per minute is spent on weapons. Today there are hundreds of millions of people who are starving and don't have enough to eat, who are malnourished. That's happening this very day, to people like us—people with eyes, ears, hands, bodies, stomachs, hearts. There are hundreds of millions of people who are so impoverished that they have little or no shelter and clothing to protect themselves from the sun, wind, and rain. There are hundreds of millions of people who are sick with diseases that we know how to cure, that just take a simple kind of medicine. But they can't afford the medicine or don't have access to it. Here today, on this small planet, these things are taking place. Clearly we must respond. We cannot hold back or look away.

At times we may have painful dilemmas about what path to take, where to put our energy. There are so many possibilities—even choosing which type of meditation to practice can be confusing. How are we to decide? It all requires an act of listening to the heart. There are two steps to this process. The first requires that we be willing to touch and feel directly the problems and possibilities in ourselves and the world around us.

This is the beginning of the teaching of the Buddha, and the beginning of our own understanding of the problem of world peace. Then the second step involves this same deep listening and touching of the heart, and from it the allowing of an immediate and spontaneous response.

To look directly at the situation is not a question of ceremonies or religion. The mandate is to look in some very deep way at the sorrow that exists now in our world, to look at our personal and individual and collective relationship to it, to bear witness to it, to acknowledge it, instead of running away. But war, ecological devastation, broken families, and even the unavoidable growing pains of our children and our own hearts are often overwhelming. The suffering is so great that mostly we don't want to look. We close our minds. We close our eyes and hearts.

Opening to all aspects of our experience is what is asked of us if we want our hearts to grow, if we want a difference. This means looking at the world with honesty, unflinchingly and directly, and then looking at ourselves and seeing that this sorrow is not just out there, but also within ourselves. It is our own fear and prejudice and hatred and desire and wanting and neurosis and anxiety. Our own sorrow. We have to look at it and not run away from it. In opening to suffering, we discover that we can connect with and listen to our own hearts.

This is the source of compassion and the basis for choosing a path with heart. Choosing our path is the second step, though it may need to be taken many times. Each time it is the same process: allowing sorrow to touch our hearts and listening to our hearts, listening to our individual response of wisdom and compassion. One of the difficulties with our busy modern culture is that we don't take time to listen to our hearts. Our immediate problems, our plans and thoughts, fill our minds and, lost in thinking, we lose our connection to our hearts and our true nature.

When we take the time to listen, from deep inside, we hear a voice that guides our journey. Some of us may respond by choosing the path of simplicity, developing an ascetic or isolated or monastic practice to purify our hearts. The hermit yogis who even today still live in caves in the North Indian Himalayas have chosen this path. And the exquisite silence and inner purity they cultivate is their powerful connection and contribution to the whole world around them. Others may choose a path of surrender and devotion, inspired by love of the Buddha or Jesus or Krishna and live a life of kindness and nonattachment through this devotion. Some may choose a path of service, of heartfelt and active social and community involvement, giving to others as their path to awakening. Others may choose a path that involves study, reflection, and a spiritual use of the intellect. There are as many paths as there are hearts to awaken. The spiritual journey does not present us with a pat formula for each of us to follow. It is not a matter of imitation. We cannot be Mother Teresa or Gandhi or the Buddha. We have to be ourselves. We have to discover and connect with our own unique expression of the truth. To do that, we must learn to listen to and trust ourselves to find our path with heart.

A great potential exists in the heart of each person for the realization of truth, for the experience of wholeness, for going beyond the shell of the ego. We can discover a wholeness of being that will express itself both through meditation and through sharing ourselves with others. When we listen to our hearts, the course to take can become clear and immediate. Whether it is an inner or outer path, it has enormous power to affect the world.

For many people service and open-hearted giving become the very vehicle for their liberation and are taken as their path or way of practice. A sense of interconnectedness leads to the realization that all our activity can be undertaken as service to the world around us. Following this path brings us face to face with selflessness and nonseparation as surely as our inner meditation does. At its best, service becomes an art of selfless giving, of acting from the heart without attachment to praise or fame or even the beneficial result of the action. To act in this way embraces both compassion in our hearts and wisdom that sees that in the end we cannot own or possess a single thing. Our service is more a spirit of acting to the best of our ability with our full being and understanding.

At its best, spiritual service is not a giving from the ego-sense of "See what I have done." It is not even a way of bettering the world through achieving desirable ends. Nor can it be a new form of attachment. It is not that these are bad. We will certainly find these kinds of mixed motivations within us when we act. But the spirit of service asks us to touch and act from a deeper place, a chord of the heart that responds to life out of connectedness and compassion, independently of results.

The sense of service and attuning our hearts to a more selfless vision can be developed and practiced like any other part of our path. Service requires us to cultivate the same quality of attention and mindfulness we have turned inward toward the world outside. It is a development of kindness and nonattachment in action. Even without knowing it, this spirit is what keeps the world alive. The insects and bees in the Amazon jungle pollinate the jungle plants, which in turn transform carbon dioxide into oxygen and replenish much of the Earth's atmosphere. Our lives depend upon those insects. The practice of service for us as humans is a process of making this interconnectedness conscious and allowing it to mindfully inform our actions. The way we drive, the way we use our money, the work we do, all of it can become a part of our path of service. As we live, whether as a plumber or waitress or physician or bookkeeper or beekeeper, we can learn to act with attention and caring. We can turn the actions of our life into the very heart of our practice. We become the server and the served, and the interconnection of it all is the heart of service.

One of the ways that our inner meditation can support and blossom into a life of service is through the cultivation of a strong and caring mindfulness and wakefulness. Equally important is the way that our inner practice brings us to look directly at the powerful facts of birth and death, at the cycling of life. From understanding this we can discover within us a place of great fearlessness.

There is a deep joy that comes when we stop denying the painful aspects of life and instead allow our hearts to open to and accept the full range of our experience: life and death, pleasure and pain, darkness and light. Even in the face of the tremendous suffering in the world there can be a joy that comes, not from rejecting pain and seeking pleasure, but rather from our ability to sit in meditation even when it is difficult and open to the truth. The work of practice begins by allowing ourselves to face fully our own sadness, fear, anxiety, desperation—to die to our limited ideas about how things should be and to love and accept the truth of things as they are. With this as our foundation, we can see clearly the source of suffering in our lives and in the world around us; that is, the factors of greed, hatred, and ignorance that produce a false sense of separation. We can look directly at how we create and enforce separation. How do we make this world of "I want this, I want to become that, this will make me safe, this will make me powerful"? How do we create a world based on race, nationality, age, sex, ideology, religion, even on the name of God? Look at yourself and see who is "us" and who is "them." Does "us" mean meditators or educated people or Americans or white people? Who is your "us"? Whenever there is a sense of "us," then there is a sense of "other." When we can give this up, then we can give up the idea that strength comes from having more than "others" or from having the power over "others." When we give this up, we give up the delusion that love is a weakness, and we find the source of true compassion in all our actions.

The inner and outer aspects of practice are illustrated by a story about an old Zen monk in China who practiced meditation for many years. He had a good mind and became very quiet, but never really came to touch the end of "I" and "others" in himself. He never came to the source of complete stillness or peace out of which the deepest transformation comes. So he went to his master and said, "May I please have permission to go off and practice in the mountains? I've worked for years as a monk, and there is nothing else I want but to understand this: the true nature of myself, of this world." And the master, knowing that he was ripe, gave him permission to leave.

The monk left the monastery and took his bowl and few possessions and walked through various towns on his way. As he left the last village behind and was going up into the mountains, there appeared before him, coming down the trail, an old man carrying a great big bundle on his back. (This old man was actually the bodhisattva Manjushri, who the Chinese Buddhists believe appears to people at the moment that they are ripe for awakening. Manjushri is usually depicted carrying the sword of discriminating wisdom, which cuts through all attachment, illusions, and separateness.) The old man addressed the monk, asking, "Say, friend, where are you going?"

The monk told his story. "I've practiced for so many years, and all I want now is to touch that center point, to know that which is the essence of life. Tell me, old man, do you know anything of this enlightenment?"

At this point the old man simply let go of his bundle, and it dropped to the ground—and, as in all good Zen stories, the monk was enlightened. That is our aspiration, our task—to let it all go, to drop and put down our whole past and future, all of our identifications, our fears, our opinions, our whole sense of "I," "me," and "mine."

At this point in the story, the newly enlightened monk looks at the old man a bit confused about what to do next. He says, "So now what?" The old man smiles, reaches down, picks up the bundle again and walks off to town.

To put our burden down requires, first, that we acknowledge all that we are carrying: that we see our sorrow, our suffering, our attachment and pain, see how we're all in it together, accept birth and death. If we do not face it, if we are afraid of death and afraid of surrendering, if we don't want to look, then we can't release our sorrow. We will push it away here and grab it again there. Only when we have seen the nature of life directly can we put it down. And once we put it down, then, with understanding and compassion, we can pick it up again. To the extent that we let go, we can act effectively, even dramatically, in the world, without bitterness and self-righteousness.

A number of years ago the Menninger Foundation sponsored a conference at which Mad Bear, an Iroquois medicine man, spoke. After several days of meetings at which scientific papers were presented, it was his turn. He said, "For my presentation I'd like us to begin by going outside." Everyone followed him outside to an open field, and he asked us all to stand silently in a circle. We stood for a while in silence under a wide open sky, surrounded by fields of grain stretching to the horizon. Mad Bear then began to speak, offering a prayer of gratitude. He thanked the earthworms for aerating the soil so that plants can grow. He thanked the grasses that cover the earth for keeping the dust from blowing, for cushioning our steps, and for showing our eyes the greenness and beauty of their life. He thanked the wind for bringing rain, for cleaning the air, for giving us the life-breath that connects us with all beings. He spoke in this way for nearly an hour, and as we listened our mindfulness grew with each prayer. We felt the wind on our faces and the earth beneath our feet, and we saw the grass and clouds, all with a sense of connectedness, gratitude, and love.

This is the spirit of our practice: love—not attachment, but something much deeper—infusing our awareness, enabling us to open to and accept the truth of each moment; and service that feels our intimate connectedness with all things and responds to the wholeness of life. Whether we are in the midst of our family life or in a remote monastery, whether we are sitting in meditation or sitting somewhere in protest, this is our practice in every moment.

28 ❀ Mindful Social Action

KEN JONES

Mindfulness is a practice of attentive yielding and accepting in the body, in the emotions, which gradually dissolves our futile root habit of conducting a kind of emotional lawsuit with everything that balks us or threatens us in any way. Energy previously blocked in controlling ourselves or wasted in negative, self-centered discharge becomes available for making appropriate and positive response (including warm, outgoing feelings) to situations we encounter. Often, when working on a project with a group of people, or when approaching an individual to try to resolve a problem, much time and energy goes into resolving "personality problems." The problem itself may receive inadequate attention because all the ritual ego dances have to be enacted before the spikier and pricklier characters have been propitiated. It is only after this we can get down to the really valuable differences of opinion, arising from different perspectives and expertise, which can make for a high-quality solution.

Consider the situation in a stormy group meeting where an important but contentious decision has to be made.

Would it not be helpful to pause, to look inward at the turbulence of one's own seething indignation and see how this—and the angry feelings of others—makes it more difficult to find a sound and acceptable solution to the problem at issue? And having looked inward, would not some fellow-feeling arise for one's gesticulating, red-faced adversaries? It is often at this point that someone suddenly sees the comedy of it all, and makes the joke that bursts everyone's inflated ego in the funniest and most undeniable way. Then the meeting can really get down to business.

Social action typically provides plenty of opportunity for a disciplined awareness practice. We usually make a voluntary commitment of time and energy to some project and to the other people who are working on it. It is likely that much of the work will be tedious and not immediately rewarding—a round of fundraising, secretarial, and committee work, leafleting on street corners, knocking on doors on dark, rainy nights to win support for a petition. Much indifference, hostility and even abuse may be experienced, creating feelings of frustration, fear and defeat. Not least, social action requires us to work in close fellowship with others, whom we may find awkward or disagreeable, and often in an emotionally loaded atmosphere of dedication and commitment not usually found in the workplace.

Moreover, if we are to be effective in our social action we have to be able to learn from hard experience even when it contradicts our deeply held assumptions and even threatens that person who at the present time we feel we are. Peace work and similar kinds of campaigning are likely to feel most comfortable and self-confirming when we distance ourselves from those with whom we are trying to communicate. If we talk with them at all, then we talk *at* them, and make sure we do most of the talking so as to retain control of the situation. Listening can be more threatening than doing the talking; expressing our own feelings or receiving someone else's is more threatening than cool, rational discussion. And yet closeness, real dialogue and shared feelings are the best ways of opening up genuine communication. And these are excellent opportunities if only we can handle them, for cultivating the mindfulness practice and hence slowly becoming the kind of person who can make effective, heartfelt response to the fear and resentment which can be invoked when people are reminded about the Bomb or some other threat.

And there are other ways, also, in which our awareness needs to be extended and informed. Thich Nhat Hanh reminds us that "Society makes it difficult for us to be awake. I am sure you know this, but you keep forgetting: forty thousand children in the Third World every day die of hunger, forty thousand of them. We know, but we keep forgetting because the kind of society in which we live makes us forgetful. That is why we need some exercise for mindfulness, for awareness. A number of Buddhists practice this— they refrain from eating a few times a week in order to be in communion with the Third World."

How self-awareness of emotional states can help others as well as oneself is illustrated in the Buddhist scriptures by a story about two travelling acrobats who performed hazardous feats on the end of a long bamboo pole. One said that their act would be accomplished safely if each watched and attended to the other. But the other and wiser one maintained that if each concentrated on doing his own part of the act safely and well he would thereby protect his friend as well as himself. Our concern to help others may conceal a need to affirm ourselves. The other person is commonly seen as "the problem," unless we have a low sense of self-identity and confidence, so that we see ourselves as "the problem." In either case increased awareness of self is the way to greater wisdom about self, and from which arises the compassion truly to help others.

Social action can throw up many "white water" situations, when the emotional rapids become too turbulent for us to paddle our little mindfulness canoe skillfully enough and it capsizes. We "go over the top" with our feelings, or screw them down with white-faced control, or slide into a wallow of self-pity, or otherwise forget where we are. Therefore it is best to learn in what is likely to be fairly calm water which does not toss us about too much. This means avoiding certain situations which cannot yet be ridden out without contributing negatively to what is happening. All mass nonviolent demonstrations tend to arouse powerful emotions which may threaten the success of the action, as well as upsetting the mindfulness practice of any militant mystics who happen to be involved! In a British pamphlet entitled *Preparing for Non-violent Direct Action* there is a section on "Forestalling Violence" in which demonstrators are advised: "Deliberately calm yourself before an action, so that you feel centered; if you start to feel wound up, concentrate on your breathing for a time." The pamphlet has warnings about doing anything which might further inflame "an already frustrated, aggressive and abusive demonstrator."

Organizations and campaigns which imply the absolute virtue and truth of their own cause and the unmitigated falsehood and evil of their opponents are probably too common to be avoided, but it is usually best to steer clear of those which go out of their way to foster their well-researched hates and which have built-in means of instilling conformity to such weighted polarization. Such is the case in many centralized, hierarchical and comparatively authoritarian organizations (including the authority of the majority), whose business it is—as with conventional political parties—to be adversarial at all costs.

A specific meditation directly related to social activism is the ancient *brahma-vihara* (sublime abidings) meditation. The meditator generates within themselves a spirit of loving-kindness (*metta*) which is directed successively to themselves, to a friend, to a stranger, and to an enemy. When he or she has become adept at this *metta-bhavana*, they extend their meditation successively to include the virtues of compassion (*karuna*), sympathetic joy (*mudita*), and equanimity (*upekkha*). On the face of it this meditation appears to be a kind of wish-fulfillment, a willing-of-virtue. Alexandra

David-Neel offers some interesting discussion of differing opinions about it which she found among Buddhists. One view was that the effect of the meditation could only be a superficial process of readily reversible auto-suggestion. However, it would be in the mainstream of Buddhist practice if it were undertaken as a simple acceptance, awareness, and befriending of the negative emotions aroused by all this willed benevolence. This in itself has the effect, over the months and years, of exposing, softening, and dissolving our deep-rooted capacity for ill will.

Daily meditation periods and periodic meditation retreats are essential for spiritual activists, as many have testified. Thus Sulak Sivaraksa of Thailand writes:

> These meditation masters [and] monks who spend their lives in the forests, are very, very important for us and for our society. Even those of us who are in society must go back to these masters and look within. We must practise daily our meditation, our prayer. We must do it at least every morning, or every evening, or both. And those of us . . . who work in society and confront power and social injustice, we get beaten every now and again and we get tired often. At least annually we ought to retreat into the forests, into the monasteries, to sit at the feet of the masters, to gain our spiritual strength, in order to come out again to confront society.

Without meditation and retreat it is difficult to remain steady and centered against the inherent ego-pull of social activism. Retreats, in particular, are laboratories for intensive spiritual practice, with a strong discipline and framework (including extra sensitivity to others' needs), freedom from everyday distractions, the support of other retreatants, and the inspiration and leadership of a teacher or facilitator.

The only transformative way to loosen the knot which our struggles continually tighten is through the work that has to be done within, opening up to recognition that we are our own problem. The follower of the Way discovers her or himself as being much the same bundle of variously knotted, ferocious, shameful, and seemingly helpless suffering as the whole of world humanity now appears to be. Each of us is a jewel in Indra's Net which replicates the whole and is the whole. Collective, cosmic karma has now unfolded to a point where it is the equal of personal, individual karma. For example, each of us has always tended to live each day heedless of our mortality, as if we were going to live forever. Our personal mortality has always been unimaginable to us. Now we have to live with the very real possibility of the extinction of the human race itself.

The argument for social activism which follows from acknowledging the line between personal and collective karma may be stepped out as follows:

1. We cannot work selflessly and fully effectively to change society so long as we are driven by divisive and delusive self-need;

2. The latter is the ordinary root response to the predicament of being human;

3. But that individual response is compounded by sociohistorical conditions which *institutionalize* alienation, ill will, aggressiveness, defensiveness, and acquisitiveness;

4. In turn, those social conditions are karmically inherited by each new generation;

5. Therefore out of *wisdom* we need to create different social conditions of a kind which nurture positive personality change, and out of *compassion* we need to create those conditions because the present ones give rise to so much gross physical and mental affliction;

6. If our work to effect these social changes is at the same time undertaken as a meditative training which ripens inner awareness then we shall at the same time contribute to our own eventual "inconceivable liberation" from self-need—or at least become a little more human!;

7. Thus we shall be more free to see clearly and act effectively so as to meet the material and spiritual needs of others, facilitating both personal and social change.

What we believe to be reality "out there" is distorted and discolored by our own fear, alienation and self-need. As we open in *acceptance* of how it is, of the powerlessness within and the terrible power without, so, paradoxically, there arises then a freedom and a clarity which enable action which is both appropriate and unquenchable. And which is beyond both hope and despair. The practice of a totally unreserved awareness is the road to absolute inner acceptance. This acceptance unblocks the space where selfless love and fearlessness are revealed. And the inner peace from which they arise is the way to effective outer peacemaking.

29 ✿ The Power of Peace

CHAGDUD TULKU

It is my wish that the spiritual power of peace
will touch the mind of every person on this earth, radiating
out from a deep peace within our own minds, across political
and religious barriers, across the barriers of ego and conceptual righteousness. Our first work as peacemakers is to clear
our minds of mental conflicts caused by ignorance, anger,
grasping, jealousy, and pride. Spiritual teachers can guide us
in the purification of these poisons, and through this purification of our own minds, we can learn the very essence of
peacemaking.

The inner peace we seek should be so absolutely pure, so
stable, that it cannot be moved to anger by those who live
and profit by war, or to self-grasping and fear by confronta-
tion with contempt, hatred, and death. Incredible patience is
necessary to accomplish any aspect of world peace, and the
source of such patience is the space of inner peace from
which you recognize with great clarity that war and suffering
are the outer reflections of the minds' inner poisons.

If you truly understand that the essential difference in
peacemakers and warmakers is that peacemakers have discipline and control over egotistical anger, grasping, jealousy,

and pride, while warmakers, in their ignorance, manifest the results of these poisons in the world—if you truly understand this you will never allow yourself to be defeated from within or without.

Tibetan Buddhists use the peacock as the symbol for the Bodhisattva, the Awakened Warrior who works for the Enlightenment of all sentient beings. The peacock is said to eat poisonous plants and transmute them into the gorgeous colors of its feathers. It does not poison itself, just as we who wish for world peace must not poison ourselves.

As you meet the powerful, worldly men who sit at the top of the war machines, regard them with strict equanimity. Convince them as effectively as you know how, but be constantly aware of your own state of mind. If you begin to experience anger, retreat. If you can go on without anger, perhaps you will penetrate the terrible delusion that causes war and all its hellish sufferings. From the clear space of your own inner peace, your compassion must expand to include all who are involved in war—the soldiers caught in the cruel karma of killing, and who sacrifice their precious human rebirth; the generals and politicians who intend to benefit but cause disruption and death instead; the civilians who are wounded, killed, and turned into refugees. True compassion is utterly neutral and is moved by suffering of every sort, not tied to right and wrong, attachment and aversion.

The work of peace is a spiritual path in itself, a means to develop perfect qualities of mind and to test these qualities against urgent necessity, extreme suffering, and death. Do not be afraid to give your time, energy, and wealth.

30 ✿ *Nowness and Enlightened Society*

CHÖGYAM TRUNGPA

From the moment you are born, when you first cry and breathe free from your mother's womb, you are a separate individual. Of course, there is still emotional attachment, or an emotional umbilical cord, that connects you to your parents, but as you grow older and pass from infancy into youth and maturity, as each year passes, your attachment decreases. You become an individual who can function separate from your mother and father.

In that journey through life, human beings must overcome the neurotic attachment of being the child-of-somebody. The principles of warriorship are connected with how individuals can develop personal discipline so that they become mature and independent and therefore experience a sense of personal freedom. But then, once that development has taken place, it is equally important to share the comradeship of human society. This is an organic expression of the greater vision of warriorship. It is based on the appreciation of a larger world. In the process of becoming a warrior, you naturally begin to feel a deep fellowship with human beings.

That is the real basis for helping others and, ultimately, for making a genuine contribution to society.

However, your connection to other human beings and your concern for their welfare have to be manifested personally, practically. Abstractly caring about others is not enough. The most practical and immediate way to begin sharing with others and working for their benefit is to work with your own domestic situation and to expand from there. So an important step in becoming a warrior is to become a family person, someone who respects his or her everyday domestic life and is committed to uplifting that situation.

You can't help society purely on the basis of your vision for the nation or the world. There are many ideas of how to organize a society so that it will fulfill people's needs. There is, of course, the popular idea of democratic rule, rule by the people. Another approach is that rule by an elite will produce a progressive society. A third idea is to take a scientific approach to ruling, in which natural resources are equally distributed and a completely balanced ecology is created. These and other ideas may have value, but they must be integrated with an individual human being's experience of domestic life. Otherwise you have a huge gap between your grand vision for society and the reality of everyday existence. To use one model of family life: a man and a woman meet, they fall in love and marry, they set up a household and then they may have children. Then they have to worry about whether the dishwasher is working or whether they have the money to buy a new stove. As the children grow up, they go to school to learn to read and write. Some children may have an ideal relationship with their parents, but the family has money problems. Or there may be lots of money but a very difficult family relationship. We go back and forth between those problems. We should respect life on that mundane level, because the only way to implement our vision for society is to bring it down to the situation of a single household.

Becoming a family person also means taking pride in the

wisdom of your family heritage. Respecting your family and your upbringing has nothing to do with separating yourself from others or becoming arrogant about your ancestry. Rather, it is based on realizing that the structure and experience of family life actually reflect the deep-seated wisdom of a culture. That wisdom has been passed down to you, and it is actually present in your everyday, domestic life. So by appreciating your family tradition, you are opening yourself further to the richness of the world. However, venerating the past in itself will not solve the world's problems. We need to find the link between our traditions and our present experience of life. *Nowness,* or the magic of the present moment, is what joins the wisdom of the past with the present. When you appreciate a painting or a piece of music or a work of literature, no matter when it was created, you appreciate it *now.* You experience the same nowness in which it was created. It is always *now.*

The way to experience nowness is to realize that this very moment, this very point in your life, is always *the* occasion. So the consideration of where you are and what you are, on the spot, is very important. That is one reason that your family situation, your domestic everyday life, is so important. You should regard your home as sacred, as a golden opportunity to experience nowness. Appreciating sacredness begins very simply by taking an interest in all the details of your life. Interest is simply applying awareness to what goes on in your everyday life—awareness while you're cooking, awareness while you're driving, awareness while you're changing diapers, even awareness while you're arguing. Such awareness can help to free you from speed, chaos, neurosis, and resentment of all kinds. It can free you from the obstacles to nowness, so that you can cheer up on the spot, all the time.

The principle of nowness is also very important to any effort to establish an enlightened society. You may wonder what the best approach is to helping society and how you can know that what you are doing is authentic or good. The only answer is nowness. *Now* is the important point. That *now* is a real *now*. If you are unable to experience *now*, then you are corrupted because you are looking for another *now*, which is impossible. If you do that, there can only be past or future.

When corruption enters a culture, it is because that culture ceases to be *now*; it becomes past and future. Periods in history when great art was created, when learning advanced, or peace spread, were all *now*. Those situations happened at the very moment of their *now*. But after *now* happened, then those cultures lost their *now*.

You have to maintain nowness, so that you don't duplicate corruption, so that you don't corrupt *now*, and so that you don't have false synonyms for *now* at all. The vision of enlightened society is that tradition and culture and wisdom and dignity can be experienced *now* and kept *now* on everyone's part. In that way there can never be corruption of any kind at all.

Enlightened society must rest on a good foundation. The nowness of your family situation is that foundation. From it, you can expand. By regarding your home as sacred, you can enter into domestic situations with awareness and with delight, rather than feeling that you are subjecting yourself to chaos. It may seem that washing dishes and cooking dinner are completely mundane activities, but if you apply awareness in any situation, then you are training your whole being so that you will be able to open yourself further, rather than narrowing your existence.

You may feel that you have a good vision for society but that your life is filled with hassles—money problems, problems relating to your spouse or caring for your children— and that those two things, vision and ordinary life, are opposing one another. But vision and practicality *can* be joined together in nowness.

Too often, people think that solving the world's problems is based on conquering the earth, rather than on touching the earth, touching ground. You can learn to live on this earth: how to camp, how to pitch a tent, how to ride a horse, milk a cow, build a fire. Even though you may be living in a city in the twentieth century, you can learn to experience the sacredness, the *nowness*, of reality. That is the basis for creating an enlightened society.

31 ❁ *Intimate Relationship as a Practice and a Path*

JOHN WELWOOD

Robert and Lynn had come into therapy because their marriage was in crisis. At first they wanted me to "fix it" for them—provide some advice or solution that would help them put their relationship back the way it was in the early days. But it was too late for that. They disagreed on too many core issues and had hurt each other too deeply during a series of arguments and power struggles to go back to the way things had been before.

Robert and Lynn had decided to get married, as so many of us do, out of deep feelings for one another. Now, four years later, they were encountering the real work of marriage—coming up against all their rough edges, having to face parts of themselves they had been ignoring for many years, and encountering some of their deepest fears. When the honeymoon glow of their marriage came to an end and they began to discover the real challenges in their relationship, they felt bewildered and discouraged. For they had no idea how or even why they should proceed with a relationship if it brought up so much pain. They needed a new vision, one that could help them see that their conflict presented them a unique opportunity—to break out of the habitual personality patterns that blocked the flow of love within and between them, to grow in new directions, and thus to connect more deeply with themselves and with life itself.

But could Robert and Lynn make use of this opportunity? That was the question. Every couple comes to a point sooner or later where they must ask themselves, in the face of the difficult challenges of intimate relationship, "Why go on?"

In previous eras, couples never had to ask themselves this question. The marriage commitment was defined and imposed on them by family and society. And every couple had a set of defined roles within an extended family, which in turn had a place in a close-knit community where people shared similar social, moral, and religious values and customs. Situated at the center of these wider networks, marriage always served a definite role and function; by providing a stabilizing influence, it supported society. In turn, society supported it; if a marriage was unhappy, community pressure held it together.

Only in the last few generations has this situation changed. Never before have couples had so little help or guidance from elders, society, or religion. Most of the old social and economic rationales for marriage as a lifelong relationship have broken down. Even many of the old incentives for having children—to carry on the family name or trade or to contribute to family work, providing an economic asset— are gone.

For the first time in history, the relations between men and women lack clear guidelines, supportive family networks, a religious context, and a compelling social meaning. Now only the intrinsic quality of a couple's personal connection can keep them going. Lacking the traditional external supports, every couple is on their own—to discover how to build a healthy relationship, and to forge their own vision of how and why to be together. Those of us who are struggling with questions of love and commitment today are pioneers in territory that has never been consciously explored before. Therefore, instead of blaming ourselves for the difficulties we may be having, we need to appreciate this unique historical situation and the new kind of opportunity it presents.

CONSCIOUS RELATIONSHIP

In former times, if people wanted to explore the deeper mysteries of life, they would often enter a monastery or hermitage far away from conventional family ties. For many of us today, however, intimate relationship has become the new wilderness that brings us face-to-face with all our gods and demons. The challenges of relationships today are calling on us to free ourselves from old habits and blind spots, and to develop the full range of our powers, sensitivities, and depths as human beings—right in the midst of everyday life.

What will allow two partners to keep moving forward together through all the ups and downs of their life together, through all the challenges, disappointments, sacrifices, and heartbreaks they may go through? What can serve as a firm basis for relationships in these uncertain times? Romantic feelings? Gratification of sexual and emotional needs? Common economic or lifestyle goals? Raising children?

I suggest that none of these any longer provides an unshakable ground for a healthy, enduring relationship. Romantic feelings continually ebb and flow. Needs change, and, once met, are no longer so compelling. Moreover, no single individual, no matter how compatible, can ever fill all our needs. Shared livelihood goals and interests change with time. Children used to contribute to family stability; however, now that they are an economic liability, rather than an economic asset, and now that the stigma of the single-parent family is disappearing, they no longer provide as strong a reason for a couple to stay together. Even love is not enough to keep two people together. How many times do people say, "I really love him (her), but I just can't live with him (her)"?

To find a solid foundation for relationship we need to consider what we most value in our connection with someone we love. What are the moments in a relationship we most cherish? Perhaps we answer: "When I feel loved." Or "When I fall deeply in love with someone." Or "When I really feel seen and understood." Yet what is really happening here that we cherish? In such moments *we become more fully present* and thus taste the richness of our being. We no longer have to prove ourselves. Something in us relaxes, our usual cares and distractions fade into the background, and we feel more awake, more alive.

Genuine love is nurturing because it affirms our being, and thus inspires us to be more present. That is why we value it so much. All the best intimate moments are those in which we are fully present, being ourselves, and sharing that with the one we love. So, beyond all the particular things two people *do* for each other, their strongest connection is the quality of being they experience in each other's presence.

Thus if intimate relationships are to flourish in these difficult times, they must reflect and promote our deepest being. Yet how many of us are really at home in ourselves? Most of us skim along the surface of our being, never bothering to explore or even wonder about the depths below. Therefore creating a healthy relationship today presents a tremendous challenge, for it means undertaking a journey in search of who we really are.

Our connection with someone we love can be one of the best vehicles for that journey. When we approach it in this way, intimacy becomes *a path*—an unfolding process of personal and spiritual discovery—*and relationship becomes, for the first time, conscious.* Through appreciating relationship as a path that can help two people develop greater awareness, depth, and spirit, we discover a larger vision and purpose that can help us persevere with our partner through the most difficult of circumstances.

The notion that relationship can help us learn important life lessons is not entirely new. Underneath our romantic ideals, most of us have some understanding that intimacy takes work and that though "you can't always get what you want" in a relationship, nevertheless if you keep at it, "you just might get what you need." I am suggesting that if we recognize and welcome this "path quality" of relationship at the very outset, we will be better prepared for the challenges we meet along love's way, instead of being totally shocked by love's outrageous demands and reluctantly forced to deal with them. Indeed, our current difficulties may allow us no other choice. Unconscious relationship simply no longer works very well.

THE NATURE OF PATH

Relationship as a path leads us on a journey of the heart— which involves becoming more fully human, more available to life as a whole. Intimate relationships are ideally suited as this kind of path because they inspire our heart to open, while at the same time showing us where we are most stuck. The more we open to another in love, the more we encounter all the obstacles that stand in the way of being fully open and present, all those habitual patterns of resistance, avoidance, and denial that we have developed as ways of coping with painful circumstances in our past. When we really love someone and discover all the ways we shut ourselves down in their presence, a desire to break out of this self-imprisonment naturally begins to stir in us. There is ferment, there is alchemy, there is the possibility for change and renewal. Our path begins to unfold.

Becoming fully human involves working with the totality of what we are—both our openness and our imprisonment, our heart and our karma. On one hand, we have become conditioned into a number of habitual patterns that cloud our awareness, distort our feelings, and restrict our capacity to open to life and to love. Our defensive postures, which we originally fashioned to shield us from pain, have become a dead weight keeping us from living as fully as we might. Yet underneath all our conditioning, the basic nature of the human heart is an unconditioned, awake presence, a caring, inquisitive intelligence, *an openness to reality*. So each of us has these two forces at work inside us: an embryonic wisdom that wants to blossom from the depths of our being, and the imprisoning weight of our karma—all those conditioned personality patterns that narrow our perception and keep us half-asleep. From birth to death, these two forces are always at work, and our lives hang in the balance. Since human nature always consists of these two elements, our journey must involve working with both of them.

If we emphasize only one side of our nature at the expense of the other, we have no path and cannot move forward in any meaningful way. And we wind up distorting our relationships as well. If we focus only on the loving side of a relationship, we may become caught in the "bliss trap"— imagining that love is a stairway to heaven that will allow us to rise above the nitty-gritty elements of our personality and leave behind all our fears and limitations: "Love is so fantastic! I feel so high! Let's get married, won't everything be wonderful!" Of course these expansive feelings are wonderful. But the potential distortion here is to imagine that love by itself can solve our problems, provide endless comfort and pleasure, or save us from facing ourselves, our aloneness, our pain, or ultimately our death. Becoming too attached to the heavenly side of love leads to rude shocks and disappointments when we inevitably return to earth and have to deal with the real-life challenges of *making a relationship work*.

The other distortion is to try to make a relationship something totally solid, safe, and familiar. This is the security trap. When we try to make a relationship serve our needs for security, we lose a sense of greater vision and adventure. Once we have lost a larger vision, we try to fill the void that remains by creating a cozy materialistic lifestyle—watching television, acquiring upscale possessions, or climbing the social ladder. And our relationship may become a kind of business deal, where everything must be negotiated. Or if we collude to play everything safe, it may become totally monotonous.

Neither of these approaches provides a path. Neither of them really goes anywhere. The heavenly bliss illusion may allow us to ascend for a while, but we eventually crash when our relationship inevitably comes back down to earth. And the security illusion keeps us glued to the earth, so that we never venture to reach out beyond ourselves at all.

Love is a transformative power precisely because it brings the two different sides of ourselves—the expansive and the contracted, the awake and the asleep—into direct contact. Our heart can start to work on our karma; rigid places in us that we have hidden from view suddenly come out in the open, and soften in love's blazing warmth. And our karma can start to work on our heart: in coming up against difficult places in ourselves and our partner, our heart has to open and expand in new ways. Love challenges us to keep expanding ourselves in exactly those places where we think we can't possibly open any further.

From the perspective of bliss or security, it's terrible that relationships force us to face so many things in ourselves that we would rather not look at. But from a path perspective, it's a great opportunity. Intimate relationships can help free us from our karmic entanglements by allowing us to see exactly how and where we are stuck. When we live alone, we are often unaware of our habitual patterns because we live inside them. But when someone we love reacts to our neurotic patterns, they bounce back on us and we can no longer ignore them.

So even though the current upheavals going on between men and women may seem daunting and perplexing, they are also forcing us to become more conscious. Looking beyond comfort and security needs, we begin to appreciate the pure essence of relationship, which is to bring together all the polarities of our existence—our buddha nature and our karmic tendencies, heaven and earth, masculine and feminine, self and other—and heal our divisions, both inner and outer.

In her struggle with Robert, Lynn was being called on to relate more directly to her vulnerability and fear of abandonment instead of denying and avoiding them through rage and blame. Robert, whose typical style was cool and logical, was being forced to face his wife's feelings, and—what was more frightening!—his own as well. The rawness he felt with his wife provided perhaps the greatest chance he would ever have to open to a deeper dimension of life. What else in his fast-paced world would call on him so powerfully to soften up, accept his own tender feelings, and expose his heart to the light of day?

If anyone else but Lynn had forced Robert to face his raw feelings, he might have simply disappeared. But since his heart was so open to her, he could not get away that easily! Because his love for her had shown him a much fuller, richer way of being, he was willing to go forth and confront his greatest fears.

What turned this couple's situation around was the growing realization that their love was asking each of them to break out of old patterns of avoidance and denial that had kept them closed all their lives. Facing and working with their difficulties called on them to cultivate deeper resources—such as patience, strength, generosity, gentleness, and courage—which helped them forge a deeper connection with themselves, with each other, and with life. This discovery gave them the vision and inspiration they most needed to persevere through this difficult period in their relationship.

Like Robert and Lynn, most of us start out imagining that if only we could get rid of the difficulties that arise in our relationships, if only we could just "get it right," we could finally get on with "the real stuff." However, since a relationship is always a living *process*, never a finished *product*, new questions and challenges continually arise. As soon as we handle one, another soon appears. When we realize that they

are there to help us keep growing and expanding, the difficulties we have with intimacy become not so much an ob-
struction as an integral part of love's path.

THREE DIMENSIONS OF THE PATH

Relationship as a path has at least three major dimensions:
evolutionary, personal, and sacred.

At the collective level, developing a new depth and quality
of intimacy in our relationships today is an important step
in healing the age-old rift between masculine and feminine
and bringing together the two halves of our humanity. Until
human consciousness can transform this ancient antagonism
into a creative alliance, we will remain fragmented and at war
with ourselves, as individuals, as couples, as societies, and as
a race. Intimate relationships are where each of us has an
opportunity to heal this collective wound. As we move in
this direction, the challenges of relationships take on a larger
meaning: They become an *evolutionary path*—an instrument
for the evolution of human consciousness.

Since we can only be as present with another person as we
are with ourselves, another important dimension of this path
involves becoming more intimate with ourselves—contact-
ing a deeper level of our being, exploring and working with
our personal barriers to love, and gaining access to a wider
range of our untapped inner resources. By helping to refine
and transform us as individuals, relationship is also an intensely *personal path*.

Beyond that, the love between two people also presents a
sacred opportunity—to go beyond the single-minded pursuit of purely personal gratifications and tap into larger
truths and energies that are at work in life as a whole. By
helping us discover what is most essential and real—the
mysteries, depths, and heights of human experience—relationship also becomes a *sacred path*.

I don't mean to suggest that intimate relationships are a
substitute for other spiritual disciplines. But if we have some

aspiration and dedication to wake up to our true nature, along with a practice that helps us do that, then in that context, relationship can be a particularly potent vehicle to help us contact a deeper kind of truth. Just as meditation practice helps us wake up from the war between good and bad, pleasure and pain, self and other *inside* ourselves, relationships help us see how we enact these same struggles outside ourselves. And they provide a training ground where we can receive immediate feedback about how deeply and genuinely we understand the principles of peace, freedom, love, and surrender.

Thus the difficulties and challenges that two people encounter in joining their energies together are not just personal travails. They are also invitations to open ourselves to the sacred interplay of the known and the unknown, the seen and the unseen, and to the larger powers born out of intimate contact with the great mysteries of life.

32 ❂ Contemplation and Intimacy

MONICA FURLONG

At first sight the contemplative principle seems inimical to relationship. Activity plays such a crucial part in meeting and getting to know people, maintaining friendships with them, or, in the case of a sexual relationship, making love, that it seems to exclude any contemplative considerations.

Yet I believe that nowhere is contemplation of more importance than in the matter of relationship. The heart of contemplation lies in a sense of "thereness" and it is often in our lack of a sense of thereness either of ourself or others that our relationship problems begin. We may have difficulty in perceiving ourselves as a real person in the eyes of others, or feel that it is only by clinging desperately to the love and affection of others that we can have any life at all. We may lack a sense of our own value, our own "richness," and be eaten up with envy for all that others have by way of looks, or success, or money or possessions, or happiness. We may feel ourselves dominated or devoured by others— our relatives or employers. We may feel put upon. We may be persecuted by our fantasies of the life we would have liked, or the satisfactions which we need and long for.

I don't want to suggest that contemplation is, or should be, the cure for these things, or that that is its function, and yet it does enter, in an important way, into all these problems. Partly because it stands for detachment. To detach ourselves, however temporarily and partially, from the heat of our desires and hopes and disappointments, gives us some perspective in an area of our lives where perspective is needed. Trying to relax into ourselves can make us aware, whatever the personality problems with which we are cursed, that however unlikely it feels at times, it really is us there standing on that particular spot and no one else. We can begin to inhabit ourselves, to have faith in the fact that we are this person, whatever the drawbacks, and no other, and that it is *this* life that is there to be lived. Some of the sense of poverty leaves us and with it the envy which can make life such a torture, or the insatiable appetite which reduces us to a state of perpetual starvation. An unexpected strength flows out of this new-found "thereness." Not the old kind of strength in which we drove ourselves on, against the grain, to do things we didn't want to do, but a new kind of strength which allows us to admit our weakness to ourselves, and sometimes to others, and live with the weakness of being human, not a superman. This love for the humanity in ourselves and others is perhaps the most costly and humiliating thing we ever have to undertake. We discover that we are "just human," not saints, not gods, not angels, not devils, not unusual, not special, not "good men," or even bad men. Progress is to grow in respect for "ordinariness" and to learn to live it gladly, accepting our weakness and failure just as much as our strength and triumph. It is the road to wholeness.

The ordinariness, despite its costliness, is disappointingly undramatic, and is a blow to the exhibitionist side of us which would love to figure in some more flattering role. Its value, however, lies in its reality. It is only interested in things as they are, not as they would be if we lived up to our idealized picture of ourselves, not as they may be at some future date. It is the reflection in the mirror before we have put on our best expression, or the photograph of us which was taken unawares.

But the reality of it is what makes relationship possible. When we are not acting, then we do not force others to act either, to take part in our private little charades. Our honesty, simplicity, and lack of guile give them the opportunity for an equally straightforward response. They become real, not part of our fantasy.

It would be foolish to pretend that we always have a choice about these things. Certain pathological states, and certain situations, enforce acting upon us as the only way of preserving our inner self from intolerable pain or destruction. But contemplation, because it is about being, makes it easier to resist that kind of seduction, easier to discover that we have a self whom we can be.

This is nowhere more important than in our sexual relationships, where the problem of integrating the self, or bringing our desire and our feeling together can be a very real one. The disintegrating effect for the individual, and for those whom he "loves," of allowing sexual appetite to be split off from any real sense of the partner as a person, is well known. Both the partners become anonymous, and are forced to accept an injury to their "being" side. Promiscuity is, in fact, activity taken to the uttermost limit, action finally cut off from its root of "being."

The great and painful effort at integration for the sexually promiscuous lies in developing their being side, partly by living in their fantasies instead of acting them out, partly by attempting the frightening feat of bringing desire and love together, of making love where they do, in fact, love. This touches upon emotional injuries of long standing which it is painful to acknowledge and seek a cure for.

For others the problem is almost the opposite one. They can banish sexual desire from their lives all too easily, and are mystified at the huge part it plays in the way others think and feel. They are sealed, virginal, in their thoughts and feelings, and may, at worst, feel superior to the suffering and struggles of others where sexual feeling is concerned. Compared to the promiscuous, they are invulnerable; they never court the rebuffs, disappointments, humiliation, and ruin which is the lot of the sexually adventurous. Yet it is their invulnerability that prohibits growth. They dread the torrents of feeling that sex can release; without, as a rule, knowing it, they cannot take the risk of abandoning themselves to experience, of "letting go." Ecstasy, the "panic" which the Greek god Pan used to inflict on unwary maidens, is the madness they fear above all others. But ecstasy is the knowledge of "being," one's own being and the being of the world about one, and not infrequently accompanies contemplative states. No one can become contemplative without leaving room for the eruption of ecstasy into their life, and the knowledge of its primacy when it does erupt. Those damaged on this side of their personality have as difficult a journey as the promiscuous.

Such sexual problems are deeply and inextricably involved with relationship problems, and these are often most painfully experienced within marriage and the family. So profound is our society's reverence for the family that we are all the victims of propaganda which almost invariably presents marriage and child-rearing as an infallibly happy process. We have only to look about us, to listen to our friends and colleagues, to read books, to know that the truth can be very different. The best arguments in favor of marriage and family life are not that they promote happiness and reduce loneliness, though at their best they do these things, but that they create a situation in which facing the truth about ourselves—our self-deceiving, touchy, vain, inflated selves—becomes more difficult to avoid than it is anywhere else. Even in marriage, and even as parents, human beings *do* manage to evade the truth for long periods, at appalling cost to everyone concerned, but it is harder to do than in most other human situations. And seeing the truth is always accompanied by pain and humiliation. No marriage and no family which rigidly excludes pain is likely to be doing its job, and most families will avoid pain if they can. The sort of marriage where the couple never have a row, cannot bear "unpleasantness," the sort of family that is endlessly and determinedly "happy" cannot lead to growth, nor any genuine form of "being." "Being" is about acknowledging one's pain, and not trying to conceal it from oneself, or inflict it upon others. For most of us there is a lot of pain inside to be acknowledged—anxiety, doubts of our own worth, moods of sadness and gloom and failure. The temptation to dodge it all by our busyness, our success, our innumerable friends and diversions, is very great.

The particular temptation of family life, the obverse of letting it help one to see the truth about oneself, is to allow it to become a prison, and oneself a helpless prisoner within it. Part of us wants imprisonment and the simplicity and lack of choice which it inflicts. It is a kind of security, notwithstanding the intense bitterness and frustration we can feel behind the bars. The humorless rigidity of the traditional Western attitudes to love and sex have made the prison exceptionally grim and the security astonishingly impregnable. The grimness of the prison has been most evident in the kind of emotional blackmail which couples have inflicted upon one another. Perhaps the worst blackmail of all has lain in the pretense that love between two people who have met when fairly young, and have usually married for unconscious reasons with a strong neurotic content, can supply all that is needed, emotionally, intellectually, sexually—for growth over what may be a period of fifty or sixty years. Because we tend to marry young and because the expectation of life is longer than it has ever been, marriage has now become a longer term contract than it ever was before. In the case of the "good" marriage, that is the marriage which allows growth, and in which there is, therefore, an awareness of freedom, generosity, sympathy, and comfort, this is an undoubted blessing. But what of the many marriages that are prisons—the ones that stifle, deny, wound and destroy— what are they but the breeding grounds of mental and physical illness and of a new generation of neurotics?

There is no slick answer to problems as grave and tragic as these. Neither the Church's quivering horror when anyone attacks "the sanctity of marriage," nor the sophisticates' glib divorcing and sleeping-around begins to reach out toward the real pain and bewilderment that men and women experience in this area of their lives. It is the very unanswerableness of it all that makes the pain so great, and drives us toward rigid solutions either of a conservative or radical nature.

I believe this is a situation to which contemplation can speak. Contemplation is about waiting, if necessarily in pain, within a fixed situation which is what marriage is. It is about finding the answers that lie not without but within, about finding freedom from the inner attitudes which bind us, with a terrible compulsiveness, into one kind of slavery or another.

Forms of slavery in marriage are not far to seek. The husband bitterly bound to the responsibilities of making money, the wife determinedly sacrificing her gifts and talents for the family, both of them bound by guilt, by what their parents thought about marriage or about life, by traditional roles of male and female, and by what the neighbors think. As slaves do, they take their pain out on one another, playing deathly games in which selfishness, anger, and hate are dressed up to look like unselfishness, patience, and love.

We can only set ourselves free from such sickness by going deeply enough into ourselves to find the courage to be what we are, and it is only when we are what we are that it will be possible for our marriage partners, or anyone else, to relate properly to us.

33 ✿ Family Life and Spiritual Practice

FRAN TRIBE

Combining spiritual practice with domestic life might have been considered impossible or even absurd two or three hundred years ago, especially for women. But the same social and technological conditions that now make it possible for women to combine having a career and a family also make it possible to combine spiritual practice and family life. This is not only possible, but desirable. Spiritual practice and domestic life can enrich each other and enable us to integrate different parts of ourselves. Together they ground us in what is fundamental about being human. My first Zen teacher, Suzuki Roshi, said that we practice Zen to become who we really are. For many of us, this process includes being householders and parents.

"When your practice is calm and ordinary," Suzuki Roshi said, "everyday life itself is enlightenment." He stressed this point over and over again in many ways, and his teaching can be particularly encouraging for people who are trying to take care of homes, jobs, relationships, and children. Yet it can be difficult to let go of our preconceptions about what spiritual practice should look like. We think that a monk working in the temple garden is practicing, but it is harder to see that a lay person taking care of his or her own garden may be practicing too. True practice does not live within any institution; it lives in the innermost part of each one of us.

It is easy to fall into a materialistic trap of thinking that meditation is some kind of answer to all of life's problems. If we sit regularly, and make great effort at it, we may imagine that our life will become smooth, free from flaws, and shiny like a well-finished table. This is a modern version of the old Puritan ethic: virtue is rewarded. If we sit for a long time and still our life is flawed (or, heaven forbid, a mess), we may feel that we have failed: "I just got it wrong. I never learned to meditate properly." Judging our practice in this way can lead to great discouragement.

We need to pay attention to our life from moment to moment, just as we pay attention to our breath in meditation. Putting one foot in front of the other, trusting that we will find our way, we find that everyday life is just pure activity. One effort. One mind. Just this mop on the floor, just this sucking baby, just this screaming baby—just this, just this—now. Any lifestyle or set of circumstances can be our training ground.

I have had the great good fortune to be able to work with several fine Zen teachers. But I have to admit that I have learned more from my children than from any of them. When my first was just a newborn, he opened my eyes to the meaning of spiritual practice. Just tending to Joshua when he cried, just cleaning up his messes, moving from one thing to another, I experienced being present in each moment. "This is beginner's mind," I said to myself. For the first time I understood what Suzuki Roshi had been talking about. "This is discipline," I felt—being one with "things as it is," as he used to say—as the days and nights grew longer and harder. My children are like little teachers crying, "Attention! Attention!" They are constantly bringing me back to this moment.

I had been sitting for seven years before my first child was born. The year before his birth I did little formal meditation, but the year before that I spent at Tassajara, San Francisco Zen Center's training monastery. Although I was struck by how similar my year at Tassajara and my first few years of mothering felt, I still assumed that the monastery was where real practice took place. I assumed that my sense that taking care of my child was also practice must be some kind of misunderstanding. My doubt and confusion grew.

For many years, taking care of my family was my main activity. The question—"How can this be practice?"—was seldom out of my mind. I did not bring it up purposely to remind myself of my commitment to Zen. It was just there in the background of everything I did. It was my koan. There were times when I found myself inventing small rituals to begin, end, or tie together my day. Sometimes when Joshua cried a lot, I found that chanting calmed us both. I structured my time carefully and took care of household chores with great attention, as if the Buddha himself were coming to dinner.

For months I did not formally meditate. The months became years. Sometimes I felt that I should be sitting, and so I'd sit a few mornings and then quit again. It felt good to sit, but meditating aroused my feelings of being isolated and alienated from the world of "real practice," the world where people got up early every morning without fail, did long meditation retreats, and kept worldly and domestic involvements to a minimum.

During the years I lived this way, caring for my family and the place where I was living, I was alone much of the time. I had few friends. My husband was a psychiatric resident for the first few years of my housewife phase, and he was not home much. He was having his own difficult time. We both felt confused and discouraged about our practice.

At some level I knew that I was practicing sincerely and intensely, but I was afraid to believe it because I looked just like any other housewife, not at all like a Zen student. I felt that Zen had brought me to a point of understanding my deep desire to raise a family and dropped me there. I missed my Zen community, but felt no one would understand me in the world of "real practice." I knew I could not go back to a community whose primary commitment was to a strict schedule of sitting, study, and work.

In the larger world, having babies and being a housewife were suspect for other reasons. The women's movement at that time (1974) attacked traditionally female activities as counter-revolutionary, reactionary, or just plain stupid. It surprised me to find so little social support for this part of my life. I had many doubts. Was I crazy? Were the feminists crazy?

I had always had doubts about my spiritual practice. Sitting for years was not supposed to lead you to discover you were a mother at heart. If I were truly committed to practice, wouldn't I be looking for babysitters and beating a path to the nearest Zen center?

Yet it felt very right taking care of home and family; I could tell it was coming from the deepest part of me. But I feared this proved I was, deep down, really not Zen student material after all. A fraud, a dilettante, just not good enough. Maybe everyone had buddha-nature except me.

Looking back on this time, I realize that I had tuned into an ancient practice, the way one might tune in a faraway radio station. For millennia women have been taking care of babies and homes, gardens, and whatever else needed care. They have worked with great care and concentration; indeed, their lives have depended on it. They invented rituals to give rhythm to their work and to appease the fearful forces that controlled life and death. They were constantly aware of impermanence because death was always close at hand. Husbands went hunting and did not return. More babies died than lived. More mothers, too. For centuries women rubbed noses with death daily; in most of the world, this is still true. We are not different from these women. In that vulnerable time after a woman gives birth, she can vividly connect with the fundamental process of life and death. It is a priceless opportunity for real spiritual practice.

Even though we can expect to survive childbirth, even though we can choose not to bear children, we are no different from the women who had to confront life and death in that way. In addition we have the opportunity to engage in spiritual practice and to become who we really are in its full sense. The options women have today are unique in history. Yet though we have more options than our grandmothers and our sisters who live in less fortunate circumstances, fundamental reality is the same for all of us. Tending our children, our garden, or domestic lives, with no thought of past or future, we can experience oneness as surely as a monk or a nun who sits facing a wall. It depends only on our sincerity. The dharma gate is open to everyone.

34 ❁ Working with Dying People

STEPHEN LEVINE

In the course of teaching meditation together, Elisabeth Kübler-Ross asked me to visit some of her dying patients. Very soon it became clear that working with the dying was a means of working on myself. In the flow of this work I met an extraordinary Dominican nun, Sister Patrice Burns, with whom I worked for a few months in the cancer ward of a San Francisco hospital. When I first came to the hospital, it was obvious to me how my practice was being put to the test. As one Zen teacher put it, "Your practice is fit for calm, but is it fit for disturbance?" And another teacher asked, "Can you keep your heart open in Hell?"

I found that a hospital is probably the most difficult environment in which to afford a really good death. Hospitals are meant to preserve life; death is an enemy there. Death is not treated with much respect, with much compassion. There's a lot of fear surrounding death. Death is a failure in a hospital.

Most terminally ill patients say they wish not to be alone when they are approaching death. They want access to people, not to feel cut off. However, in many hospitals, because of a lack of understanding of how to work with the dying and how to accept their own dying, nurses and doctors and technicians are often not available in any meaningful way to a dying patient. Studies have shown that, not willfully, but because of our subtle psychological tendencies, the call-light of a terminal patient takes longer to be answered by the nursing staff than that of a patient whom the nurses sense they can "do something to help." Therefore, at the time of our greatest hope for contact with life, we have the least opportunity. Not such a good place to die.

It became clear to me that the problem in hospitals is the same as the problem in ourselves: ignorance. A lack of understanding of the ongoing process. It's fear and resistance personified, concretized in attitudes and in separation from some part of ourselves we don't comprehend: our dying.

I saw that a good nurse on a ward became a blessing to her patients, and made a great deal of difference. Actually "good nurse" is not the right term. What I mean is a nurse who is in touch with herself enough to allow herself to care. In many nursing schools, and in much medical training, it's very common to hear, "Don't get involved with your patients." However, it is that quality of caring, of involvement, that is the essence of healing. Essentially what is happening in hospitals and in the medical profession in general is that healing is taken out of the human realm, out of the realm of the transmission of energy, and put into the chemical-electrical realm of medicines and devices.

I experienced how difficult it is to care with as much ignorance as we usually carry with us most of the time. How easily we identify with our conditioning about dying and how painful it is when we lose our perspective about suffering. I know very few people who work with the dying who aren't deeply affected and often fatigued by it. It is very demanding work. Only when we can see life and death as not so separate, as part of an ongoing process of maturation, of coming home, of returning to God, of returning to the source—whatever terms we try to define this process with—

can we stay mindful of the context in which the pain and dying are occurring. Then, when working with someone who's in pain, we honor their difficulty, we see how difficult it is for them, but we don't reinforce their resistance to that pain by saying how awful pain is and therefore intensify their affliction.

Nor do we say, "Oh the pain is just due karmic process," because that is not compassion. We're just talking off the top of our head, we're not working on ourselves by encouraging that state of mind which maintains separation. It *is* their karma, but that understanding has to come from a deep experience of the moment, from the heart, not from the head. We have to feel it as our karma, not just as their karma. We have to discover karma in ourselves, not as a concept, but as an ongoing experience, as an unfolding. Our unfolding, their unfolding: all part of the same process. The content of our life and their life might be different, just as the content of our mind and another person's mind is different, but the process is precisely the same. The natural laws governing cause and effect and the laws governing how the mind and body relate are precisely the same. And it's that sameness that is the way into understanding, the way not to get caught in content, our content or their content. In fact, it is on the level of that sameness where contact can be made.

That sameness exists when I walk into the room of a person who is in great pain, and I feel it in my gut, but the feeling is surrounded by a spaciousness which is just with it as it is, which is willing to allow it to follow its natural course. It can be psychological pain like anger or fear or great doubt, or it can be cancer eating their nervous system. In the room there is extreme discomfort, extreme dissatisfaction with the present. And I sit with them, and let myself go into that feeling. But I go into it taking with me the understanding of the context in which we all exist. And entering that experience as much as I might, I pass through it, allowing them to pass through it when they can. These words certainly don't convey the experience. But as I'm sitting with somebody, I can let go into them, I seem almost to become them. I'm not someone separate from them; the distance between me and the person I'm with is not an obstacle to my ability to be available to them. Which means giving up some image of myself as some great white knight, as Captain Karma, come to heal the sick and dying, with some subtle denial in my head that I am sick and dying, that I am riddled with clinging and ignorance. I am wise; they are not. I am healthy; they are ill. This is delusion.

Buddha said that fortune changes like the swish of a horse's tail. Two beings are in that room and they're there karmically. One is down and heading out of this life, the other one's there because there's nowhere else he can be of more use to himself or someone else. We both have work to do on ourselves. If we're in that room under any other pretext, we are not getting the most out of the situation. It's the same whatever we're doing; it's just more evident when we're with ourself dying.

A person's in the room with me who is very close to dying, and afraid. I can feel the fear of death in myself. In working through my fear, I give them an opportunity, silent though it may be, to work through theirs. If I come into a room, saying, "Oh, there's nothing to be afraid of: we go through death and then into another rebirth," that's not very useful. That's a way of not dealing with the power of the moment—the suffering in that room in the fellow on the bed, and the suffering in the mind of the fellow next to the bed.

It's the ability to suffer, the ability to experience my own unsatisfactory mind, my own unfortunate resultant karma—that is the ability to purify and get done. Working with the dying is like facing a finely polished, very fierce mirror of my own reality. Because I see my fears, and how much I dislike pain. The conditioned dislike of pain, of uncomfortable mental and physical states, is very great—it's going to be something we're working with much of the time. The judging mind is leaning over my shoulder, telling me how uncooked I am, how much work I have to do on myself. If I stay open to it, sometimes it gets quite painful but it's obviously the work that is to be done, so I stay with it, and sometimes find myself very open-minded, soft, compassionate, and very present.

The attachment which wants someone to die some other way than the way they are dying is of no use to them; that's my problem. I learned not to make someone else die my death for me. Not bringing my problems into the room became the process for further purification. Sometimes if I'm with a person and I'm stuck, I just have to say, "I'm stuck now," but that's more honesty than that person may experience all day. There's a lot of pretense in hospital rooms. The person lying in bed is often pretending, the people visiting are pretending. My work in that room is simply one of being. No pretense. And to be, I must be present. I have to be able to accept all of myself. And part of me is suffering and lying in that bed. In truth there are two deaths occurring right then.

Honesty doesn't mean forcing my truth on someone. It means being present, being real. I could feel that the more open I was, the more accepting of the human condition, of the suffering that comes with our involuntary grasping, from our immense forgetfulness, the more space I was able to allow for our growth. And the more compassion I had for even my own projections and fears. I could see that compassion is not interference. It is not forcing someone into my karma. Compassion comes from feeling another's suffering and transcending it in myself, leaving them the open space into which to grow, or even die, as they see fit, as they can, as they're karmically able.

I found that compassion meant not saying, "Oh, how nice you look today," when they were getting grayer and thinner, but rather letting them be sick when they *were* sick. Letting them accept themselves. Not to reinforce their aversion for their sickness because their sickness is what they have to work with. It's their method.

I saw how much we underrate the capacity of the human

heart, how we think we can only be of service through knowing something. But the intuitive understanding of the wisdom mind can allow us to be available to another without
getting lost in a lot of "doing." We're just there, because
we're open to be there. Which means someone is deathly ill
and we accept their sickness and take that, too, into our
heart. When the pain in the room is so great it pries open the
heart, by not holding onto things being any way other than
they actually are we seem almost to disappear at that point
where the heart and mind coincide—we experience ourselves within the open heart of understanding. We feel the
other person as ourselves, and speak to them as though
speaking to ourselves.

At those moments when I was no longer being "the giver,"
or even giving, but was just there as two aspects of myself,
one dying and one watching, I was reunited with my completeness, and all fatigue vanished. I was fed from the same
source, from the no-mind spaciousness of something greater
than my limited "me" which was feeding another.

When we're giving from the source and we come out of
the room, we don't even know who we are. There is so much
spaciousness of mind, we just don't know. The person dies,
and we don't even know if we helped. We did what we could
and learned from it, but we don't even know what we
learned. All we know is that there was a process going on, a
process of moving toward our vastness, toward our potential, toward being who we hardly even imagined we are.

35 ❀ Facing Death

DAININ KATAGIRI

We must all face the reality of impermanence. It is a difficult situation because we don't know how to deal with birth and death. We don't know how to deal with the person who is going to die, as well as we don't know how to deal with ourselves. Today I would like to make a few points.

The first point is that we have to deeply understand human suffering. Suffering and pain never go away. Even though you attain enlightenment—even though you become a Buddha, a bodhisattva, or a saint—suffering and pain never go away. The more deeply you are a bodhisattva, the more you see the minute vibration of suffering coming up from the depths of your heart.

There are certain preconceptions that when you become a Zen priest you have to die peacefully or in a sitting position. However, I think that there is, strictly speaking, no particular pattern of how to die. It is completely free. You may have an idea of how to die or an image of what is a happy death. But there are no guarantees when you really face death itself. No guarantees. At that moment there is no space for you to look at death objectively, because you are right there. You must be alive there. So you still have to understand how to live from moment to moment. It is not easy for us.

When you face death as it really is, you may compose a poem. This expression of death in a poem is really an exquisite scream. It is very beautiful, and it touches our heart, but still it is nothing but a scream. So human suffering is not something you try to create or try to remove—it's already there. Particularly at one's last moment, deep suffering really comes up and is conspicuous. That is why it is very difficult to be with it.

There are many complicated emotions in the person who is going to die: feelings of despair, sentimentality, and anger. This is very natural. Finally the person reaches the stage where they completely give up. Finally the person realizes that there is no solution and nothing to grasp.

Even though you say, "I am ready to die," there are no guarantees. Maybe you will still struggle and scream "help!" Probably. There was one Zen master whose disciples asked him, "What do you think about death?" The Zen master said, "I don't want to die." But the disciples did not expect such a statement because they believed that their teacher was a great Zen master. They thought that a Zen master should say, "I am happy to die." I don't think it is so happy, you know. The Zen teacher is very straightforward toward death. This is to say that you should understand really deep human pain and suffering. Otherwise you cannot be there.

The second point I would like to make is that you should have the feeling of togetherness. When you think about death, when you examine your idea of death, you feel some separation. But that is just an idea. In terms of true reality there is no separation. You and the person who is dying are exactly one. That is why you want to be there and serve him or her. If the person wants a cup of water you can give it. You can do it.

There was a person who was going to die who wanted to see Zen master Ikkyu. This person asked Zen master Ikkyu, "Am I going to die?" Ikkyu said, "Your end is near. I am going to die. Others are going to die." This is very important. Zen master Ikkyu said nothing particular to make the person feel comfortable. Still they can share. The person who is going to die can share his or her suffering with us. We can share our suffering with him or her.

You are going to die. I am also going to die and others are going to die. Zen master Ikkyu's statement comes from deep understanding of human suffering. When a person is facing his or her last moment, then you can really share your life and death. This is why I say that you should have the feeling of togetherness. You should *do* it. This is practice. You can hold the hands, massage the back, serve the cup of water, or just be present by him or her. This is actual practice of the feeling of togetherness.

If your heart is very warm and compassionate, even though you don't say anything, your presence very naturally affects the person. However, this quality of feeling cannot be gotten overnight. You have to practice this day to day. This is why I always mention everyday life. Even though you do not like it, you have to do it. Even though you do not like him or her, you have to take care of human beings with compassion. This practice really affects your life and makes your personality mature. Everyday life is made up of innumerable, small, seemingly trifling things we can do. This day-to-day practice is very important for us.

The third point I would like to make is that we should constantly be in the realm of oneness. The Buddhist way of understanding the world is a little different from our usual way of understanding the world. According to the ordinary conception of human knowledge, we first separate and classify all the entities in the world. In Buddhism, before we separate—trees, pebbles, mountains, rivers, oceans, skies, all sentient beings, all things visible and invisible—all are originally one.

In terms of our usual, commonsense understanding of human knowledge, if I say "this is one," at the same time another being is over there separated from this one. But in terms of the Buddhist way of understanding, if I say "this is one," that means I already accept oneness completely from the very beginning. All beings are one, before you poke your head into the concept of separateness.

The Buddhist way of understanding the world makes it clear that it is not necessary to have a certain view about life and death. This means that we shouldn't have a particular idea of what is a happy death. One person is struggling and screaming in his or her last moment, another person is praying to God, another person is chanting the name Buddha, another person is expressing anger and hatred. That is fine. Whatever way a person dies is fine.

The point is that our mental or psychological framework of death must be very light and flexible, no matter what type of death we are in. In other words, we must be right there in the middle of the broad scale of the universe. This universal realm of oneness is completely beyond our speculation, beyond good or bad, right or wrong. It is nothing but an endless stream or dynamic flow of energy. All we have to do is just be there. This is the last moment. This is why the last moment is very quick. This is it. This is why when you are exactly in the last moment you don't know it. In Buddhism this is call dharma, or totality, or the whole universe.

You should understand that oneness needs you. Dharma, totality, really needs you, whoever you are. Oneness is naturally open to everyone, and it needs you always. This is why we have to deal with it and make it alive. The moment when totality appears in your life is called *ki* in Japanese. *Ki* is usually translated as dynamic work, or device, or vital opportunity. Still we don't understand. There are no English words. *Ki* means . . . Oh, how can I say it? Do you know the television series *Bewitched?* Oh, I love it! This woman is supposed to be a witch. Whenever she wants to do something, she always moves her nose, like this. At that time, I always feel that I want to pinch that nose before she does it. At that very first movement of her nose, I want to pinch it. This is called *ki!*

We always have to return to the first moment of our

activity—meditating, bowing, moving the nose. When we come back to the first moment, if we can grasp it, pinch it, that is called *ki*. At that moment you can really experience sameness or wholeness. This is very simple practice. Already, we are there, but usually we don't pay attention to it. This is why everyday practice is important. Moment to moment you have to deal with all sentient beings, then all sentient beings are coming back to you and are supporting your life. You need all sentient beings; all sentient beings need you. This is our practice.

So when the time comes for you to face death, you have to return to the very first moment of death. Dogen Zenji says, "This birth and death is the life of the Buddha." We should practice this again and again. We have to return to the silent source of our life and stand up there. We have to come back to the realm of oneness and make it alive, with a feeling of togetherness with all sentient beings and deep understanding of human suffering.

✿ Acknowledgments

I would like to thank my wife, Jennifer Welwood, for helping me edit my selections in this book, Peter Turner of Shambhala Publications for his help and advice along the way, and Connie Zweig for planting the original seed-idea of this book in my mind. I am also grateful to the authors and publishers who granted permission to excerpt and reprint copyrighted material in this book.

CHAPTER 1 is comprised of excerpts from *The Sun My Heart* by Thich Nhat Hanh. Copyright © 1988 by Thich Nhat Hanh. Reprinted by permission of Parallax Press.

CHAPTER 2 is comprised of excerpts from *The Way of Transformation* by Karlfried Graf von Dürckheim. Copyright © George Allen & Unwin (Publishers) Ltd., 1971, 1980, 1985. Reprinted by permission of the publisher.

CHAPTER 3 is from *The Myth of Freedom* by Chögyam Trungpa. Copyright © 1976 by Chögyam Trungpa. Reprinted by permission of Shambhala Publications.

CHAPTER 4 is comprised of excerpts from *Everyday Zen* by Charlotte Joko Beck. Copyright © 1989 by Charlotte Joko Beck. Reprinted by permission of HarperCollins Publishers.

CHAPTER 5 is an excerpt from *The Wisdom of No Escape* by Pema Chödrön. Copyright © 1991 by Pema Chödrön. Reprinted by permission of Shambhala Publications.

CHAPTER 6 is comprised of excerpts from *Krishnamurti's Notebook.* Copyright © 1976 by Krishnamurti Foundation Trust Ltd. Reprinted by permission of HarperCollins Publishers.

CHAPTER 7 is from *Diamond Heart, Book Three: Being and the Meaning of Life* by A. H. Almaas. Copyright © 1990 by A-Hameed Ali. Reprinted by permission of the author.

CHAPTER 8 is comprised of excerpts from *The Zen of Seeing* by Frederick Franck. Copyright © 1973 by Frederick Franck. Reprinted by permission of Alfred A. Knopf Publishers Inc., a division of Random House, Inc.

CHAPTER 9 is comprised of excerpts from *Writing Down the Bones* by Natalie Goldberg. Copyright © 1986 by Natalie Goldberg. Reprinted by permission of Shambhala Publications.

CHAPTER 10 is excerpted from "Meditation and Poetics," in *Spiritual Quests: The Art and Craft of Religious Writing,* edited by William Zinsser. Copyright © 1988 by Allen Ginsberg. Reprinted by permission of the author.

CHAPTER 11 is excerpted from *Just Being at the Piano* by Mildred Chase. Copyright © 1985 by Mildred Chase, Creative Arts Book Co., 833 Bancroft Way, Berkeley, CA 94710. Reprinted by permission of the publisher.

CHAPTER 12 is an original article, written with the help of Jude Patterson. Published by permission of the author.

CHAPTER 13 is comprised of excerpts from *Zen in the Art of Archery* by Eugen Herrigel. Copyright © 1953 by Pantheon Books Inc. Reprinted by permission of Pantheon Books, a division of Random House, Inc.

CHAPTER 14 is comprised of excerpts from *The Unfettered Mind* by Takuan Soho, translated by William Scott Wilson. Copyright © 1986 by Kodansha International Ltd. Reprinted by permission of the publisher.

CHAPTER 15 is comprised of excerpts from *Zen Driving* by Kevin Berger and Todd Berger. Copyright © 1988 by Kevin Berger and Todd Berger. Reprinted by permission of Ballantine Books, a division of Random House, Inc.

CHAPTER 16 is a revised version of material that originally appeared in *The Work of Craft* by Carla Needleman (Knopf,

1979). Copyright © 1979 by Carla Needleman. Printed by permission of the author.

CHAPTER 17 is from *A Way of Working*, edited by D. M. Dooling. Copyright © 1979 by Parabola Books. Reprinted by permission of the publisher.

CHAPTER 18 is a revised version of an article that originally appeared in *Pilgrimage*, 1990. Copyright © 1990 by John Welwood.

CHAPTER 19 is a revised version of an article that originally appeared in *The Journal of Contemplative Psychotherapy*, Vol. 5, 1988. Printed by permission of the author.

CHAPTER 20 is excerpted from *How Can I Help?* by Ram Dass and Paul Gorman. Copyright © 1985 by Ram Dass and Paul Gorman. Reprinted by permission of Alfred A. Knopf Publishers Inc., a division of Random House, Inc.

CHAPTER 21 is an excerpt from an article that originally appeared in *The Sun*, March, 1988. Copyright © 1988 by *The Sun*. Reprinted by permission of the author.

CHAPTER 22 is comprised of excerpts from *Nourishing Wisdom* by Marc David. Copyright © 1991 by Marc David. Published by Bell Tower. Reprinted by permission of Harmony Books, a division of Random House, Inc.

CHAPTER 23 is an excerpt, originally titled "Taking Tea by the Fire," from *Healing into Life and Death* by Stephen Levine. Copyright © 1987 by Stephen Levine. Reprinted by permission of Doubleday, a division of Bantam Doubleday Dell Publishing Group, Inc.

CHAPTER 24 is comprised of excerpts from *Being Peace* by Thich Nhat Hanh. Copyright © 1987 by Thich Nhat Hanh. Reprinted by permission of Parallax Press.

CHAPTER 25 is an excerpt from an article that appeared in *ReVision*, spring, 1990. Copyright © 1990 by Deena Metzger. Reprinted by permission of the author.

CHAPTER 26 is an excerpt from *World as Lover, World as Self* by Joanna Macy. Copyright © 1991 by Joanna Macy. Reprinted by permission of Parallax Press.

CHAPTER 27 is comprised of excerpts from *Seeking the Heart of Wisdom* by Joseph Goldstein and Jack Kornfield. Copyright © 1987 by Joseph Goldstein and Jack Kornfield. Reprinted by permission of Shambhala Publications.

CHAPTER 28 is comprised of excerpts from *The Social Face of Buddhism* by Ken Jones. Copyright © 1989 by Ken Jones. Reprinted by permission of Wisdom Publications, Boston, MA.

CHAPTER 29 is reprinted from *The Path of Compassion*, edited by Fred Eppsteiner. Copyright © 1985, 1988 by Buddhist Peace Fellowship. Reprinted by permission of the publisher, Parallax Press.

CHAPTER 30 is an excerpt from *Shambhala: The Sacred Path of the Warrior* by Chögyam Trungpa. Copyright © 1984 by Chögyam Trungpa. Reprinted by permission of Shambhala Publications.

CHAPTER 31 is an original article, parts of which appeared in *Journey of the Heart: Intimate Relationship and the Path of Love* by John Welwood (HarperCollins, 1990).

CHAPTER 32 is an excerpt from *Contemplating Now* by Monica Furlong, published by Hodder & Stoughton Ltd., London. Copyright © 1971 by Monica Furlong. Reprinted by permission of Sheil Land Associates Ltd.

CHAPTER 33 is a revised version of material that originally appeared in *Not Mixing Up Buddhism*, published by White Pine Press, 1986. Printed by permission of the author.

CHAPTER 34 is an excerpt from *A Gradual Awakening* by Stephen Levine. Copyright © 1979 by Stephen Levine. Reprinted by permission of Doubleday, a division of Bantam Doubleday Dell Publishing Group, Inc.

CHAPTER 35 is comprised of excerpts from a talk given by the late Dainin Katagiri Roshi. Edited by John Welwood. Reprinted by permission of the Minnesota Zen Meditation Center.

✿ About the Contributors

A. H. ALMAAS is a teacher who founded the Ridhwan school. His books include *The Pearl Beyond Price*, *Essence*, and *The Void*.

CHARLOTTE JOKO BECK is an American Zen teacher who has a center in San Diego. She is the author of *Everyday Zen: Love and Work*.

KEVIN AND TODD BERGER are co-authors of the book *Zen Driving*. Kevin is a journalist and Todd is a psychotherapist.

STEPHEN BUTTERFIELD is a professor of English at Castleton State College in Castleton, Vermont. His books include *Black Autobiography in America* and *Amway: The Cult of Free Enterprise*.

CHAGDUD TULKU, a Tibetan Buddhist lama, is founder and president of the Mahakaruna Foundation in Oregon. He is a meditation master, artist, and Tibetan doctor.

MILDRED CHASE was a concert pianist, teacher, and author of *Just Being at the Piano*.

PEMA CHÖDRÖN is an American Buddhist nun who is Director of Gampo Abbey, a monastic center for men and women in Cape Breton, Nova Scotia. She is author of *The Wisdom of No Escape*.

MARC DAVID is a nutritionist, teacher, and consultant. He is the author of *Nourishing Wisdom: A New Understanding of Eating*.

KARLFRIED GRAF VON DÜRCKHEIM is a philosopher and psychotherapist who has lived in Japan and studied Zen extensively. His books include *Hara, The Way of Transformation,* and *The Call for the Master.*

FREDERICK FRANCK is an artist, teacher, and writer. His books include *The Zen of Seeing, To Be Human Against All Odds,* and *A Little Compendium on That Which Matters.*

MONICA FURLONG is a biographer, novelist, and poet. Her books include *Contemplating Now, End of Our Exploring,* and biographies of Thomas Merton and Alan Watts.

ALLEN GINSBERG is a renowned American poet and a founder of the poetics department at the Naropa Institute in Boulder, Colorado. His works include *Howl, Kaddish,* and *Collected Poems.*

NATALIE GOLDBERG is a writer, poet, and teacher. Her books include *Writing Down the Bones* and *Wild Mind.*

PAUL GORMAN is Vice President for Public Affairs at the Cathedral of St. John the Divine in New York City, and has worked in public affairs for much of his life.

KEN JONES has been a social activist for many years. He is the author of *The Social Face of Buddhism.*

THICH NHAT HANH, Vietnamese Zen teacher, poet, scholar, and peace activist, was nominated by Martin Luther King for the Nobel Peace Prize. He is the author of many books, including *Being Peace, The Miracle of Mindfulness,* and *Peace Is Every Step.* He lives in Plum Village, a small community in France, where he teaches, writes, gardens, and works to help refugees worldwide. He also lectures and leads retreats throughout the world on the art of mindful living.

EUGEN HERRIGEL was a German professor who taught in Tokyo between the world wars. One of the first Westerners to study and penetrate Zen training, his books include *Zen in the Art of Archery* and *The Method of Zen.*

DAININ KATAGIRI was a Zen master in residence at the Minnesota Zen Meditation Center until his death in 1990. He was the author of *Returning to Silence.*

JACK KORNFIELD is a psychotherapist and meditation teacher. He is the founder of the Insight Meditation Society in Woodacre, California, author of *Living Buddhist Masters*, and coauthor of *Seeking the Heart of Wisdom*.

J. KRISHNAMURTI was a spiritual teacher who followed no tradition but challenged people to inquire for themselves into the nature of their experience. Among his many books are *Freedom from the Known*, *The Awakening of Intelligence*, and *The First and Last Freedom*.

STEPHEN LEVINE is a writer and teacher who has worked extensively with people who are dying. His books include *A Gradual Awakening*, *Who Dies?*, and *Healing into Life and Death*.

JOANNA MACY is a writer and teacher active in movements for peace and social justice. Her books include *World as Lover, World as Self*, *Dharma and Development*, and *Despair and Personal Power in the Nuclear Age*.

DEENA METZGER is a writer, psychotherapist, and teacher. Her books include *The Woman Who Slept with Men to Take the War out of Them* and *Looking for the Faces of God*.

CARLA NEEDLEMAN is a writer and an occasional potter. Her writings include the book *The Work of Craft*.

RAM DASS [Richard Alpert] is a teacher and writer. His books include *Be Here Now*, *The Only Dance There Is*, and *How Can I Help?*

TAKUAN SOHO was a seventeenth-century Japanese Rinzai Zen master. *The Art of Sword* is taken from letters he wrote to a famous samurai of his time.

DENISE TAYLOR, teacher of meditation and theater/movement improvisation, lives in New York City. She is founder and director of the Theatre of Life.

FRAN TRIBE is a psychotherapist who specializes in working with cancer patients and their families, and is also a Zen priest.

CHÖGYAM TRUNGPA was a meditation master, scholar, poet, and the founder of the Naropa Institute. One of the most influential Buddhist teachers to come to the West, his books include *Shambhala: The Sacred Path of the Warrior, Cutting Through Spiritual Materialism,* and *The Myth of Freedom.*

KAREN KISSEL WEGELA is a psychotherapist and Director of the Contemplative Psychotherapy program at Naropa Institute in Boulder, Colorado.

JOHN WELWOOD is a writer, teacher, and psychotherapist in San Francisco. His books include *Awakening the Heart: East/West Approaches to Psychotherapy and the Healing Relationship, Challenge of the Heart,* and *Journey of the Heart: Intimate Relationship and the Path of Love.*